Hawkeye Greats,
By the Numbers
Nos. 1 through 50

Lyle Hammes
Neal Rozendaal
Kevin Hammes

Order this book online at www.trafford.com
or email orders@trafford.com

Most Trafford titles are also available at major online book retailers.

Cover design by Niki Reynolds and Lyle Hammes

Printed in the United States of America.

ISBN: 978-1-4269-4303-4 (sc)
ISBN: 978-1-4269-4302-7 (e)

Library of Congress Control Number: 2010913337

*Our mission is to efficiently provide the world's finest, most comprehensive book publishing
service, enabling every author to experience success. To find out how to publish your book,
your way, and have it available worldwide, visit us online at www.trafford.com*

Trafford rev. 09/30/2010

 www.trafford.com

North America & international
toll-free: 1 888 232 4444 (USA & Canada)
phone: 250 383 6864 ♦ fax: 812 355 4082

A Roster For the Ages

Acknowledgements

There are many thanks to give out for the production of this book. First, I thank Neal Rozendaal and Kevin Hammes for their contributions. We've made a good team. I especially thank Phebe, Sophia, and Ben for their support and patience; both are appreciated more than you know. I thank my father for instilling in me a love for Hawkeye sports. Our afternoons and evenings spent watching games together will never be forgotten. I want to thank each of the approximately 60 media members and athletes we interviewed for this book. A special thanks goes to Gary Dolphin for writing the foreword. I am also very appreciative of Bob Rasmus for providing many of the photos. Thanks to Barb Schendel and Harris Seidel for their help. Lastly, I thank you, the Iowa fans, for your avid support of all things Hawkeye.

- Lyle Hammes

First, I must thank my parents, Bill and Norma Rozendaal, and my siblings, Seth, Jolie, and Jill, for enduring an endless stream of stories about Hawkeye history with understanding smiles. I want to acknowledge my grandparents, John and Jennie Van Maanen and Wilbur and Elinor Rozendaal, for shaping my life at an early age. I would also like to thank Lyle Hammes for giving me the opportunity to participate in this project. Sincere appreciation goes to Ashley Ackerley for her steadfast support and Matt Fall for his valuable research on historical Hawkeye rosters. Thanks also to Mark Bond, Rob Tanzer, Michael McGinley, Andy Ver Woert, David and Luana Long, and Jeff, Laurie, Ben, and Krystal Terpstra for their friendship and support. To all of my family and friends that I failed to mention, you know how much I appreciate you, and I promise I'll list you by name next time. Finally, to all the players, coaches, administrators, and fans of the University of Iowa Hawkeyes, this book would not exist without your devotion and loyalty, so you have my sincerest gratitude.

- Neal Rozendaal

Introduction

Many of my eleven older siblings enjoyed sports to some degree, but none of them grew up with the passion for Iowa sports that I did. The first football season I remember well was Iowa's 1981 Rose Bowl team. My dad, brothers, and I listened with surprise and joy as Iowa beat Nebraska. Then, to prove that wasn't a fluke, Iowa went on the road to beat mighty Michigan. It was exciting to me, but it must have been even more satisfying to my dad, who had suffered through two decades of losing seasons. You see, I didn't know the history of Iowa sports yet; I just knew what the Hawks were doing that season was a first during my lifetime. Now I've lived long enough to enjoy the Big Ten football championships, NCAA wrestling championships, and one basketball Final Four appearance for both the men and women. I've also suffered through the Rose Bowl disappointments, patiently waited for another Big Ten basketball championship, and witnessed the decline of the wrestling program prior to Tom Brands' resurgence. Through it all, including a move to Ames of all places, I've remained loyal and looked forward to each new season all over again.

In 2004, I was given a number of old basketball and football programs from the second-biggest Hawkeye fan in Ames. As I looked through the rosters, I began to appreciate all over again the players I had seen, and even more so, those I had not. My "real" job is working as an engineer, so I'm a numbers person. Naturally, at least for me, I began to wonder who the greatest Hawkeye player was to wear each jersey number in either basketball or football. I started to go through the rosters I had and compiled a list. Even given that number of rosters, it was like looking at the ocean through a porthole window. I needed a bigger perspective and more rosters. Thus began *Hawkeye Greats, By the Numbers.*

As stated, I knew I needed a bigger perspective to go with the additional rosters. Who better to contact for a historical Hawkeye perspective than Jim Zabel? I wrote him in 2005 about my project and asked him what he thought of the idea and whether he'd provide me some quotes on these players to include in the writing. Months passed without hearing a response. Quite frankly, I had almost forgotten about it until I received a phone call at work from my wife, Phebe. She said, "You wouldn't guess who just called for you. Jim Zabel wants you to call him back."

So I called him back and asked him what he thought of the idea. He responded, "I love it!", as only Jim can say it. Given Jim's initial reaction, I convinced myself the project had potential, but I needed advice on how to actually produce a book. The next person I contacted was George Wine. He also liked the concept and thought it was a great idea for a book. I then posted a message on HawkeyeReport.com, asking who people thought was the best athlete at a few of the numbers. The message post received over 300 replies. I realized that this type of project would hold interest with Hawkeye fans of all ages and backgrounds.

I began to interview more and more members of the media and the athletes themselves. It was a great joy to sit down with Bob Brooks for over an hour, learning his thoughts on the greatest Iowa players going back to the Ironmen of 1939. I spoke to Ken Ploen and Forest Evashevski, then Murray Wier and Greg Stokes. I then spoke to Danan Hughes, Gary Dolphin, and Chuck Hartlieb. Quite frankly, it didn't matter where the project went because I was enjoying the first-hand accounts from each of the players and members of the media. I even sat down with Dan McCarney in his Iowa State football office to speak about players he had coached (at Iowa) and coached against (at Wisconsin and Iowa State). Talk about being out of my element! It was all cardinal and gold in that building.

One day, my brother, Kevin, called, and I mentioned what I was doing. He showed interest in helping with the book. As much as I wanted to do it, the thought of putting an entire book together by myself was a bit daunting. Kevin soon began conducting interviews with players also. He spoke to two of the 1939 Ironmen, then Wally Hilgenberg (who has since passed away), Randy Duncan, Mike Haight, and others. It was definitely a boost to the prospects of my book coming to fruition.

By June 2006, I had interested Tom Kakert into doing a piece on my project for HawkeyeReport.com. We did a quick interview, and he published it on his web site. In the interview, I made a statement that I thought Iowa began using jersey numbers around 1938. Neal Rozendaal, who I had never heard of at the time, emailed me soon after, stating that he did not think that year was accurate. And he had the rosters to prove it! At the same time, Bob Devine contacted me with information on what number his uncle, Aubrey Devine, wore in 1921.

Neal became particularly helpful in researching football rosters all the way back to 1914 and basketball rosters back to 1926. He's a collector of old Iowa programs – exactly what I needed at that time to finalize some of the jersey numbers still in question. He was able to find roster lists that were not even available at the Iowa Sports Information Department. It became evident that Neal also had ambitions of someday writing a book about Hawkeye athletics, so he became an integral contributor to the writing and research, more and more so as the project progressed.

As we moved forward with our research, the University of Iowa developed a renewed interest in historical rosters for Hawkeye football and basketball. Within the past few years, the University began to provide, for the first time, a listing of jersey numbers worn for both football and men's basketball in their annual media guides. Our research had been completed by this time, but it was interesting to check our historical rosters with the University's. It confirmed that our background research was right on. And which players at each number were the best? Well, that was entirely up to us to make our case.

With the number of books that have been written about Iowa football and Iowa basketball, we knew we had to dig deep for new aspects about the athletes' lives and bring new stories to light. As the manuscript grew, it became apparent that the entire list of jersey Nos. 1-99 was going to be too much for one book. Therefore, we split the manuscript into two volumes. Volume One has jersey Nos. 1-50. Volume Two will have Nos. 51-99, plus additional material to make that book even more unique.

I tell people that this project is a convergence of three things I enjoy: numbers, history, and, most of all, Iowa sports. *Hawkeye Greats, By the Numbers* is not a "top 50 athletes" book or list that you've seen many times before. These are the actual jersey numbers worn, rather than a ranking with no historical significance. For the reader, it is a somewhat random and curious stroll through the people responsible for Iowa's rich sports tradition.

Introduction

The definition of a "great" or the "best" athlete is different to each person. It's a subjective list, but we have searched through Iowa sports history as objectively as one can. Even doing so, it's nearly impossible to pick a most outstanding player at certain numbers.

Take jersey No. 7 for instance. How do you define the "greatest" of these players? Is "greatest" defined as the athlete who produced some of the most memorable field goals in Iowa football history? Is "greatest" the All-American basketball player from the 1940s? Is "greatest" the All-American punter who also had a stellar professional career? Or is "greatest" the one-year starter who led his team to an undefeated Big Ten championship and nearly won the Heisman Trophy? In the end, it doesn't matter. The debate is the fun part. *This is the essence of the book.* Five years of research and effort have culminated in what you're holding. We hope you enjoy the book.

- Lyle Hammes

Foreword

What's in a number?

Plenty if you're an Iowa Hawkeye fan. Whether casual or passionate, if you follow the Hawks, you have a favorite in football or basketball. I do. Now comes, *Hawkeye Greats, By the Numbers,* an encyclopedia of Hawkeye favorites, literally, by the numbers. Lyle Hammes, an avid Iowa fan himself, has come up with one of the most unique insights for your "best of" bookshelf.

Who was or is your favorite Iowa Hawkeye? What sport did they play? Now you can do a mix and match. You can agree or disagree as the authors, following interviews with historians and other experts, select their *Hawkeye Greats, By the Numbers.*

Who wore number one? Aubrey Devine was one of the all-time football greats of the 1919-21 era along with Gordon Locke and Fred "Duke" Slater who make the list at numbers 2 and 15, respectively. Legendary Michigan player and coach Fritz Crisler called Slater the greatest offensive tackle he played against. But look who else wore number 15: Don Nelson, Willie Fleming, and Jimmy Rodgers. That's the joy of the read. This book will have you stretching your memory as to which number your favorite player donned. Is Ronnie Lester number one with the number 12? What about number 16 – Chuck Long or Paul Krause? Did you know former Iowa basketball player, NBA champion Chicago Bull, and my current basketball play-by-play analyst Bobby Hansen wore the same number as Nile Kinnick? In addition to Ed Podolak, who wore number 14?

From Murray Wier to Jack Dittmer, Roy Marble and Kenny Ploen, Larry Station or Reggie Roby, this book truly evokes the "number one in our Hawkeye hearts, number _____ in your program."

In addition, this book goes beyond players and personalities. Hammes is clearly a mathematical junkie. He runs through Hawkeye history 1-99 with a fact, figure, or happening. Did you know there are 61 words in the school song, "On Iowa"? There were 98 consecutive Big Ten wrestling meet wins by Iowa from 1975-89. What are the numbers of the two retired football jerseys at Iowa? You'll chuckle at what sits behind the number 50.

This is one of those "can't put it down 'til the end" books.

As important as University of Iowa athletics is to this state, one would think every angle had been covered in print. Not quite – until now perhaps. *Hawkeye Greats, By the Numbers* is a tremendous reference for me. It'll be much more to you, the fan.

- Gary Dolphin

#1: A DEVINE HAWKEYE

"Aubrey Devine gets my vote as the greatest Iowa football player of the 20th century."
- George Wine

Who's the greatest player in Iowa football history?

Ask many Iowa football fans that question, and they'll answer almost instinctively, "Nile Kinnick." Most Iowa fans already know the story of Iowa's only Heisman Trophy winner and his remarkable year in 1939. Even novice fans have heard of Kinnick, since Iowa's home field bears his name.

However, if you had asked someone who watched the early years of Iowa football that same question, you might not have received the answer you were expecting. Most fans of that generation swore that Iowa's greatest football player ever was not a man of iron, but one who bordered on divine. There was no Heisman Trophy in 1921 when Aubrey Devine ruled the football fields of the Big Ten; if there had been, he just might have won it. Even without the Heisman Trophy, few athletes in school history can match Devine's accomplishments.

Aubrey Arthur Devine was born November 21, 1897, the youngest of nine children born to William and Elizabeth Devine of Des Moines. Aubrey was a standout football player in high school for West Des Moines. He led West Des Moines to a mythical state championship game in 1914, and he was named an All-State back in 1916 and 1917. Before college, Devine joined the U.S. Marine Corps for a year. He was stationed at Parris Island off the coast of South Carolina during World War I.

In January 1919, Aubrey Devine, and his older brother, Glenn, enrolled at Drake University in Des Moines. Within a week, the Devine brothers reversed field and transferred to the University of Iowa.

Both Devine brothers were named starters as sophomores for the 1919 Iowa football team. Glenn Devine started at the right halfback position, and Aubrey Devine started at left halfback. Aubrey also played defensive back, punter, kicker, punt returner, and kick returner. The third game of that 1919 season would help shape Aubrey Devine's college career.

Iowa traveled to play Minnesota, and the Hawks had never defeated their northern rivals in Minneapolis. Iowa's quarterback, Bill Kelly, had been hospitalized all week with a nagging injury, but Kelly made the trip and started the game. Aubrey scored a touchdown to open the second quarter, but Minnesota responded with a touchdown to tie the game, 6-6, at halftime.

Kelly was too hurt to continue, so Coach Howard Jones shifted Aubrey to the quarterback position for the final half. Devine directed the offense and repeatedly pinned Minnesota deep in their own territory with his punts. He also rushed the ball six times for 52 yards in the second half, including a 30-yard burst which set up Iowa's final drive. With seconds remaining, Aubrey Devine drop-kicked a 27-yard field goal to give Iowa the 9-6 victory.

Kelly soon recovered, but Aubrey was now Iowa's quarterback of the future. Devine accounted for all of Iowa's points in key wins over Northwestern and Iowa State as the Hawkeyes won three of their final four games in 1919. As a result, Devine was selected to the All-Big Ten team as a sophomore.

As a junior in 1920, Aubrey first teamed up with sophomore fullback Gordon Locke. Locke's powerful inside runs were a perfect complement to Aubrey's quick, elusive sprints to the outside. In the final game of the 1920 season, Devine passed for a touchdown, rushed for a touchdown, and intercepted three passes in a victory over Iowa State. As in 1919, Iowa finished the season with a 5-2 record. Devine led the Big Ten in scoring and was again named All-Big Ten.

In his senior season, Aubrey Devine was unanimously elected captain of the 1921 Hawkeyes, arguably the greatest team in school history. In their second game of the season, Iowa faced Notre Dame, coached by Knute Rockne. It was Iowa's first meeting with the Irish, and Notre Dame had not lost a game since 1918, a span of 20 straight games. Devine's first-quarter 45-yard field goal was the difference as Iowa shocked Notre Dame, 10-7.

The Hawkeyes had won a fierce, physical game. Aubrey later recalled, "It seemed that the Iowans were trying to play a joke on me because when I would start on a play, the whole Notre Dame team hit me from all sides. I did not feel like running off the field after the whistle blew. The next morning, Glenn had to help me out of bed."

The following week, Iowa defeated Illinois, 14-2. Hall of Fame coach Bob Zuppke, who coached Illinois to seven Big Ten titles, remarked, "You can say for me that Aubrey Devine is the greatest backfield man in the United States today. I have watched him for three years against my team, and he is better than ever." But the signature game of Devine's career would come two weeks later against Minnesota.

In his return to Minneapolis, Devine accounted for 464 total yards and six touchdowns as Iowa annihilated the Gophers, 41-7. Aubrey rushed for 162 yards and four touchdowns; passed for 122 yards and two touchdowns; had 200 return yards on kicks, punts, and interceptions; and kicked five extra points. It was then the most points ever scored by a team against Minnesota, a record that stood through the first 60 years of Minnesota's program. It was also the first time a school had defeated the Gophers four consecutive seasons.

> Hall of Fame Minnesota coach Henry L. "Doc" Williams, who had coached Minnesota to eight Big Ten championships at Northrop Field, called Aubrey Devine "the greatest player who ever stepped on our field."

The next week against Indiana, Devine rushed for 183 yards and four more touchdowns and passed for 102 yards before leaving the game in the third quarter. Devine had accounted for 57 points in consecutive weeks. Iowa ended the year with a 7-0 final record and a perfect 5-0 mark in the Big Ten. It was Iowa's second Big Ten title and the first outright Big Ten title in

Hawkeye history. Not only did Iowa not lose a game, but also the 1921 Hawkeyes never trailed an opponent all season.

Aubrey Devine led the conference in scoring for the second time and was named All-Big Ten for the third straight year. He was a consensus First Team All-American in 1921, just the second in school history.

Devine's 895 yards rushing in 1921 is still an Iowa season record for a quarterback, and he led Iowa in rushing, passing, and scoring each of his three years in uniform. His 1,961 career rushing yards was a school record until Dennis Mosley broke it 58 years later.

Devine was more than just a great football player. He was the fourth person in Iowa history to gain nine varsity letters, as he was a three-time letter winner in basketball and track (where he competed in the pole vault) as well as football. Devine also won the Big Ten Medal for excellence in athletics and academics.

He credited athletic success to a few factors, including a strong work ethic. "College football isn't all glory, although some people and players seem to entertain such an impression…It takes lots of hard work and plenty of ability to make the grade," Devine wrote.

Aubrey also felt that real football stars love the game. "A genuine liking for football is a most necessary quality if a player hopes to be a real star. With the liking for the game goes the determination or will to do," he wrote. "Success in college football rests upon the same broad foundation as does success in any other line of endeavor. If a man does not enjoy playing football for its own sake and is not possessed of the willpower to perfect himself in the game to the very limit of his capacity to do so, he can no more expect to reap the rewards of a successful football career than he could expect to be successful in any other line of work in which he might engage in a half-hearted manner. In other words, he must be willing to pay the price."

Minnesota had so much respect for Devine's work ethic and passion for the game that he was rumored to be a candidate to succeed Williams as Minnesota's head football coach in 1922. Devine, who wanted to practice law and had no interest in professional football, instead agreed to serve as a freshman coach and assistant varsity coach under Howard Jones while attending law school at Iowa. After one season, Aubrey left for the University of Denver, where he was an assistant football and head basketball coach in 1924 and 1925. Devine later rejoined Coach Jones as his assistant coach at Southern California before retiring from coaching in 1936 to become an attorney.

So who is Iowa's greatest football player ever? Today, all great football players find themselves measured against the legacy of Nile Kinnick. But when Kinnick had completed his masterful season of 1939, *The Cedar Rapids Tribune* ran an article with the headline, "Iowa Now Likens Kinnick to Famed Aubrey Devine."

For fans of his generation, Aubrey Devine set the standard.

Accolades

- Consensus First Team All-American (1921)
- All-Big Ten (1919, 20, 21)
- One of six Hawkeyes to earn nine varsity letters at Iowa
- Selected to the all-time University of Iowa football team (1989)
- Inducted into the College Football Hall of Fame (1973)

How He's Remembered

"Aubrey Devine of Iowa is the best triple-threat back I ever saw."

Fielding Yost, former Michigan coach

"As far as Aubrey Devine is concerned, I would be willing to take ten or twenty years and put him on an All-American team for that period. He is an excellent performer in all things which make a great backfield man. I have never seen his equal in forward passing. He is a first-class drop-kicker, punter, and open-field runner."

Howard Jones

"Aubrey Devine, the Iowa captain, is one of the most unusual men who ever played football...Devine can take the ball and advance it six or seven straight times, pick or make holes and go around ends, and come right up for the next play as unweary and as hard to stop as ever. He deserves any honor as a player that football can heap on him."

Henry "Doc" Williams

"There was little about football which Devine could not do and do just a little better than most players of his day. He was fast and a clever dodger. He was an accurate handler of the ball in receiving forward passes and catching punts. As a field general, he was far superior to any of his day in the Middle West. He was quick to discern weaknesses in an opponent's defense, and he pounded them relentlessly. He was about the best exponent of the triple threat the Middle West has had since the coming of the forward pass in 1906. The fact that he could run, kick, or pass made him a dangerous player at any stage of the game, while his field goal kicking ability also demanded respect. Defensively, he played in the fullback's position and rarely permitted an opposing player to make much ground after he had passed the scrimmage line...Considering his all-around offensive and defensive ability, combined with a football instinct, Aubrey Devine is rightfully entitled to be considered the greatest football player in Iowa's football history."

Walter Eckersall

Jersey #1 Honorable Mention

Quinn Early – Football (1983-87)

Arguably Hayden Fry's most talented wide receiver in the 1980s, Quinn Early replaced Robert Smith as Iowa's "go-to" receiver. His All-Big Ten senior season was one of the best ever by an Iowa receiver, with 1,004 yards receiving and ten touchdowns. Early set an Iowa record with a 256-yard, four-touchdown performance versus Northwestern in 1987. He also set Iowa's longest pass reception of 95 yards and ranks in the top ten all-time for yards received. Early's success extended beyond football, as he also starred for the Hawkeyes in track and field. Off the field, he was an accomplished artist. In a 2006 interview, Early stated that Iowa's art program was a factor in his decision to attend Iowa over teams such as Penn State, Boston College, and Syracuse.

"Quinn was just a stud. I remember coming in and just watching the guy run his routes. You knew with his size and speed he was destined to play on Sunday."

Brad Quast, former Iowa teammate

Adam Haluska – Basketball (2004-07)

After committing to Iowa State as a freshman in high school, Adam Haluska played one year in Ames before transferring to Iowa. At 6'5", he was a versatile guard who made a living from behind the three-point line and driving to the basket. He helped lead Iowa to two NCAA Tournaments and a second-place Big Ten finish as a junior. As a senior, he led the conference in scoring with 21 points per game and earned First Team All-Big Ten honors. Adam finished as Iowa's seventh-leading all-time scorer after only three years with the Hawkeyes. He started every game of his career at both schools and was named First Team Academic All-American his senior season. A native of Carroll, Iowa, Haluska also garnered eight individual prep state track titles for the Tigers.

#2: TAKING IT TO THE HOUSE

"It's interesting to be around the men who played with Gordon Locke and see the adoration they hold for him yet...his magnetism is amazing, and you can see at a glance why the Hawkeyes of that period fought so valiantly as a unit."

- Tait Cummins

At its core, football is a simple game. The team that scores the most points wins. If you have a player who consistently finds the end zone, your team will win a lot of football games. No player in Iowa or Big Ten history illustrates that better than Gordon Locke, Iowa's fullback from 1920-1922.

Gordon C. Locke was born in Denison, Iowa, on August 3, 1898. After starring for four years at Denison High School, Locke enrolled at Iowa as a freshman in 1919.

He made the move to the varsity team in 1920, where he was slated to be the backup fullback and defensive back behind Fred Lohman. As a junior in 1919, Lohman had been team captain and an All-Big Ten selection. However, just before fall practice began, Lohman announced that he had been accepted into Iowa's school of medicine, and Lohman had decided to forgo his senior season of football to concentrate on his studies. Locke was pressed into emergency service as a sophomore, and he was named a starter for 1920.

Locke's powerful charges into the teeth of the opponent's defense were a successful complement to quarterback Aubrey Devine's quick dashes to the outside. Locke scored four touchdowns as a sophomore and improved greatly throughout the season. Academically, he was so highly regarded by his classmates that they elected him sophomore class president.

In 1921, the Hawkeye football team could not be stopped. The most highly anticipated game of the season was a non-conference tilt with Notre Dame. It was Iowa's first meeting with Notre Dame, and the Irish had not lost a game since 1918, a span of 20 consecutive games. Early in the game, Iowa drove down the field to the Notre Dame two-yard line. It was fourth down and goal to go. Aubrey Devine called for Duke Slater to block Notre Dame's Hall of Fame guard, Hunk Anderson.

Devine later wrote, "Slater missed the block on Hunk and as I watched the play, Anderson was directly in front of Locke. I never saw a better exhibition of ball carrying with two yards to go for a touchdown, fourth down, as Locke did on that play. Locke swerved just enough to keep Anderson from hitting him straight on and he was over the goal line." That was Iowa's only touchdown as the Hawkeyes pulled a stunning 10-7 upset.

The game with Notre Dame took a physical toll on all of the players but none more so than Locke. Locke was twice knocked out of the game, the last injury coming late in the game when he was clipped by a Notre Dame player. He injured his back so badly that he had to be carried off of the field, and Locke spent the night in the hospital. He was questionable to play the following week after he missed the entire week of practice.

With many of Iowa's players hurt and Locke a game-time decision, the Hawkeyes were in trouble. The next game was Homecoming against Illinois, winners of four of the last seven Big Ten titles. Illinois had also defeated Iowa each of the last three seasons, and it looked as though the elation from Iowa's win over Notre Dame would be short-lived.

Locke turned in one of the greatest performances in school history, considering his condition and the strength of the opponent. He not only played, but he carried the ball 37 times for 202 yards and scored both of Iowa's touchdowns in a 14-2 victory over the Illini. Locke returned to the hospital the next week, and for the rest of the year, he was largely overshadowed by the brilliant play of Devine. Still, his game against Illinois in 1921 was a sign of things to come.

Locke finished the year with over 700 rushing yards and finished second in the Big Ten in scoring behind Devine. Iowa posted a perfect 7-0 record in 1921 and won its first Big Ten title in 21 years. Locke was a consensus All-Big Ten selection and a First Team All-American in 1921, largely due to his performances against Notre Dame and Illinois.

> **As he reflected on Iowa's 1921 victory, Notre Dame coach Knute Rockne said, "We had heard so much about Devine, but the guy who hurt us the most that day was Locke."**

Aubrey Devine and his brother Glenn, Duke Slater, and Lester Belding all departed after the 1921 season, and they left tremendous voids on the team. Aubrey Devine, Slater, and Belding had all been named as First Team All-Americans in their careers. Gordon Locke was the biggest "star" that returned for 1922, and the senior was unanimously elected the captain of the 1922 Hawkeyes.

For the first few games of the season, Leland Parkin, who replaced Aubrey Devine at quarterback, stole the show while teams keyed on stopping Locke. It was Parkin who scored Iowa's only touchdown in the Hawkeyes' biggest win of the year, a 6-0 victory over then-powerhouse Yale.

However, before Iowa's fourth game of the season against Purdue, it was announced that Parkin would not be able to play due to injury. Coach Howard Jones was having a difficult time finding someone to take Parkin's place. Locke piloted the team in Parkin's absence and started the only game of his career at quarterback. Locke scored two touchdowns and ran the team effectively, guiding the Hawks to a 56-0 rout of the Boilermakers. It is still the largest margin of victory ever by any team over Purdue in 123 years of Boilermaker football.

The *Chicago Post* noted, "Howard Jones in one season completely changed Locke's style this year, converting him from simply a battering ram into a fully developed all-around football player. He crashed and slid off the tackles, even tore wide around the ends, got into the forward pass game and did part of Iowa's punting. His defensive skill improved over last year. Locke was almost a flawless football player, entitled to all the honors that went to Aubrey Devine of Iowa last year."

After a three-touchdown performance against Minnesota, Locke led the Hawkeyes into Columbus for Iowa's first-ever meeting with Ohio State at Ohio Stadium. Parkin was again injured, and the Buckeyes knew that if they stopped Locke, they would win the game. Ohio State scored first; for the first time in two seasons, Iowa was trailing in a football game. But Locke would not be stopped. He rushed for 126 yards and both Iowa touchdowns, and he returned three kickoffs for 91 yards as Iowa defeated Ohio State, 12-9.

Locke ended his career at Iowa by notching four touchdowns in a victory over Northwestern. The win clinched another undefeated season for the Hawkeyes in 1922 and a second straight Big Ten title. It is the only time that Iowa has ever won consecutive conference titles in football.

> **Gordon Locke was named a consensus First Team All-American in 1922. He is the only Iowa football player to be named First Team All-American for two Big Ten championship teams.**

Gordon Locke was a tremendous student, earning the Big Ten Medal for scholastic and athletic achievement his senior year. In addition to football, Locke lettered three times for the baseball team. After graduation, he served as an assistant football coach at Iowa while he attended law school. He later graduated in the top three of his law school class at Iowa.

When his studies were completed, Locke moved to Cleveland, Ohio, where he was associated with a prominent law firm. He also coached football at Western Reserve University in Cleveland for five years. He later served as general assistant law director for the city of Cleveland. During World War II, Locke completed 18 months of combat duty with a bombing group in the Mediterranean. When he returned from the war, he lived in Washington, D.C. as general counsel for the Committee for Oil Pipe Lines.

Locke scored a total of 30 touchdowns in his career at Iowa. He totaled 16 touchdowns in 1922, including 12 in Big Ten play, a conference record. Shortly after Locke's career ended, Illinois star Red Grange took aim at Locke's season record of 12 touchdowns in conference play. But even Grange could never catch Locke's mark. It would stand for 21 years before it was broken against the weak wartime teams of 1943. No Hawkeye after Locke would exceed his mark of 16 touchdowns in a single season until Tavian Banks scored 19 touchdowns in 1997.

Locke's teams were 19-2 in his three years at Iowa. After starting his career 2-2, Locke would never lose another game as a collegian. When his career ended, Iowa was on a 17-game winning streak, which would reach a school-record 20 wins before being broken.

Gordon Locke is remembered as one of the greatest scorers in Iowa history. It should come as no surprise that he is remembered as one of the school's greatest winners as well.

Accolades
• Consensus First Team All-American (1922)
• All-Big Ten (1921, 22)
• Broke Big Ten record for touchdowns in a single conference season
• Selected to the all-time University of Iowa football team (1989)
• Inducted into the College Football Hall of Fame (1960)

How He's Remembered

"I do not believe that there is any other fullback in the West or East who has carried the ball as consistently as Locke."

Howard Jones

"Tacklers climbing aboard Locke invariably get a two- or three-yard ride before they bring him down. Despite his hefty build, Locke is fast and agile, running with a sort of corkscrew gait that is very deceiving. His powerful legs rip through the arms of the tackler who neglects to get his shoulder into play."

Waterloo Evening Courier (Oct 12, 1922)

"Gordon Locke has won praise from coast to coast and in every part of the Middle West. We imagine there is not a youngster in the Middle West who cannot tell you about the greatest plunging fullback the West has boasted in years...In every game, he has been a consistent gainer. Even when the line was slow and at times when the forward wall failed to make a hole, Locke managed to get through some way. And if there was a hole, he always found it and went through like a bullet, his momentum often carrying him ten to fifteen yards beyond the line of scrimmage."

Iowa City Press-Citizen (Dec 6, 1921)

"Powerful is an inadequate adjective to use in describing his strength and ramming talents. He had the legs that gave the drive the momentum of a battle tank."

John W. Heisman

Jersey #2 Honorable Mention

Robert Smith – Football (1983-86)
Hayden Fry had speed in mind when he signed Robert Smith, from Dallas, Texas, to his 1983 recruiting class. A high school All-American in track, Smith saw action his freshman year and became a three-year starter at wingback. He averaged over 20 yards per catch in his career, including receptions of 86 and 89 yards. Smith also returned 76 punts, breaking Nile Kinnick's career record of 71. Smith helped lead the Hawkeyes to bowl games four straight years and also lettered in track.

Fred Russell – Football (2000-03)

One of the quickest running backs in Iowa football history, Fred Russell was a native of Inkster, Michigan. He came to Iowa via Milford Academy in Connecticut and led Iowa's 2002 Orange Bowl team and 2003 Outback Bowl team in rushing. Behind one of Iowa's most dominating offensive lines, he totaled 1,264 yards (5.7 yards per carry) in 2002. He followed that up by adding 1,355 yards his senior season.

"The quintessential scat-back, he originally signed with Michigan and then came back in 2002 to help deliver a signature win of the Kirk Ferentz era at the Big House."

Steve Deace, WHO-Radio

Jeff Horner – Basketball (2003-06)

Like Dean Oliver a few years before him, Jeff Horner played prep ball for Mason City High School. After committing to Iowa as a high school freshman, Horner became a fan favorite because of his pinpoint passing and long-range shooting. Horner helped lead Iowa to two NCAA Tournament appearances and a second-place Big Ten finish his senior year. He is Iowa's all-time leader in three-point field goals and assists and ranks 12th all-time in scoring. Horner is the only Iowa player to amass more than 1,000 points, 600 rebounds, and 500 assists during his career.

"It seems like Horner committed to Iowa when he was still in the crib. When he reached high school, he always drew a crowd...often times standing room only. Jeff played his heart out. That's all you can ask."

Keith Murphy, WHO-TV

#3: ANGEL IN THE END ZONE

"One of the best all-around athletes to ever wear a Hawkeye uniform. He could do anything. Well, I'm not sure about the pommel horse."

- Keith Murphy

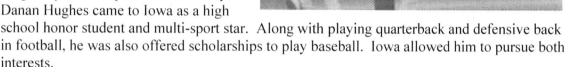

It's nice to have options. Should a person play college football at Iowa, Nebraska, or Penn State? Play offense or defense? How about playing baseball also? Try both professional football and baseball, or just stick with one?

Those are the kinds of questions that only elite athletes realistically need to ask themselves, and those are the exact questions Danan Hughes faced throughout his college years.

Originally from Bayonne, New Jersey, Danan Hughes came to Iowa as a high school honor student and multi-sport star. Along with playing quarterback and defensive back in football, he was also offered scholarships to play baseball. Iowa allowed him to pursue both interests.

"I was recruited by East Coast schools like Penn State, Maryland, Syracuse, and Boston College, and then as far west as Nebraska and Iowa," said Hughes. "It really came down to those schools, and Nebraska was running the wishbone at the time. They actually wanted me to play defensive back. Once I made the decision I wanted to play receiver, that kind of nixed Nebraska."

"I chose Iowa for a couple different reasons," Hughes recalled. "Iowa had a very solid tradition, especially in the 1980s with Chuck Long, Chuck Hartlieb, and receivers like Quinn Early. I looked at that, and then one of the main things was that they were very open to me about playing baseball. Although there were other schools and coaches who said it, nobody was as convincing and trustworthy as Coach Fry was. With those components, I knew Iowa was the place for me."

Danan's primary recruiter, however, was assistant coach Bernie Wyatt. Wyatt had a proven track record of bringing talent into Iowa from the East Coast. Players such as Ronnie Harmon, Tony Stewart, Devon Mitchell, Owen Gill, and Nate Creer all hailed from New York. College roommates Leroy Smith and Danan Hughes were from New Jersey. All were led to Iowa by Wyatt and were key components to Hayden Fry's success at Iowa.

After redshirting in 1988, Danan Hughes shared receiving duties his freshman year with Travis Watkins. Despite the Hawkeyes struggling through their first losing season since 1980,

Hughes set an Iowa freshman record with 471 yards receiving. He caught a pass in every game – a feat not duplicated at Iowa for another decade.

His sophomore season brought both individual and team success. The Hawks bounced back in a big way and earned a ticket west to Pasadena for the third time under Coach Hayden Fry. Iowa secured a share of the Big Ten championship along with Michigan State, Michigan, and Illinois, but the Hawkeyes claimed the Rose Bowl berth by defeating all three of the other conference co-champions on the road. Hughes played a key role in two of those contests, with five catches against Michigan and two touchdowns in the 54-28 blowout of Illinois.

> **Danan Hughes threw a 66-yard pass to Nick Bell on one of Coach Hayden Fry's "exotics" in the 1991 Rose Bowl.**

Having re-established themselves on the national scene, Iowa's 1991 season brought even more wins than the previous year. The Hawkeyes ended the season with a 10-1-1 record and a No. 9 national ranking. Hughes had clearly developed into Iowa's featured receiver, finishing the year with a career-high 757 yards and earning All-Big Ten honors.

Fans' most vivid memory when recalling Hughes' career may have occurred in a snow-covered Kinnick Stadium in 1991. A foot of snow fell the night before Iowa took on Minnesota to end the regular season. In all, 32,000 fans braved the miserable conditions to see quarterback Matt Rodgers throw for nearly 400 yards and three touchdowns. After one of the scores, Danan Hughes dove in the end zone, rolled on his back, and made a snow angel imprint. Iowa fans loved it, and even some Gopher fans may have found the humor given the situation. The win gave Hayden Fry 100 wins at Iowa and some brave fans a memorable experience.

The infamous "Snow Angel" play was an audible made at the line of scrimmage. Rodgers recognized man coverage by the Gophers. In the snow, it was difficult for the defender to turn and run deep, so he audibled to "White 5 G.O. (Get Open)." This gave Hughes the option to run a Post or a Post/Corner based on how the defensive back played. Hughes went to the Post, and the rest is history.

"Out of all the years since that game," Hughes stated, "there has hardly been a time where I've ever stepped into the state of Iowa and not heard that story. If I was just passing through Iowa at my daughter's soccer tournament, somebody would recognize me, pull me aside, and say, 'I remember the snow angel.' The funny thing is all those guys that jumped on me in the end zone were my Iowa baseball teammates standing down in the snow watching the game. They showed a clip of Minnesota in the huddle, and they were just getting pummeled by snowballs from every angle."

Each spring, Hughes was also enjoying success away from the football field. His role as center fielder for the Iowa baseball team was interrupted, however, by an injury his junior year. While hitting over .400 early that spring, Hughes suffered a broken finger that caused him to miss significant time.

"I was smashing the ball at the beginning of the season," Hughes recalled. "I hit about four or five home runs in the first four or five games. I had just hit a home run the previous at-bat, and they asked me to bunt. I squared around, and the pitcher threw a high and inside pitch that hit my finger, so I was out for 20 or 30 games."

By August 1992, the 6'2", 200-pound senior was ready to begin his final football season as a Hawkeye. North Carolina State was the opponent in the 1992 Kickoff Classic, held in his home state of New Jersey. Unfortunately, the Hawks fell to the Wolfpack, 24-14, and began a disappointing 5-7 season. Hughes battled injuries his final season but still produced enough to become Iowa's all-time leading receiver in yardage and touchdowns.

> **In a 23-22 victory over Wisconsin in 1992, Danan Hughes broke Ronnie Harmon's school record of 2,045 career receiving yards.**

With his collegiate football now over, Hughes was approaching another career decision. He had already been selected by the Milwaukee Brewers in the 1992 MLB Draft after being selected by San Diego in the previous year's draft. A few months after Iowa's football season ended, Kansas City chose him in the 1993 NFL Draft. After spending time in the Brewers organization, Hughes finally opted to make a career of it in the NFL. There, he played six seasons, all with the Chiefs, before he retired in September 1999.

Today, Danan Hughes still lives in the Kansas City area with his wife and children. After leaving the Chiefs, he began working in home mortgage lending and is currently a sales manager for US Bank. He has stayed involved in sports recently by working as a television commentator for both football and baseball.

Hughes recalls fondly his playing days at Iowa. A few games stand out in particular almost 20 years later. "Obviously, the Rose Bowl in 1991 was memorable just because of the history there," Hughes said. "We played Ohio State in 1991 the day after a University of Iowa student shot a number of people on campus. [To honor them], we stripped the stickers off our helmets and then upset the Buckeyes. Michigan was always a big game, and I played well against them."

"My brother-in-law went to Michigan, and I worked with a guy that went to Iowa State," Hughes continued. "I always [joked] with them and said that if it wasn't for Michigan and Iowa State, I would have never made the NFL." Hughes, in fact, did set the stage against the Cyclones with long first-quarter touchdowns in both 1989 and 1991. In his final in-state battle, Hughes caught eight passes for 133 yards and a touchdown.

Danan Hughes didn't have the open field speed of Iowa's Robert Smith, but he was fast. He may not have been as elusive as Ronnie Harmon, but he had moves. He didn't have the explosiveness of Tim Dwight, but he could leave a guy behind him.

What made him great was his combination of all of the above traits. He was the complete wideout, and the player who carried the torch from Quinn Early to Tim Dwight as Iowa's go-to wide receiver.

Accolades
• All-Big Ten (1991)
• Broke school record for career receiving yards
• Holds school record for career touchdown receptions
• Played both football and baseball professionally

No. 3 DANAN HUGHES

Year	Recept	Yds	Avg	TDs	Long
1989	28	471	16.8	2	37
1990	29	410	14.2	5	35
1991	43	757	17.6	8	52
1992	46	578	12.6	6	29
Totals	**146**	**2,216**	**15.2**	**21**	**52**

How He's Remembered

"Danan and I were together for a year. He was a classy guy. I still run across him, and I think the world of him. I love stories where kids come in and learn a new position. Danan was a quarterback-turned-wide receiver and turned out to be one of Iowa's all-time great wide receivers."

Chuck Hartlieb

"I'll match Danan against anybody one-on-one. If I just put it in the area with Danan, he's going to come down with it every time."

Jim Hartlieb

"Danan Hughes was just an absolutely gifted wide receiver. As a receiver, the quarterbacks loved to throw to him, because he ran the routes perfectly. They could throw the ball before he even made the break, because they knew Danan Hughes was going to run the route exactly the way it was drawn up."

Frosty Mitchell

"I think some athletes would have trouble making the transition from baseball to football, but not Danan Hughes. He thinks he's King Kong. I don't think he'll miss a lick."

Hayden Fry

Jersey #3 Honorable Mention

Tom Nichol – Football (1981-84)

The first of three kickers listed in *Hawkeye Greats*, Tom Nichol played a large role as Hayden Fry's Hawkeyes of the 1980s took flight. Nichol was given his opportunity when Iowa's starting kicker, Lon Olejniczak, broke his leg early in Nichol's freshman season. He left an indelible mark in Iowa football history with three field goals in a shocking 9-7 upset at Michigan that same year. He helped lead Iowa to four consecutive bowl games and concluded his career in Iowa's 55-17 win over Texas in the 1984 Freedom Bowl. Nichol shattered Iowa's all-time scoring record with 277 career points, 145 points ahead of the previous record. Nichol currently lives in his native state of Wisconsin.

Kerry Burt – Football (1984-87)

Kerry Burt shared team captain duties in 1987 while earning All-Big Ten honors. He currently ranks eighth on Iowa's all-time interceptions list. He had seven interceptions and two recovered fumbles in 1987. Burt started his career as a wingback and kick returner before switching to defensive back his sophomore year. He attended high school in Waterloo, Iowa.

Damien Robinson – Football (1993-96)

Originally from Hillcrest High School in Dallas, Texas, Damien Robinson came to Iowa as a 6'2", 185-pound defensive back. He left Iowa as a four-time letter winner with All-Big Ten honors in 1996. He currently ranks fourth all-time on Iowa's career interceptions list with 14 and 16th on the all-time tackles chart with 291. Robinson helped lead the Hawkeyes to wins in the 1995 Sun Bowl and the 1996 Alamo Bowl. In his senior year, he intercepted a pass in the end zone with 30 seconds remaining to preserve a 37-30 victory over Michigan State. He ranked fifth in the nation in interceptions as a senior.

"Senior free safety Damien Robinson left his calling card all over the field in the form of bruised and battered Nittany Lions. Not long ago, Robinson wasn't regarded as the most physical or most effective defensive back on Iowa's roster. Now, he's a veritable hit man."

Mike Hlas, *Cedar Rapids Gazette* (Oct 20, 1996)

#4: A SWEET ENDING

"The total package from class, talent, integrity, work ethic, and faith perspectives. Were it not for the bad back, he might have gone down as the best Iowan ever to wear the Iowa basketball uniform."

- Steve Deace

Jess Settles grew up like many Iowa sports fans in the early 1980s. He recalls watching Steve Carfino on winter evenings and thought he was larger than life. He was there when No. 1 Iowa defeated No. 2 Michigan in 1985, and he wondered what it would be like to wear the black and gold. Jess Settles was no different than many young children today.

He wanted to be a Hawkeye.

There was one difference between Jess and most other children. He had the right mix of desire, work ethic, and God-given ability to realize his athletic dreams. Jess helped lead the Winfield-Mt. Union Wolves to two appearances in the state high school basketball tournament. After being named Iowa's "Mr. Basketball" in 1993, he was off to Iowa City to play for Dr. Tom Davis.

"One of my most memorable moments," Settles recalled, "was [my first] Black and Gold Blowout Game which was the intra-squad scrimmage. I came into Carver-Hawkeye from parking in the back…and into the locker rooms. I walked around the corner and there's my uniform, which I had never put on before, and it's all pressed. It looked like a pot of gold there. Our team was wearing gold. With the flash right in front of you, all your dreams came true. Everything you worked for growing up watching the Hawkeyes, living half-an-hour south of Iowa City. Right there, that's your moment.

"Just putting that uniform on that day was a tremendous feeling of accomplishment," Settles explained. "You know how it is in high school – your mom has to wash your socks, your white uniform ends up turning a little faded because it got mixed in with a red uniform. When you get [to Iowa], you just show up and all that's taken care of for you."

> **Jess Settles' freshman scoring average of 15.3 points per game is the second-highest for a freshman in Iowa history behind Dick Ives' 18.1.**

If getting ready for the first game was exciting, the game itself was breathtaking – literally. "I remember going out and playing in that game," Settles said. "I was so nervous that I could hardly breathe going up and down the court. I told my parents after the game that I'm just not in good enough shape, and I don't know if I can do this. But it was just nerves. I just couldn't get my wind."

Jess was a breath of fresh air for a team in need of some good news. The fall of 1993 brought the departure of Kevin Smith, the team's senior point guard. The previous January, the team tragically lost their inspirational leader in Chris Street. That left undersized center James Winters as Iowa's only senior. Along with fellow starters Kenyon Murray, Jim Bartels, and Mon'ter Glasper, Settles became an immediate contributor to the team. Despite the team struggling to a 5-13 record in conference play, Settles averaged over 15 points per game and earned Big Ten Freshman of the Year honors. He credits what success the team did have that year to team MVP James Winters.

"James did a phenomenal job mentoring us under just brutal circumstances," Settles recalled. "Chris Street was James' roommate and teammate. He loses Chris, and then Kevin Smith ends up quitting the team before his senior season. So you think about James – here he is losing two starters and friends and then having to deal with us knuckleheads who had never played. He did a phenomenal job of working us all through that."

Again with only one senior, the team bounced back in the 1994-95 season. Bolstered by the addition of sophomore Andre Woolridge, the team improved its record to 21-12 and advanced three games into the NIT Tournament. Settles again averaged over 15 points per game. Chris Kingsbury, also a sophomore, led Iowa in scoring with 16.8 points per game. With three sophomores leading the team in scoring, the future looked bright. For Settles, however, all was not well. As they entered conference play, he began developing back problems and played in only 26 of 33 games that season.

Team expectations were higher for Settles' junior season of 1995-96. The trio of Settles, Kingsbury, and Woolridge were now upperclassmen, while the senior class consisted of Kenyon Murray, Russ Millard, and Mon'ter Glasper. They returned to the NCAA Tournament for the first time in three years.

"We played George Washington in the first round of the [1996] NCAA Tournament," teammate Ryan Bowen recalled, "and we were down about 18 points with seven or eight minutes to go. Jess singlehandedly brought us back and won that game for us. He just wasn't going to let anything stop him from winning that game."

Two days later, however, Iowa was defeated by Lute Olson's Arizona Wildcats, 87-73. Settles' junior season came to a close, and he was now faced with a very difficult decision. Should he play through his senior season at Iowa or take a chance on the NBA one year early? He had finally helped return Iowa to the NCAA Tournament, and he had just finished a third straight year of scoring over 15 points per game. The case could definitely be made that he was ready for the next level.

Both Settles and teammate Chris Kingsbury decided to make themselves available for the 1996 NBA Draft. Neither would see their names called. Settles eventually withdrew his name from the draft and decided to return to Iowa. Kingsbury went undrafted, and his Iowa career was over.

The following season was an injury-riddled and frustrating one for Settles. Instead of enjoying the final year of a stellar career, Jess was sidelined with lingering back and hip injuries. He played in only three games and eventually decided to redshirt the season. Even after an off-season of treatment, the pain would not subside. Settles was forced to the sidelines for the second straight season in 1997, and in October of that year, he declared that his injuries might cost him the rest of his basketball career.

"It just hit me in college," Settles said about the injuries. "It started out gradually, and it kind of got out of hand. I just could never get it figured out. Injuries are the one thing that you can't control."

It was announced in April 1998 that the next season would be Dr. Tom Davis' last as head coach of Iowa. A disappointing end to the 1998 season and declining attendance were two factors given in the decision. Some players thought Coach Davis had not received fair treatment in the decision, and they resolved to send him out on a positive note.

Settles was one of them. He received news that the NCAA had granted him a rare sixth year of eligibility, and Jess decided to give it one last shot. It paid off. The return of Settles gave the Hawkeyes instant experience and depth. Though still not 100 percent, he was well enough to average 10 points per game and play in 28 of the 30 games his final year.

Perhaps the most memorable win that year came in December in Lawrence, Kansas. Trailing by 18 points with 12:50 remaining in the game, Iowa made a memorable comeback and defeated Kansas, 85-81. It was the Jayhawks' first loss in Phog Allen Fieldhouse in 62 games. The 1998-99 Hawkeyes made it all the way to the Sweet Sixteen before losing to eventual champion Connecticut.

"The thing I remember about Jess is his toughness," said Gary Dolphin. "He really was the catalyst for that Sweet Sixteen team. What I really liked about him was the way he played through pain. He had a very debilitating back that to this day gives him all kinds of problems, and he never really was the player he could have been because of injuries. But that also showed me how tough of a player he was.

"He made an interesting comment one time," Dolphin continued. "He felt that if Sam Okey…had not broken his wrist in [1999], they could have won the national championship with that team that got beat by Connecticut in Phoenix. But they just didn't quite have the rebounding and strength in numbers that they had when Okey was with them."

> **Jess Settles was a three-time recipient of the Chris Street Award, which goes annually to "a Hawkeye player who best exemplifies the spirit, enthusiasm, and intensity of Chris Street."**

As his career finally came to an end, it became clear that Settles had left an indelible mark on the Iowa basketball program. He was a three-time All-Big Ten selection and was also named team MVP three times. He currently stands in sixth place on Iowa's all-time scoring list. Off the court, he represented the program well by earning Academic All-Big Ten honors four times and All-American honors once. By every measure, Jess Settles had an outstanding career.

Since leaving the Iowa basketball program, Settles has made numerous speaking appearances around the state. He published a book in 1999 entitled "The Next Level: Maximizing Potential." In churches, youth groups, schools, and businesses, he speaks about his experiences and how he has realized goals in his life. He also runs "The Next Level Basketball Camp" each summer for kids. Jess and his wife Joanna currently live in southeast Iowa, where Jess is employed as a pharmaceutical salesman for parts of southern Iowa and northern Missouri.

"He doesn't sit and moan and talk about 'what if'," said Ryan Bowen of Settles. "He'll be the first to say he's very fortunate to have been able to play basketball at Iowa and basketball has been great to him. I don't think he would ever say, 'I should still be playing if it wasn't for this.' He would definitely focus on the positives and the great career that he had rather than the negatives."

Just like Jess watching Steve Carfino over 25 years ago, thousands of young Iowans grew up watching Jess Settles play for the Hawkeyes. He also seemed larger than life to this new generation of Iowa fans. And, like Settles, they want to be Hawkeyes.

Accolades
• Big Ten Freshman of the Year (1994)
• First Team All-Big Ten (1996); Third Team All-Big Ten (1994, 95)
• Team MVP (1995, 96, 99)
• Ranks sixth in school history in career scoring
• Led team in rebounding (1994, 96, 99)

No. 4 JESS SETTLES

Year	GP	FG-FGA	FG%	FT-FTA	FT%	Reb	Avg	Pts	Avg
1994	27	156-272	.574	86-109	.789	203	7.5	414	15.3
1995	26	138-294	.469	97-121	.802	162	6.2	405	15.6
1996	32	179-375	.477	86-116	.741	239	7.5	484	15.1
1997	3	10-20	.500	13-14	.929	10	3.3	34	11.3
1999	28	98-225	.436	54-69	.783	133	4.8	274	9.8
Totals	116	581-1,186	.490	336-429	.783	747	6.4	1,611	13.9

How He's Remembered

"Is he still playing at Iowa? I enjoyed watching Jess all 11 seasons he wore the Hawkeye uniform. I know, I know, it only seems like Settles played for a decade. It's too bad Jess was so banged up because he was on his way to a great career. Even nursing a sore back, he was better than most. And what a great guy. We had Jess on our Sound-Off show once, and he agreed to take live phone calls. A couple of people took cheap shots, but it didn't phase Settles. He knows who he is."

Keith Murphy

"Talking with him a little bit after games, you saw a guy play with a lot of pain. I remember watching him play at times and thinking that I have no clue how he can get out there and do it, knowing the back problems and everything he was going through. There would be a lot of guys who would just get down, and I'm sure at times Jess did. But I almost think that made his faith greater. To me, his 1999 season was just a fitting end, especially how that season played out for the Hawkeyes."

Mark Allen

"Jess would be a guy that probably had his career tarnished a bit just because of his injury. He probably never really played to his potential after his sophomore year. Between back problems and other injury problems he had, he just was not able to go. But he played with great representation of his school and made a lot of people feel very good that he stayed at Iowa."

Mac McCausland

"I think Settles was star-crossed with all his injuries, but when he was right, he was really good. He's like a lot of Iowa power forwards from Chris Street on to the present day like [Greg] Brunner – just 'blood and guts' guys. Not pretty players, but guys who just night after night would mix it up with anybody and give supreme effort."

Mike Hlas

"Settles' toughness was so prominent. He could score, he could shoot, he could take it to the basket, he was a great free-throw shooter, but just his overall mental toughness as well as his physical ability really set him apart."

Gary Dolphin

"Jess has always been someone I've tried to be just like. We scrimmaged against each other in high school one time, and I couldn't get over how good this guy was, how big he was, how strong he was, and just how hard he worked. And I thought to myself, 'That's what I need to get to if I want to play college basketball.'"

Ryan Bowen

Jersey #4 Honorable Mention

Chris Pervall – Basketball (1965-66)

Chris Pervall was the first of many outstanding junior college players that head coach Ralph Miller brought to Iowa. Pervall, a guard, arrived from Coffeyville, Kansas, and made an immediate impact on Miller's first Iowa team. He averaged over 21 points per game in his first season at Iowa, which included a 38-point performance against Illinois. Pervall helped the Hawkeyes achieve their first winning season since the Don Nelson era ended in 1962. In his final season, he helped lead Iowa to a third-place Big Ten finish. In 1966, both Pervall and teammate George Peeples were selected by the NBA's Baltimore Bullets.

#5: TEXAS TWISTER

"[Sedrick] could take punishment and dish it out. He liked to run inside as much as outside, through people or around them. You never knew what he was going to do when he got the ball. He had great moves and spins, which is what made him such an exciting player."

- Hayden Fry

Coming from the state of Texas, Sedrick Shaw was used to big things. He left Iowa in 1996 with rushing statistics to match.

Getting him in an Iowa uniform wasn't easy, so two native Texans went down to convince him. Both Carl Jackson and Hayden Fry made their case to Shaw that Iowa was the place for him.

Fry wrote about Sedrick's mother, Sandrea, in his autobiography, *A High Porch Picnic*. "She wanted to know everything about the University of Iowa and the other schools recruiting her son, and I mean everything," he stated. "I wish more mothers were like her. She wanted what was best for her son and we had to convince her that Iowa was the best school for Sedrick, but it wasn't easy."

Shaw attended high school in Austin, where he earned Second Team All-State. He was named All-American by SuperPrep and was rated the sixth-best prep recruit in Texas. As a senior, he rushed for 1,120 yards and seven touchdowns. He had a very successful track career as well. He ran a leg on the school's national championship mile relay team the previous year.

Shaw played at Iowa as a 6'1", 195-pound freshman in 1993, and he made an instant impact. The first time he touched the ball as a Hawkeye, he returned a kickoff 75 yards for a touchdown against Tulsa in the season opener.

> **Sedrick Shaw led the Hawkeyes with 989 all-purpose yards as a freshman, and his 561 rushing yards were a school record for an Iowa freshman.**

As a sophomore, Shaw took center stage in Iowa's offense. He averaged nearly six yards per carry and gained over 1,000 yards for his first of three straight years. Iowa experienced another season without a bowl game, however.

After three straight subpar seasons, Coach Hayden Fry needed the Hawkeyes to come back strong in 1995. Iowa needed a solid start to the Big Ten season in particular, as Iowa had only won one of their last eight conference openers. In 1995, they opened the Big Ten season in East Lansing against Michigan State. Shaw rushed for 250 yards on a school-record 42 carries to lead Iowa to victory. The 250-yard outburst was the second-most in school history behind Ed Podolak's 286-yard game against Northwestern in 1968. "He's a reckless runner. He runs hard," Spartan coach Nick Saban said. "He runs with power. We missed 36 tackles in the game. Most of them were against him. That says something about his ability and his power."

Iowa started the season 5-0, but the Hawks then lost four straight games. In their fourth loss, Shaw rushed for 135 yards against Northwestern to surpass Tony Stewart as Iowa's all-time leading rusher. At 5-4, though, the Hawkeyes needed to win their final two games to qualify for a bowl game. In the next game against Wisconsin, Shaw got Iowa back on the winning track with 214 yards and three touchdowns in a 33-20 victory. He set the school season record for rushing attempts and rushing yards in the process. The Hawks followed that by beating Minnesota, 49-3, to earn a berth in the Sun Bowl.

Fry set an NCAA record by returning to coach in the same bowl 32 years after his SMU Mustangs lost the 1963 Sun Bowl. This time, the Hawks were matched up against the Pac-10 co-champions from Washington, who had defeated Fry in two of his three Rose Bowls. The Huskies were heavily favored, but Shaw set the tone with a 58-yard touchdown run less than two minutes into the game. He finished with 135 rushing yards and that touchdown, and Iowa pounded Washington, 38-18. Shaw was named the game's MVP, as the Hawkeyes won their first bowl game in eight years.

As a senior, injuries took their toll and limited Shaw to 224 carries. Nevertheless, he still gained over 1,000 yards to distance himself from Tony Stewart on Iowa's career rushing charts. Shaw earned All-Big Ten honors as a senior and was named MVP of the team for the second straight season. With an 8-3 record, the Hawks were invited to play Texas Tech in the 1996 Alamo Bowl.

Shaw had been held to just 14 yards as a freshman in the inaugural Alamo Bowl, which Iowa lost, 37-3. This time, he squared off against Texas Tech's Byron Hanspard, who had won the Doak Walker award as the nation's top running back. In his final game as a Hawkeye, Shaw rushed for 113 yards and was named the game's MVP, and Iowa held Hanspard to a season-low 64 yards en route to a 27-0 triumph. Fry said later, "[Texas Tech coach] Spike Dykes told me after the game, 'I thought we had the best running back in the country, but I was wrong. You do.'"

> **Sedrick Shaw became just the eighth player in Big Ten history to rush for over 1,000 yards in three different seasons.**

After his college career concluded, Shaw was selected in the third round of the 1997 NFL Draft by New England. He played three seasons in the NFL and then played in the CFL for the Saskatchewan Roughriders.

Shaw has fond memories of his time at Iowa but has never been one to draw attention to himself. "Sedrick is a super human being," Coach Fry said. "He's very humble. This kid can't be less concerned about his statistics. He just wants to win."

Shaw still keeps in touch with his former Hawkeye teammates. "We probably talk about once a month," Shaw told Rob Howe of HawkeyeNation Magazine in 2008. "The guys that I played with in college – I can honestly say they're friends for life. The relationship with those guys goes far beyond just football. Football is just something we all did together, but that was just a small part of the relationship. I really value those guys as people and friends."

Accolades
- All-Big Ten (1996)
- Team MVP (1995, 96)
- Holds school career records for rushing yards, attempts, and touchdowns
- Left school ranked eighth in Big Ten history in career rushing yards and attempts

No. 5 SEDRICK SHAW

Year	Att	Yards	Avg	TDs	Long	Recept	Yards	TDs
1993	127	561	4.4	2	22	14	115	0
1994	170	1,002	5.9	7	80	7	100	1
1995	316	1,477	4.7	15	58	16	144	0
1996	224	1,116	5.0	9	50	14	79	1
Totals	837	4,156	5.0	33	80	51	438	2

How He's Remembered

"I think of Sedrick Shaw, and I remember that game versus Michigan State. Did he rush for 500 yards or did it just seem that way?"

Keith Murphy

"For all of his yardage and touchdowns, he was one of the stronger inside runners I can remember at Iowa. He was a big guy, and he ran with such authority inside the tackles. He had good speed, and he could get to the outside."

Gary Dolphin

"Sed was just tough; and that guy could run. Growing up in the Quad Cities, I knew how talented Tavian Banks was, and he couldn't unseat Shaw from the starting lineup. He wasn't going to run away from you, he wasn't going to juke you out of your shoes, but he'd sure as heck run you over. I thought he was well-deserved to be the all-time leading rusher because he would punish people and he wasn't afraid to take the rock 30 or 40 times."

Tom Kakert

Jersey #5 Honorable Mention

Andre Woolridge – Basketball (1995-97)

Andre Woolridge was a decorated three-year starter for the Hawkeyes. He began his career at Nebraska where he was named to the Big Eight all-freshman team. After transferring, the 6'0" point guard made an instant impact in Iowa City, earning team MVP and All-Big Ten honors as a sophomore, junior, and senior. His career highlights include two NCAA Tournament appearances, including a 29-point performance in his final game against Kentucky in the second round. As a senior, Woolridge became the first Big Ten player to lead the conference in both points per game (20.9) and assists per game (6.1). He also led the Big Ten in assists as a junior. His total of 575 career assists ranked first in school history and eighth in Big Ten history. Woolridge still ranks ninth at Iowa in career scoring. In 1997, he became the first Hawkeye to earn All-American honors since Ronnie Lester in 1980.

Drew Tate – Football (2003-06)

Drew Tate came to Iowa as a highly touted, record-setting quarterback from Baytown, Texas. He initially committed to Texas A&M as a high school senior before choosing Iowa. While not a prototypical running quarterback, Tate had the distinct ability to sense pressure in the pocket and evade would-be tacklers. Tate gained the starting quarterback role for Iowa's magical 2004 season, a year in which five running backs were lost to injuries. The heady sophomore led Iowa to the Big Ten championship and the 2005 Capital One Bowl. There, Tate made his most lasting memory as a Hawkeye by connecting with Warren Holloway on an improbable 56-yard touchdown pass to end the game and give Iowa a 30-25 win over LSU. In three years as Iowa's starting quarterback, Tate led the Hawkeyes to 23 wins and three bowl games. He is second only to Chuck Long in career passing yardage.

"Now they gotta call time out! They wind the clock! Nine seconds to play and Drew Tate doesn't know that! The game's gonna end on this play! He fires downfield – it's caught – AND INTO THE ENDZONE! TOUCHDOWN IOWA! TOUCHDOWN IOWA! NO TIME ON THE CLOCK! I DON'T BELIEVE WHAT I JUST SAW! TOUCHDOWN IOWA! OH MY GOD, I CAN'T BELIEVE WHAT I JUST SAW!"

Gary Dolphin's radio call to end the 2005 Capital One Bowl

#5 – Sedrick Shaw

#6: TD

"Superman wears No. 6 and he plays for the Iowa Hawkeyes!"

- Wayne Larrivee

There are fan favorites in sports, and then there are true, homegrown fan favorites. Many in this book are the former; few are the latter. Tim Dwight is one of those few.

Punters kicked away from him; opposing punt returners feared him; teammates fed off his energy; fans loved him. "I watched him play football in high school and obviously at the University of Iowa," said WHO-Radio's Mark Allen. "Whenever Dwight touched the ball, you saw the backs of 70,000 fans become straighter because you never knew what was going to happen each and every time he touched the football."

The legend of Tim Dwight began early. He ran 92 yards for a touchdown the first time he carried the ball as a freshman at Iowa City High School. "Even when he was a freshman, he had so much respect from the juniors and seniors on our football team," stated Larry Brown, former head coach of Iowa City High.

He was a three-year football starter at tailback and safety for the Little Hawks. One of his best performances came in his junior season when second-ranked City High met top-ranked Bettendorf High School in the state quarterfinals. Dwight had 185 combined yards rushing and receiving and four touchdowns, but future Hawkeye teammate Tavian Banks ran for 245 yards and three touchdowns to help Bettendorf to a 31-28 win. "They just put on the greatest show on turf," Tom Kakert recalled.

As a senior, Dwight scored a state-record 43 touchdowns, averaged 12.5 yards per carry, and led City High to that elusive state championship. In track, Dwight won 12 state titles and was twice named the outstanding high school male athlete at the Drake Relays. He was even the school's homecoming king.

> **Tim Dwight scored 80 career touchdowns for the Iowa City High Little Hawks.**

Dwight was recruited nationally coming out of high school, and he considered schools such as Stanford and Nebraska. Colleges of all sizes came to Iowa City High to talk with Coach Brown and inquire about Tim's intentions. "There was a coach from North or South Dakota who came into my office," recalled Brown. "He asked me if he could look at some film on Tim. I politely said, 'I'd be very happy to set you up with some film, but I can tell you right now Tim's going to play Division I football.'

"The visiting coach said, 'Well, that's what I've heard, but I know that he's not very big.' Well," Brown continued, "I saw him after my seventh period class and the coach said, 'He will be a Division I player.'"

In the end, Dwight's rapport with the Iowa staff kept him home. Though he wanted to play tailback, he knew that likely wouldn't be his college position. He talked openly about taking a redshirt year in 1994 to get acclimated to college football, but the competitor in him won out. "I didn't want to wait a year," Dwight said. "I mean, Hawkeye football is on the rise now, and I want to be part of that."

As a true freshman, Dwight spent time as a return specialist, reserve running back, and reserve defensive back. Although he rushed for a touchdown in the first game of the season and threw for a touchdown in the last game of the season, it almost seemed as though Coach Hayden Fry didn't know how best to utilize the multi-talented Dwight. With Sedrick Shaw and Tavian Banks sharing time at the running back position, Fry moved Dwight to wide receiver after his freshman year.

> **As a freshman, Tim Dwight once left the sideline to run water bottles out to the Iowa huddle.**

Dwight settled in at wide receiver, and he made an instant impact as a starter. In Iowa's first game in 1995, Dwight had 191 all-purpose yards and two touchdowns. He led the team with 816 receiving yards that season, the seventh-highest total in school history. His receiving and returning skills helped Iowa to an 8-4 record and a Sun Bowl victory.

Despite the accolades, Dwight avoided the media for most of his first two seasons. "I came out of high school and was highly recruited this and that," he said. "I get singled out because I'm from Iowa City, and they want me to say something. But I wanted to prove myself first. You shouldn't get rewards unless you've done something for them."

Tim Dwight started his junior season with a bang. On Iowa's first punt of the year, he sprinted down the field and obliterated Arizona's Rodney Williams. That hit set the tone for the season. Five weeks later, Iowa carried a 4-1 record into Happy Valley against tenth-ranked Penn State. Dwight returned a punt 83 yards for a touchdown, the fourth-longest punt return in school history. He also set up another touchdown with a 65-yard reception, as Iowa upset the Nittany Lions, 21-20. "He can run like a deer. He's a great return man, great on reverses, and he can beat you deep like that," Penn State coach Joe Paterno said with a snap of his fingers. "He's a little faster than anyone we've played."

The following week, Dwight returned a punt 86 yards for a touchdown against Ohio State. Four plays later, he broke several tackles and returned a punt 43 yards to set up another touchdown. "I don't know if I've ever seen a punt returned in college football the way Dwight did it. He was magnificent," Ohio State coach John Cooper said.

"Dwight's a guy I refer to as 'Mr. Excitement,'" said former Iowa announcer Ron Gonder. "I thought that he was the most exciting Iowa football player in my time. He was certainly the most outstanding kick returner of any player that I've followed or covered. I think the thing that made him so great as a kick returner was the fact that, when he took the ball either on a punt return or a kickoff return, he went into immediate action. He didn't dance around and wait for blockers. Certainly, he followed his blockers, but his primary thing was that he took the ball and did something with it right away, right now, and I thought that's what made him great. He was making his own blocks. He was that kind of a player."

Tim Dwight broke the school season record for punt return yards in 1996, set by Nile Kinnick as a sophomore in 1937. It was the oldest individual record in the school's record books. Dwight finished second in the nation in punt return average with 18.9 yards per return and was named First Team All-American. Iowa finished with a 9-3 record and a victory in the Alamo Bowl.

> **Tim Dwight's competitive nature surfaced during one of Iowa's annual spring games. The rules of the scrimmage stated that punt returners must make a fair catch on punts caught in the air, so Dwight let the ball bounce first, picked it up, and ran 70 yards for a touchdown.**

The Hawkeyes were tabbed as Rose Bowl contenders in 1997, and Dwight was a pre-season Heisman Trophy candidate in his senior season. While the team fell short of the Big Ten title, it was a record-setting season for Dwight. He returned a punt for a touchdown as time expired in the first half in a road game against eventual mythical national champion Michigan. Wolverine coach Lloyd Carr remarked, "He's a great football player. The best blocking wide receiver I've ever seen. He kills people. The great ones take pride in their blocking, and that's why Dwight's a great one."

Dwight returned a punt for a touchdown the following week against Indiana. In Iowa's next game, Purdue had consecutive punts of 11 and 22 yards, as the Boilermakers tried to keep the ball out of Dwight's hands. That was the kind of impact he had on the team. Dwight surpassed 1,000 career yards in kickoff returns, punt returns, and receiving. He led the team in receiving for the third straight season and surpassed Danan Hughes as Iowa's all-time leading receiver.

In his final home game against Minnesota, Dwight returned a punt 44 yards for a touchdown. That helped him set Big Ten records for punt return touchdowns in a season (three) and career (five) and career punt return yardage (1,102). Dwight led the nation in punt return average and led the Big Ten in that statistic for the third time. He was a consensus First Team All-American as a senior, the 14th in school history and the first ever from Iowa City.

Though some doubted whether Dwight's skills would translate to a professional career, he was a fourth-round draft choice of the Atlanta Falcons and played ten years professionally. Atlanta made their first Super Bowl in Dwight's rookie year. Despite losing to Denver in Super Bowl XXXIII, he provided Atlanta's lone highlight by returning a kickoff for a touchdown. Dwight is currently the only Hawkeye to score a touchdown in the Super Bowl.

"They always said that he was too small to play in the NFL," said Gary Dolphin, "that physically he would be unable to put up with the pounding. He has certainly suffered his share of injuries, but there aren't many guys his size who've lasted ten years in the NFL like he has."

After his rookie year with the Falcons, Dwight chose to use his remaining college eligibility and return to the Iowa track team. He led the Iowa 4x400 meter track relay team to the 1999 NCAA championship finals race. Two other Iowa football players, Bashir Yamini and Tim

Dodge, were also in the relay. Coaches and fans alike were appreciative of the attention and enthusiasm Dwight's return brought to the program.

Tim Dwight left quite a legacy at the University of Iowa. He finished seventh in the Heisman Trophy voting. He was a consensus First Team All-American. He was All-Big Ten in two sports. But his most lasting legacy seems to be the adoration Hawkeye fans had for him when he played for Iowa. It lasts to this day. "I think if I would have gone somewhere else, I probably wouldn't have gotten what I've gotten here," Dwight said. "I'm not trying to say I'm special, but I'm from Iowa City, and the fans here and from Iowa support their players."

He was special, talented, competitive, and easy to support. Most of all, Hawkeyes everywhere are fortunate that Tim Dwight was one of us.

Accolades
• Consensus First Team All-American (1997)
• Holds school records for career punt return yards, receiving touchdowns, and receiving yards
• Broke Big Ten record for career punt return touchdowns and punt return yards
• Finished seventh in the Heisman Trophy balloting (1997)
• Meet MVP of the Big Ten Outdoor Track Championships (1999)

No. 6 TIM DWIGHT

Year	Rec	Yds	Avg	Punt Returns	Return Avg	KO Returns	Return Avg	TDs
1994	-	-	-	13	12.4	14	19.9	1
1995	46	816	17.7	16	7.4	22	19.0	11
1996	51	751	14.7	24	18.3	12	18.9	9
1997	42	704	16.8	23	16.7	10	27.3	11
Totals	139	2,271	16.3	76	14.5	58	20.6	32

How He's Remembered

"One of the best all-around football players I've seen in college football, whether I've been at Iowa, Iowa State, or Wisconsin. He was a big play waiting to happen as a punt returner, kick returner, and receiver. I know he was one of Coach Fry's all-time favorites. His explosiveness as a player...I mean, he was a guy that could take any play to the house. That gets tossed around frequently sometimes about players, but Tim Dwight was the leader of that pack."
Dan McCarney

"He was a great competitor. He had a great work ethic and a great personality. He had the whole package. Tim was a very special athlete, that's for sure. I feel very fortunate that I had an opportunity to coach him."
Larry Brown

"Tim Dwight was your consummate 'Mr. Everything.' I don't know if there's a sport out there that he couldn't have played. I think football happened to be his overall best sport, but I think he'd have been a great soccer player, and he'd have been a tremendous wrestler. His toughness set him apart from a lot of competitors. He was a rare combination of speed, power, and instinct."

Gary Dolphin

"Tim Dwight was, other than maybe Tavian Banks, the most exciting football player at Iowa I've ever witnessed during my time. He was, without question, the best competitor. I know Hayden Fry has said that Tim Dwight is the best competitor he had in over four decades of coaching. Dwight was just a rare breed. A lot of guys are born with speed, but he was the total package other than his lack of height. He had speed, power, finesse, but I think it was his courage and his toughness that really separated him."

Pat Harty

"Maybe my favorite Hawkeye. I don't have mancrush or anything, but I think Tim approaches life the way we all should – he has fun! I remember the first time I interviewed him at the Drake Relays. I couldn't believe how small he was – 5'8" is generous – but man, could he run. I think he's the only guy I've ever seen who seemed faster in a football uniform than without one. When he touched the ball at Iowa, everybody leaned forward and waited for a jolt of electricity. Like many people, I thought he should have had the ball in his hands a lot more, but he made the most of his opportunities. I still interview Tim at least once a year, and he never disappoints. The guy loves life and lives it up every day."

Keith Murphy

Jersey #6 Honorable Mention

Leland Parkin – Football (1922-24)

Leland Parkin was a football and track star at Waterloo East High School. He succeeded Aubrey Devine at quarterback for the Hawkeyes in 1922 and scored Iowa's only touchdown in an upset victory over Yale that season. While the Hawks won the Big Ten title in 1922, injuries limited Parkin's effectiveness for much of his first two seasons. However, he had an excellent senior season in which he was Iowa's 1924 team MVP and the All-Big Ten quarterback. Parkin led Iowa to a 6-1-1 record that year under new coach Burt Ingwersen. He had a 163-yard rushing performance against Minnesota in 1924, and he followed that up weeks later with a 170-yard performance, including a 63-yard run, against Wisconsin. Parkin was a Third Team All-American as a senior. Walter Eckersall of *The Chicago Tribune* called Parkin "a natural leader and an excellent field general. He knows the game thoroughly, catches punts well and is dependable as a safety man."

Ben Stephens – Basketball (1937-39)

Ben Stephens was a superstar forward for Coach Rollie Williams' basketball squad from 1937-1939. Stephens scored 168 points as a sophomore, one of the highest season totals in school history. In his junior season, he scored 23 points against Indiana on January 9, 1938, to set the school record for points in a game. Stephens finished the year with 185 points, which set the single-season record at Iowa and earned him a Second Team All-Big Ten nod. Despite missing several games due to illness as a senior, Ben Stephens became the first Hawkeye to top 200 points in a season, notching 215 points and earning a First Team All-Big Ten selection. He then played three seasons in the National Basketball League, a forerunner to the NBA. Stephens finished in the top six in scoring in the league all three seasons, leading the NBL in scoring in 1941. He was a two-time First Team All-League pick before ending his athletic career to serve in the U.S. Navy during World War II.

#7: SHOTS HEARD 'ROUND THE STADIUM

"Roby was 'Mr. Thunder.' There is no kicker certainly in my time that could make the football thunder like he did. From high in the press box when Reggie kicked there was a large audible sound. It was much louder than any other player who ever kicked the ball."

- Ron Gonder

The man who has been described as "Mr. Thunder," whose legendary punting exploits thrilled Hawkeye fans, almost had his football career derailed by his other passion – baseball. While still in high school, Reggie Roby was drafted by the Cincinnati Reds organization as a pitching prospect. Thankfully for Iowa fans, Reggie's older brother, Mike, who played a couple of seasons in the minor leagues, convinced him that he should pursue college instead. Reggie took his brother's advice, and Coach Hayden Fry and the Hawkeye faithful were in for a treat.

Reginald Henry Roby, a native of Waterloo, Iowa, graduated from Waterloo East High School in 1979. During his four years at East High, he was a three-sport standout in baseball, football, and basketball. Roby was an All-State selection in the first two sports, respectively, and a three-year letterman in basketball. He was a versatile player on the football field, playing linebacker, tight end, place-kicker, and punter for the Trojans.

> **As a child, Reggie Roby would practice by kicking soccer balls back and forth over his house.**

It was as a punter that Roby truly excelled. He had to kick toward the south end of his high school field because school buildings were adjacent to the field on the north end. "When he kicked at the [north end], the footballs ended up on the roof of the school," his high school coach, Roger Kittleson, recalled. "By the end of warm-ups, we'd be out of footballs. We lost a lot of balls when he was kicking."

Hayden Fry was hired by the University of Iowa after the 1978 season. As a new coach in the area, he needed to put his stamp on in-state recruiting. "Recruiting is difficult for a staff in its first year, especially when taking over a program that hasn't been winning," Fry noted. "We needed a punter badly, and we wanted to make a statement that we could land a top in-state recruit, so we really went after Reggie." Roby was recruited by Dan McCarney, one of Fry's assistants at the time. "It was between Iowa and Wisconsin," McCarney said. "We were sitting on pins and needles."

Roby waited to announce his college choice on signing day. Fry took no chances. "The night before the signing date, we took our whole coaching staff to Waterloo to show Roby how much we wanted him," Fry said. Just before midnight, Roby called McCarney and told him that he had some bad news. "My heart went up to my throat," McCarney recalled. Then Roby said that he was going to be a Hawkeye, and the coaches had a wild celebration. "That was about as high as I ever saw Coach Fry's boots get off the ground – when I told him we got Reggie," McCarney said.

"I was never so happy to sign a punter," Fry said. "Getting Reggie helped us convince Iowa kids that playing for the Hawkeyes was the thing to do. And he helped give us one of the best kicking games in college football for the next four years." Roby said that the visit helped sway him toward the Hawkeyes. "They said he was coming, and I didn't really believe it," Roby recalled. "When Fry walked into my house, I felt like I must be the most important guy in the world. I thought, 'I've got to do this. I've got to follow this guy.'"

Early in his career, Roby handled more than just the punting duties; he also handled kickoffs and some field goals. As a high school senior at Waterloo East, he had kicked four field goals of 35 yards or more, including a 51-yard field goal against Waterloo West. However, Roby soon developed into the nation's top punter, and Fry had Roby focused solely on that.

"Hayden wanted to establish the kicking game, and he had a great weapon in Roby," said longtime Iowa announcer Bob Brooks. "In fact, Reggie could have played other positions in football very easily, but Hayden wasn't gonna trust that leg to any injury."

> **Twenty-six of Reggie Roby's kickoffs at Iowa went through the uprights.**

Reggie Roby spent much of his career chasing the perfect punt. The closest he came was during a practice at Iowa. Roby reminisced, "It was 95 degrees and no wind. The ball was on the goal line, and I was standing at the back of the end zone. The ball landed at the other 20, rolled through the end zone and bounced into the stands." The coaches were astonished at the sight of a 130-yard punt and asked him to try it again, but his next punt "only" went 40 yards. "After that [130-yard] punt, I realized I could do it. I want to do it every time. Until I do, I won't be satisfied," Roby said.

Roby's signature game came in Iowa's opening game of the 1981 season. The Nebraska Cornhuskers were ranked No. 6 in the country and had beaten Iowa 57-0 in Lincoln the previous year. In 1981, however, Iowa pulled a dramatic 10-7 upset using the same formula that they would rely on throughout their magical Rose Bowl season. The offense was opportunistic, coming out in an unexpected formation and scoring ten quick points. The defense was tremendous, yielding only 234 total yards to the Cornhuskers. Finally, Reggie Roby was nothing short of spectacular. He averaged 55.8 yards per punt on five punts against Nebraska, setting a school record and leaving the 'Huskers with miserable field position all game long.

Roby was a consensus First Team All-American in 1981, breaking a 32-year-old NCAA record by averaging 49.8 yards per punt. It remains the NCAA record for punting average in a season with a minimum of 40 punts. The Hawkeyes broke a 20-year drought without a winning season and shot into the Rose Bowl. McCarney summed up the season by saying, "Our 1981 team went to the Rose Bowl with a fantastic defense, an okay offense, and the best punter in college football."

Reggie set a Rose Bowl record with a 51-yard average on four punts. He led the nation in punting again as a senior with an average of 48.1 yards per punt, which ranks sixth in NCAA history for punting average in a season with a minimum of 40 punts. He was named a First Team All-American in 1982 for the second straight time. Roby is one of only three players in NCAA history to lead the nation in punting in consecutive seasons. Roby's career average of 45.6 yards per punt is second in NCAA history for a minimum of 150 punts.

Roby continued his legacy for high, booming punts into the NFL. He was drafted in the sixth round of the 1983 NFL Draft by the Miami Dolphins, and he played in Miami for ten of his 16 NFL seasons. "Often on walkthroughs in domed stadiums the day before the game, he always would try to hit the top of the dome with a punt," Hall of Fame Dolphins coach Don Shula recalled. In one pre-season game, Roby hit the roof of the Metrodome, which was 186 feet high. He also hit the scoreboard that hung from the roof of the Superdome in New Orleans three times before a game. The scoreboard was about 200 feet above the field. "Reggie helped define the position, and even after he retired, every time I saw a long, high punt, it always reminded me of his kicks," Shula said.

Roby was well-known for wearing a wristwatch and also popularized the two-step punting approach, which allowed him to get his punts away more quickly. "He really could turn around a field," former Dolphins teammate Kim Bokamper remarked. "It's a testament to the type of player he was how long he lasted in the league. He was really at the cusp of the new era of punters."

During Roby's long career, he made the Pro Bowl three times, and he still holds the Pro Bowl record with 10 punts in the 1985 game. As a member of the Dolphins, he played in Super Bowl XIX against San Francisco. In ten of his 16 seasons, he ranked in the top ten in punting average in the NFL. In addition, he was just the third African-American punter in the history of the NFL.

Roby had other skills as well. He displayed his cooking talents by opening Reggie Roby's All-Pro Cookies in 1995, and he ran his business until his bakery was destroyed by fire a few years later. Roby then transitioned into working as the marketing and development director for Backfield in Motion, a non-profit group designed to help inner-city boys.

His fans were stunned in 2005 when Reggie Roby passed away of an apparent heart attack at the age of only 43. Several former Hawkeye players and teammates have established a memorial fund in his name, and the proceeds are earmarked for several projects in his hometown of Waterloo. In addition, during the fall of 2006, Waterloo East High School named their football practice field in the memory of Roby. Roby was inducted into the Iowa High School Football Hall of Fame in 2009.

Reggie Roby will always be remembered fondly by Hawkeye fans as a key member of the 1981 Rose Bowl team. He was quite possibly the greatest punter who ever lived. For Roby, he made a living doing what came naturally to him, all the way back to when he was kicking those soccer balls over his family home as a boy. "Punting is my hobby," Roby said. "A lot of people don't make their profession a hobby, but I do. I just love to kick."

Iowa fans were lucky enough to be able to watch him do it.

Accolades

- Consensus First Team All-American (1981)
- Led nation in punting average (1981, 82)
- Broke NCAA records for punting average in a season and career
- Selected to the all-time University of Iowa football team (1989)
- Played 16 seasons in the NFL; First Team All-Pro (1984, 94)

No. 7 REGGIE ROBY					
Year	Punts	Avg	Long	FG	PATs
1979	35	42.6	61	5-11	22-25
1980	41	40.6	69	6-15	6-9
1981	48	49.9	68	0-0	0-0
1982	56	47.2	66	0-1	0-0
Totals	180	45.4	69	11-27	28-34

How He's Remembered

"Reggie Roby was the greatest punter I ever saw – period – at any level. I never saw a guy who could kick the ball ten stories high. It wasn't so much the length with Reggie down the field, although there wasn't anybody better, but what made him stand out was his hang time. He could kick the ball as high as he could far. He had just an unbelievable right leg. People forget Reggie Roby was the first big signee for Hayden Fry. He was the guy that really got it started for Hayden back in the late '70s. When he committed out of Waterloo East, that really started the crescendo or the funnel of Iowa high school stars to Iowa."

Gary Dolphin

"A guy I knew very well and considered a friend. He was just the type of person who lit up a room when he entered it, and that's tough for a punter to do. He had charisma, and he cared about the community as well. He was taken too early and leaves quite a legacy behind for his children."

Steve Deace

"I didn't know Reggie when he played, but he joined us on Sound-Off one night to promote his cookies. He was so nice. I remember watching Roby play, and he could change a game with his punting. You remember those booming punts that seemed to hang in the air forever. Roby would never leave the ground but his right leg would be about a foot over his head, and he always wore that watch."

Keith Murphy

"He was the best punter in the history of college football. I remember people coming to pre-game warm-ups just to watch Reggie. They weren't there to watch my defensive line or Kirk Ferentz's offensive line; they were there to watch Reggie Roby warm up. Punters would hit the ball, and there was a little bit of a thud. Then Reggie would hit it, and there was an explosion. That was the difference. He's in a class by himself. God had other plans for Reggie. But loyalties ran deep. He came over and worked my camp at Iowa State three or four different summers because of the loyalty we had through all those years. He was phenomenal. I think he and Ray Guy are the best punters in the history of college and the NFL."

Dan McCarney

Jersey #7 Honorable Mention

Dick Ives – Basketball (1944-47)

Dick Ives came to Iowa without a scholarship from Diagonal, Iowa, but he was soon awarded one his freshman year. He became the first freshman in Big Ten history to lead the conference in scoring, and he set an Iowa freshman record with 18.2 points per game that still stands today. He set a Big Ten record by scoring 43 points against the University of Chicago in 1944; it remains the third-highest scoring performance in school history. Ives then led Iowa to a Big Ten championship as a sophomore in 1945. He and teammate Herb Wilkinson were the first players in Iowa history to be named First Team All-American in 1945. Ives was also a Third Team All-American in 1944 and 1946. He led Iowa in scoring his first three seasons, and he was named to Iowa's All-Century Team in 2002.

Rob Houghtlin – Football (1985-87)

Rob Houghtlin will forever be known as the man who made "The Kick." In 1985, his 29-yard field goal as time expired beat Michigan in a battle of No. 1 versus No. 2. This former walk-on scored 290 points during his prolific career. He connected on over 63 percent of his attempted field goals and 95 percent of his PAT attempts. He kicked many memorable field goals for the Hawkeyes including a game-winning kick against Minnesota in 1986 and also one against San Diego State in the 1986 Holiday Bowl. Houghtlin finished eighth in the nation in scoring in 1985 and ranks second in career scoring at Iowa.

Brad Banks – Football (2001-02)

Brad Banks came to Iowa as a junior college transfer from the state of Florida. As a senior in 2002, he quarterbacked the first Hawkeye team to win 11 games in a single season. Individually, he had one of the most decorated seasons an Iowa player has ever had. He was the 2002 Heisman Trophy runner-up, Walter Camp First Team All-American, AP Player of the Year, and Big Ten MVP and Player of the Year. During the 2002 season, Banks threw for 25 touchdowns and led the nation in passing efficiency. He was a threat both running and passing the ball, and he totaled 2,996 total yards of offense. That ranks as the third-highest total in Iowa history. His memorable moments from the 2002 season include a key fourth-quarter run and touchdown pass against Purdue and a ten-for-ten passing day against Northwestern.

#8: A FAMILY AFFAIR

"The Hartlieb brothers really were a special lot coming here from Marion Central Catholic. Chuck got Iowa out of many, many a jam in third and long. He and Chuck Long were a lot alike, but sometimes it's tough following the great one. Hartlieb had to do that, and he did it with authority. I would dare anybody to find a guy who followed the numbers of Chuck Long and performed as well as Chuck Hartlieb. There aren't many of them out there."

- Gary Dolphin

Iowa football has proven at times to be a family affair. Six Hilgenbergs earned twenty letters over a span of four decades. The Haight brothers were mainstays on each side of the ball. A trio of defensive backs named Stoops patrolled Hayden Fry's defensive secondary. Another set of three brothers hailed from Woodstock, Illinois. Leading that trio was Iowa's record-setting quarterback of the late 1980s, Chuck Hartlieb.

A self-described late-bloomer, Hartlieb attended a small, Catholic high school of about 400 students. Going into his senior year, the two-way starter struggled to attract attention from larger college programs. Upon leading his team to the 1983 state championship his final year, things changed.

"I probably ended up with 15 scholarship offers," Hartlieb explained. "My four visits were Indiana, Wisconsin, Duke, and Iowa. I felt they were all great academic schools, but Iowa was clearly the better football program at the time and they threw the ball well. So I committed in late December and obviously never regretted my choice.

"I was a good example of a kid you never wanted to give up on because I had a very average junior year. I kind of came into my own my senior year and caught some attention. It was [typical] of a consistent style of recruiting at Iowa. They don't necessarily always go for the flash and the glitz. They just look for players, and I think I kind of fit that mold for them," said Hartlieb.

> **Brothers Chuck, Jim, and John Hartlieb all lettered for Iowa. A fourth brother, Andy, lettered at Wisconsin.**

Hartlieb did not letter as a freshman in 1985, and with the Chuck Long era ending after that season, Mark Vlasic and Tom Poholsky earned the starting role throughout 1986. Hartlieb first saw game action that year against Iowa State. Going five for six in a back-up role, he came off the field finally convinced he could play at the college level.

In 1987, the starting quarterback position was very much up for grabs with Dan McGwire, Tom Poholsky, and Hartlieb all vying for the role. McGwire earned the starting nod versus

Tennessee in the Kickoff Classic. All three quarterbacks saw action in the 23-22 loss to the Volunteers. Poholsky started the second game against Arizona. Hartlieb then started the annual intrastate battle in Ames. He won the starting role for good a few weeks later in a win against Wisconsin. That day was also notable for another reason.

"In 1987, we played Wisconsin with all kinds of family there, and my brother Andy was on the other side of the ball facing me as a linebacker," Hartlieb recalled. "I've always felt that was a really unique, special experience. Not many situations occurred in Big Ten football where you have your brother on the other side of the ball. To win that game and go up against him was a great experience."

After a 37-10 loss to Michigan, the 4-3 Hawkeyes finally found their stride and won their next six games. This included an offensive clinic at Northwestern. Hartlieb threw for a Big Ten-record seven touchdown passes (by the end of the third quarter) and finished with 471 yards. Quinn Early hauled in ten catches for 256 yards and four touchdowns, including a 95-yard touchdown reception.

"I thought that would have been broken by now, but I'm still holding on to that one," Hartlieb said about the record-setting day. "Drew Brees had a couple games that were six [touchdowns] and there was still some time left in the fourth quarter. I thought he was going to do it, but he never quite got there. It'll certainly get broken some day but not yet."

> **Chuck Hartlieb still owns nine school records at Iowa.**

Late in the 1987 season, the Hawkeyes faced a November showdown at Ohio State. Just two years earlier, the Buckeyes knocked Iowa from an undefeated record and college football's No. 1 ranking. Hayden Fry had yet to win in Columbus. In fact, Iowa had not won there since 1959.

Earle Bruce's Buckeyes would trade leads with the Hawkeyes six times that afternoon. With 2:45 left in the fourth quarter, Ohio State again went ahead 27-22. Hartlieb now had to lead the charge against a Buckeye defense that featured All-Americans Chris Spielman and Eric Kumerow.

After key passes to Mike Flagg and Marv Cook, Iowa was in a fourth down and 23 situation with only 16 seconds remaining. Evading a strong rush, Hartlieb threw a pass to Marv Cook for a game-winning, 28-yard touchdown. To Hawkeye coaches, fans, and players, it remains one of Hartlieb's most memorable moments.

Hartlieb said that the play to Cook was called "Lion 75 Wide Trail." "It was called in a timeout. Coach Fry asked me what I had the most confidence in. I really felt I wanted to get it to our best playmaker, and that was Marv," Hartlieb said. "Even though we had Quinn, Marv was such a big target and knew how to get open. I was thinking if we could just get the ball to him about 20 yards downfield, then hopefully he could get the first down. It turned out a lot better than that."

With plenty of momentum going into Hartlieb's senior season of 1988, expectations were high. Iowa had won ten games in 1987, culminating in an exciting victory over Wyoming in the Holiday Bowl. Hartlieb ranked third in the nation in passing as a junior. The Hawks were generally seen as a top ten team in pre-season polls in 1988. Two publications even had them picked as the No. 1 team in the nation.

However, the Hawks never found their stride and ended with an unusual 6-4-3 record. It was a season of ups and downs, with no consecutive wins nor consecutive defeats. At one point, after a 17-17 tie with Michigan, Hayden Fry said, "This is the longest season I've ever put in as a coach."

There were high points, such as Hartlieb's 558 passing yards in a loss to Indiana, which set a single-game school record. There were low points, such as a season-ending loss to North Carolina State in the Peach Bowl. Chuck Hartlieb had undergone arthroscopic knee surgery immediately after the regular season ended, yet he was able to play in the Peach Bowl. He threw for 428 yards, a Peach Bowl record, in his final game as a Hawkeye.

Despite the up-and-down season, Hartlieb finished his senior year second only to Chuck Long in career passing yards. He was the first Iowa quarterback to pass for over 3,000 yards in two separate seasons. For the fifth time in six seasons, Iowa's quarterback was the All-Big Ten selection. He passed the Iowa quarterback duties down to Matt Rodgers as well as Chuck's younger brother, Jim Hartlieb.

Today, Chuck still resides in the Hawkeye State, working as a wealth manager for a Des Moines financial company. Outside of work, he spends time with his wife and four children. Hartlieb still follows his alma mater quite closely each fall.

To Chuck Hartlieb, wearing the black and gold as an Iowa Hawkeye is something special. To play in Kinnick Stadium and win multiple letters is something to be proud of. To share that distinction with your brothers is something to cherish.

Accolades
• Honorable Mention All-American (1987, 88)
• All-Big Ten (1987, 88)
• Left school ranked second in school history in career passing yards
• Holds school records for passing yards, completions, and attempts in a game and season

No. 8 CHUCK HARTLIEB							
Year	Att	Comp	Pct	Yds	Int	TDs	Long
1985	Did not play						
1986	8	7	.875	104	0	1	42
1987	334	217	.650	3092	8	19	95
1988	460	288	.626	**3738**	13	17	59
Totals	802	512	.638	6934	21	37	95

How He's Remembered

"Hartlieb was a great passer. Most fans remember Chuck Long as being the all-time great. Well, Hartlieb came right after him and was just as good. He was deadly accurate, and he threw seven touchdown passes in one game against Northwestern. He was very good, and a real nice guy, too. He was an exceptional quarterback. Boy, Iowa was lucky in those years. Iowa had the All-Big Ten quarterback five out of those six years."

Buck Turnbull

"Chuck is a great guy, and I'm glad he's not in TV because with his knowledge, looks, and charisma, I could be out of a job."

Keith Murphy

"Chuck was almost a coach on the field. If a play wasn't there, he could almost always come up with one. And of course, his great play at Ohio State to his tight end was the one people will always remember. Chuck was a handsome kid, but he was a total gentleman. In an interview, he would say, 'Yes, sir,' or 'No, sir.' And he never called me Frosty; he'd call me Mr. Mitchell."

Frosty Mitchell

"I think Chuck Hartlieb never really got his due for how good a college quarterback he was because he immediately followed Chuck Long. But Hartlieb had some tremendous games while he was a starter."

Mike Hlas

"Chuck is always extremely accurate in a game. He has the unique ability to find a way to get points on the board. He's not as impressive from technique – he's a semi-sidearm passer, but he gets the results…He's got all the leadership qualities you look for in a quarterback."

Hayden Fry

Jersey #8 Honorable Mention

Leroy Smith – Football (1988-91)

Undersized at only 6'2" and 214 pounds, Leroy Smith had perhaps the most dominating senior season a Hawkeye defensive end has ever had. His season-ending statistics in 1991 included 18 sacks (a Big Ten and Iowa record) and 22 tackles for loss. Most notably, he had five sacks in a single game at Ohio State, a game the Hawkeyes won, 16-9. Originally from Sicklerville, New Jersey, Smith came to Iowa as a running back. He ended his Iowa career as a consensus First Team All-American defensive end and helped lead Iowa to a 10-1-1 record in 1991. He was also named the Big Ten Defensive Player of the Year as a senior.

"I was gone for Leroy's junior and senior year but was there when Bernie Wyatt recruited him. He was a guy we knew was going to be a really good football player. It was just a matter of where. We didn't know what position he'd play. I think he was a running back when Bernie recruited him. He was going to be a dominant, impact player someday. One of the nicest kids off the field, one of the most tenacious players on the field."

Dan McCarney

#9: GLEN ELLYN GREATNESS

"Obviously, any time you're perceived as a leader, you have to be able to handle adversity. You have to."

- Matt Bowen

Right place, wrong time. Sometimes a great player, through forces beyond his control, is a leader on a very bad team. Though the late 1990s weren't the best of times for the Hawkeye football program, Matt Bowen established himself as one of the toughest, hardest hitters the program had ever seen.

Bowen, who hails from Glen Ellyn, Illinois, committed to Iowa partly out of a fondness for assistant coach Bob Elliott. "He used to tell me that he could get me a date whenever I wanted," Bowen laughed. "He came to school one day at my high school in suburban Chicago. I said, 'You're going to ask this girl to the prom for me.' You should have seen his face! But I gave him some flowers and he did it…He came through on his word!"

Bowen broke onto the scene as a sophomore in 1997 against Indiana, when he intercepted a second-half pass and returned it 70 yards for a touchdown. It is the seventh-longest such scoring play in modern school history. He became a full-time starter as a junior, but as Bowen's game rapidly improved, the team's fortunes rapidly deteriorated. He led the Hawkeyes with 92 tackles in 1998, and the following year, he became the 46th Hawkeye in history to record 200 career tackles. But the Hawks went just 4-18 in Bowen's last two seasons.

Matt Bowen did what he could to help the Hawks win. In Iowa's only victory in 1999, Northern Illinois trailed just 10-0 with less than ten minutes to play. The Huskies attempted a chip shot field goal, but Bowen blocked the kick, and LeVar Woods ran the ball 87 yards the other way for the game-clinching touchdown. After the game, Bowen gave Coach Kirk Ferentz the game ball to commemorate his first win as Iowa's head coach.

> "It was a real special moment for me personally, to be able to hand him that football and be a leader of that team and say, 'You know, Coach, we're behind you and this game ball's for you and we're glad you're here,'" Matt Bowen said.

After graduation, he had 15 tackles in a playoff game for the Green Bay Packers against Atlanta in 2002, and he signed with Washington that off-season. In 2003, Bowen started all 16 games for the Redskins and had 94 tackles with three interceptions, two forced fumbles, and two fumble recoveries. He appeared to be well on his way to a long pro career as a starting safety. But the following season, Bowen tore his ACL, and soon knee and leg injuries would force him to retire from football.

In 2008, Bowen was invited by Ferentz to serve as the team's honorary captain for their game against second-ranked Penn State. Bowen talked to the team about his experiences dealing with adversity – not so much about his team's college record or his NFL injuries, but mostly about his son, Matthew, who was born with Down's syndrome. When he received his son's diagnosis, Bowen drew strength from Hawkeye defensive coordinator Norm Parker, whose son, Jeff, also had the condition. "You'll always need your teammates, in your thirties and in your forties and in your fifties," Bowen advised. "And you're going to need them Saturday against Penn State."

When he played, his Hawkeye teams struggled to win, but as an honorary captain, Bowen's record is spotless. As the Hawks shocked Penn State with a last second field goal to win, 24-23, Matt Bowen could enjoy the success of the program he helped rebuild. "It was one of the greatest football games I've ever seen in my life. Fans are rushing the field. It was just cool to be a part of it," Bowen said.

For a tough player who had persevered through some tough situations, it finally all came together. Right place, right time.

Accolades
- Team captain and MVP (1999)
- Recorded 222 career tackles
- Led team in tackles (1998, 99)
- Played seven seasons in the NFL

No. 9 MATT BOWEN							
Year	Solo	Asst	Total	PBU	Int-Yds	TD	Forced
1996	1	2	3	0	0-0	0	0
1997	11	7	18	2	2-126	1	0
1998	54	38	92	2	2-0	0	1
1999	76	33	109	5	1-0	0	0
Totals	142	80	222	9	5-126	1	1

How He's Remembered

"Matt Bowen is another favorite of mine because he was a guy that really was not expected to be the player that he was. He's a guy that overcame a lot of adversity. He wasn't heavily recruited but is a guy that has gone on now to play outstanding in the NFL also because of his toughness. Toughness will overcome a lot of things. With Matt Bowen, he is certainly in that category."

Gary Dolphin

"I felt Matt Bowen wasn't fully appreciated because the teams he played for weren't very good. He certainly in the NFL has had a long career and showed what he's made of. It's a shame he didn't have a chance to showcase his skills better in college."

Mike Hlas

"To say the least, Matt Bowen has been a versatile player at Iowa. He was recruited as a quarterback, [but] now plays strong safety...[He's] gaining a reputation as one of the team's most ferocious hitters. This season, he's considered the heart and soul of the defense."

Greg Smith, *Associated Press*

"Strong safety Matt Bowen likes to hit anything that moves in practice."

Don Banks, *Sports Illustrated*

"I still love being a Hawkeye. It's the best decision, outside of marrying my wife, that I ever made in my life. It really is."

Matt Bowen

Jersey #9 Honorable Mention

Ben Selzer – Basketball (1932-34)

Ben Selzer, who hailed from Passaic, New Jersey, came to the Hawkeyes to play guard for Coach Rollie Williams' basketball team. Selzer had academic issues that limited his playing time as a sophomore in 1932, but he became a star in his junior season. He was named First Team All-Big Ten in 1933, Iowa's first All-Big Ten selection in six seasons. As a senior in 1934, he helped lead Iowa to a 13-6 record and was named Second Team All-Big Ten. He was also selected as a Second Team All-American, becoming the first Hawkeye basketball player to earn All-American honors. In 2002, the University of Iowa named him as one of 20 players on their All-Century Team.

Maurice Brown – Football (2002-03)

Maurice "Mo" Brown played high school football in Fort Lauderdale, Florida, and he helped lead his team to a state championship his junior season. He came to Iowa in 2000 and struggled early. Brown saw limited action as a freshman and was suspended for most of his sophomore season. But he worked his way back onto the team as a junior in 2002, and he made the most of his opportunity. Brown led the Hawkeyes that season in receptions, yards, touchdown catches, and yards per catch. His 966 yards receiving that year ranks fourth all-time, and his touchdown catch in the 2003 Orange Bowl set the school record for touchdown receptions in a season. He suffered an ankle injury as a senior in 2003 and missed five games, but he still led the team in receiving, finishing his career with 96 yards and a touchdown catch in the 2004 Outback Bowl.

#10: THE FOUNTAIN OF YOUTH

"Does this guy ever age? Seriously. He looked 14 when he played at Iowa and finally looks 22 now. I'll have whatever he's having."

- Keith Murphy

For many Iowa fans, it was that infectious smile. For others, it was his quiet yet steadfast leadership. For all, he made them proud to be Hawkeye fans. For those and many other reasons, B.J. Armstrong stands atop the list at jersey No. 10.

"B.J. was one of the first really outstanding recruits George Raveling had, and he made himself into a talented point guard," said Iowa announcer Mac McCausland. "As you could see, he was really a terrific shooting guard, which proved to be true in the NBA. Although he was only about 6'2", he went on and became an outstanding shooter in the NBA. But at the college level, he made himself into an awfully good point guard."

Armstrong was a big part of Coach George Raveling's best recruiting class at Iowa, which also included Ed Horton, Roy Marble, Kevin Gamble, and Les Jepsen. B.J. was an All-State player out of Detroit, Michigan, but when he arrived in Iowa City, he had much to prove. The skinny 175-pound point guard played in 29 games as a freshman, averaging 2.9 points per game. While he had a few promising performances, his freshman year was a work in progress overall as he learned the point guard position. Quietly, some Iowa fans wondered if he could live up to the others in his class. Coach Raveling himself was rumored to question his recruitment of Armstrong.

> **B.J. Armstrong once scored 51 points in a high school game and made 26 of 27 free throws in another.**

However, Raveling left Iowa City in 1986 for USC, and Dr. Tom Davis became Iowa's new head basketball coach. "When Coach Davis came in 1986, he put everybody at the same level going into the training camp for the China trip," said teammate Les Jepsen. "I think it was in late July when we started training to go to China. On day one, I think he basically put the five guys that worked the hardest that summer in the starting five. Basically, he said, 'Look, here's the deal. We're all starting from square one, and you have to prove you belong in the top eight.' He was a real big advocate of the top eight players."

"I think it really helped B.J. to know this wasn't the same level [as high school]," continued Jepsen. "You have to beat out Michael Reaves, Michael Morgan, Bill Jones, and Jeff Moe. [Coach Davis] was considering everybody for point guard. It did help B.J. because he worked his butt off that summer through the fall. I mean, it was ridiculous how hard he worked. He would get up in the morning and work on his shot. He'd get to practice early to work on his shot. He would practice hard, and then after practice he would work on his shot as well. He made himself the player he was by his work ethic."

As one of Armstrong's closest friends, Jepsen could certainly attest to Armstrong's work ethic. "One of [B.J.'s] best friends on the team was Les Jepsen, and that was kind of the odd couple," Tom Kakert recalled. "A 7'0" guy from Bowbells [North Dakota] and a kid from Detroit who's a point guard. They were great friends, hung out together; and kind of Felix and Oscar if you will – the odd couple. Their personalities were really similar."

The departure of Andre Banks in 1986 opened a starting role in the Hawkeye backcourt. A number of players were vying with Armstrong for the starting point guard spot. "Point guard is where the action starts in Davis' system and the potential starters are B.J. Armstrong and Michael Reaves," wrote *Iowa City Press-Citizen* columnist Al Grady. "Armstrong, an exciting sophomore, would seem the heir apparent, but Davis promises to give both Armstrong and Reaves, a junior, equal opportunity. Armstrong might be a more skillful passer and a better shooter, but Reaves probably is better defensively. Davis says it's 'nice' if a point guard can contribute some points, but not essential."

An early-season knee injury to Reaves cleared the way for Armstrong, and he made the best of it. The Hawkeyes participated in the Great Alaska Shootout in 1986 and were paired up with No. 17 N.C. State in the semifinals. With one second left in regulation and the Hawks trailing by two points, Armstrong was fouled on a drive to the basket. B.J. calmly sank both free throws and sent the game to overtime. Iowa eventually defeated N.C. State in overtime, 90-89, behind Armstrong's team-leading 26 points.

"If not for an injury to Michael Reaves before the Great Alaskan Shootout, B.J. might not have been the starter," Kakert said. "They go up to the Shootout, and B.J. played tremendously well. He hit some clutch free throws against N.C. State. That was B.J., really – that was the hard work he had put in. Michael Reaves gets hurt, and B.J. Armstrong basically makes him look like Wally Pipp because he never came out of the lineup after that."

Armstrong's sophomore year was special for the Hawkeyes, and he played a large role averaging over 12 points per game. Dr. Tom Davis' inaugural squad won their first 18 games and rose to No. 1 in the nation before a home loss to Ohio State. After a nineteen-point, first-half lead evaporated against UNLV, Iowa ended the season four points away from the Final Four.

While neither his junior nor senior season could duplicate the success of the 1986-87 team, the Hawkeyes did make the NCAA Tournament both years. B.J. was a Second Team All-Big Ten selection in 1988, and Iowa finished tied for third in the Big Ten. Armstrong scored a career-high 35 points in an opening-round, NCAA Tournament win over Florida State, and then the Hawkeyes avenged their loss to UNLV the previous season by defeating the Runnin' Rebels for a spot in the 1988 Sweet Sixteen. However, a 99-79 loss to Arizona ended their season.

As a senior, Armstrong was again a Second Team All-Big Ten choice and led the Hawkeyes to their fifth consecutive NCAA Tournament appearance. Armstrong averaged 18.6 points and 5.4 assists per game. He climbed to first on the career assists chart, and his career-high of 35 points against Rutgers in the NCAA Tournament placed him third on Iowa's career scoring list. The 35-point performance was his final win at Iowa.

> **B.J. Armstrong recorded an Iowa-record 15 assists versus Minnesota in February 1989.**

When his collegiate days ended, Armstrong set his sights on a professional career. Three Hawkeye seniors were selected in the 1989 draft; Marble went to Atlanta, Horton to Washington, and Armstrong to the Chicago Bulls. B.J. had developed from a seldom-used freshman to a first-round draft choice in four years.

"I remember B.J. developed a really good strong relationship with the Iowa athletic trainer John Streif," said Tom Kakert. "Streif got him ready for the NBA Draft. He just kind of put a whole program together and got him a first-round draft pick because of the hard work he put in. Then watching him play on those great Bulls teams was fun."

Armstrong's hard work had paid off with some good fortune. The Bulls were the up and coming team of the NBA. Led by Michael Jordan and Scottie Pippen, they began a decade of dominance by winning their first NBA title in 1991. B.J. moved into the starting lineup in 1993 when Chicago won their third straight championship. In 1994, Armstrong was voted to start the All-Star game in Minneapolis. He is the only Hawkeye letterwinner to start an NBA All-Star game. B.J. played six years for Chicago and concluded his professional career after 11 seasons.

Armstrong returned to Chicago and spent five years in the front office as assistant general manager. He followed that experience with a brief stint as an ESPN analyst. He currently works as a sports agent and is also active in charity work.

In 1992, Iowa honored Armstrong by retiring his No. 10 jersey. He was placed on Iowa's All-Century team with 19 other outstanding Hawkeyes a decade later.

Armstrong summarized his time at Iowa in a 2008 interview with sportswriter Michael Tillery. "It was a great experience," Armstrong explained. "As a young kid coming from Detroit, Michigan, I had the chance to experience a side of life I hadn't previously growing up in the city. Going to school at the University of Iowa was an interesting experience. It was so opposite of how I grew up.

"I went there with an open mind with the mindset that I didn't know what to expect. When I had the opportunity to visit, I saw that the people were what made it a place I wanted to be a part of. The people stood out to me. They were outstanding, and looking back on it I'm glad I made the decision to attend the University of Iowa."

Accolades
- Second Team All-Big Ten (1988, 89)
- Ranks fourth in school history in career scoring and career assists
- Played 11 seasons in the NBA; won three NBA championships with the Chicago Bulls
- Selected to Iowa's All-Century basketball team (2002)
- No. 10 retired by Iowa basketball in his honor

No. 10 BJ ARMSTRONG									
Year	GP	FG-FGA	FG%	FT-FTA	FT%	Reb	Avg	Pts	Avg
1986	29	32-66	49	19-21	91	16	0.6	83	2.9
1987	35	153-295	52	100-126	79	89	2.5	434	12.4
1988	34	203-421	48	124-146	85	74	2.2	592	17.4
1989	32	195-403	48	160-192	82	79	2.5	596	18.6
Totals	130	583-1185	83	403-485	83	258	1.9	1705	13.1

How He's Remembered

"One of the nicest guys around. There was no arrogance to B.J. Armstrong. That baby face and infectious smile are something you'll always remember about him. He was just an infectious personality."

Tom Kakert

"B.J. Armstrong, in my opinion, is the best point guard in the country. I think he's outstanding. We've played against him all these years, and I think he's just a great player."

Lou Henson

"He just was the ultimate perfectionist. He worked as hard as anybody did coming through Iowa. B.J. was phenomenal. We played at Northwestern my freshman season and John Streif, who's our trainer, had B.J. come over to our team meal the night before the game, and I got to sit at his table. I just sat there and grilled him with questions. A lot of it was just how critical it is to take care of your body as far as the foods, nutrition, and rest. Then he gave me a few pointers on how to scout an opposing player and their tendencies and things."

Jess Settles

"I told him we haven't played anybody better. Horton and Marble are good players, but Armstrong just sticks out above other people. I have a fascination with the way B.J. Armstrong plays."

Bob Knight

Jersey #10 Honorable Mention

Dave Danner – Basketball (1944, 1946-47)
Dave Danner started his career off with a bang, averaging 14.4 points as a freshman. That 1944 team began the year 12-0 and featured a starting lineup of Dick Ives, Lloyd Herwig, Ned Postels, Jack Spencer, and Danner. The team finished 14-4 in Pops Harrison's first year as head coach, and Iowa achieved second place in the Big Ten Conference with a 9-3 record. Danner was named First Team All-Big Ten and Second Team All-American. He then spent a year in military service, and his starting spot was filled by the legendary Murray Wier. Danner returned to the team in 1946 and spent his final two seasons as a reserve.

#11: THE GREAT PLOEN

"We had a great game out at the Rose Bowl; there's no question about that. It was the thrill of a lifetime because it was the dream of a lifetime to go out there and play in it and win and get the MVP and the whole shootin' match. You couldn't ask for anything better."

- Ken Ploen

In spring football practice of 1956, the Iowa football program was at a crossroads. A few months earlier, a 3-5-1 season ended back-to-back winning campaigns. Consecutive winning seasons is a modest milestone at best, but for a program which had not achieved that since before the Great Depression, it was clearly progress. Iowa's 37-year-old head coach, Forest Evashevski, had begun the process of improving the mindset and raising expectations for a program mired in mediocrity.

The question remained, however, as to whether Iowa could take the proverbial "next step." With the departure of several key players including consensus First Team All-American and Outland Trophy winner Calvin Jones, football pundits and prognosticators had no reason to expect more than a middle-of-the-road Big Ten finish from the Hawkeyes. But armed with a new offense and dazzling senior quarterback Ken Ploen, Evy's Hawkeyes would reach heights never before attained by Iowa football and blaze a trail to the Rose Bowl.

A native of Clinton, Iowa, Ploen was a multi-sport star in high school, earning football and basketball All-State honors in 1952-53. He was a standout baseball player and a state champion track hurdler his senior year. In the classroom, Ploen earned a Nile Kinnick Scholarship to study civil engineering at the University of Iowa. After playing three sports his freshman year at Iowa, Ploen eventually settled on a football career, much to the approval of Coach Evashevski.

"I learned after my freshman year that you can't do it all," Ploen said, "so I participated my sophomore year in just football and spring track. Then I just went with football my junior and senior years."

> **The first time he touched the ball as an Iowa Hawkeye, sophomore Ken Ploen threw a seven-yard touchdown in 1954.**

Although Ploen received some playing time as an underclassman, he had yet to see extended minutes behind team MVP Jerry Reichow at quarterback. Ploen finally took over the role of Iowa's starting quarterback as a senior with Reichow's departure after the 1955 season. To better utilize personnel in 1956, the Hawkeye coaches opted to move away from an unbalanced line offense to the balanced Wing-T offense. This innovative offense was being used at the University of Delaware by a former Michigan teammate of Evashevski and had commonly become known as the "Delaware Wing-T."

Iowa's Wing-T offense used counters, reverses, and bootlegs; all were perfectly suited for the all-around athleticism of Ken Ploen. He had a sharp mind and was able to grasp the new offense quickly. After only a few spring practices, Evy felt as though his Wing-T was in good hands.

The first game of the 1956 schedule sent Iowa to Bloomington, Indiana. The Hawkeyes made quick work of the Hoosiers with a balanced rushing game and touchdowns by four different players. Ploen said, "With the type of personnel we had there, it fit to a 'T', so to speak. The Big Ten had never seen it. Against Indiana, they couldn't figure out what the hell was going on."

"The whole offense is really based on single-wing blocking, but they don't have a tailback," Ploen continued. "The quarterback goes up underneath center, and they have a wingback and flankers if you want to put them out and also a fullback. I spun, rolled out, bootlegged, and did all the different types of things that a tailback would do in the single-wing with that type of blocking."

The first home game would be significant for a reason not realized until later that year. With Ken Ploen out for the second half of the game due to a knee injury, Iowa needed to score twice in the fourth quarter to edge Oregon State, 14-13. Three more wins brought Iowa to 5-0, and Evashevski quietly sensed something special. A 17-14 loss to Michigan the following week would be Iowa's only blemish on the season.

A game with undefeated Minnesota next awaited the Hawkeyes. The powerful Gophers brought with them a nationwide television audience and a chip on their shoulders from a 26-0 pasting by the Hawks the year before. Minnesota would clinch a Rose Bowl berth with a win, and the Gopher faithful had gone so far as to completely book one airline of all their tickets from Minneapolis to Pasadena for the last week of the year.

Minnesota fumbled on their first possession of the game, however, and Iowa took over on the Gophers' side of the field. Ploen led the team down the field, but Iowa faced a fourth down with four yards to go from the Gopher eight-yard line. Evy decided to go for it, and Ploen drifted back and floated a pass which skimmed off of a Minnesota defender's fingertips and into the waiting arms of receiver Jim Gibbons. Though Gibbons was marked down inches shy of the goal line, the Hawkeyes scored on the next play and grabbed an early 7-0 lead. Iowa's defense would force six Minnesota turnovers on the day, and the Hawks prevailed in a defensive battle.

That victory set up the Big Ten finale with Ohio State back in Iowa City. Iowa would go to the Rose Bowl with a win, but Ohio State was a formidable foe. The Buckeyes had won 17 straight Big Ten games, a conference record. They were the back-to-back defending Big Ten champions from 1954 and 1955, and a win would give Ohio State their third straight outright Big Ten title, a conference record. The week before the Iowa game, the Buckeyes put on an incredible display against Indiana, setting the Big Ten record with 465 team rushing yards. Still, the Hawkeyes were aware of the stakes. A sign in the locker room read, "You have 60 minutes to play the game Saturday, and the rest of your life to remember it."

Just like the week before, the Ohio State game was a hard-fought, low-scoring affair. After a scoreless first half, Iowa took the second-half kickoff and drove down the field. On second and seven from the Ohio State 17-yard line, Ploen floated a touchdown pass to Jim Gibbons that is etched forever as one of the most significant plays in Iowa football history.

"The touchdown pass was a corner pattern," Ploen recalled. "It was a fake sweep to the right side. I came back and faked the ball to our halfback going to the right side and bootlegged out to the left. We had set that up a bit with the running going down there. I kept noticing that defensively the end wasn't paying a hell of a lot of attention to me when I faked the bootleg. The deep back was running over a bit, too. Gibbons went down and just took the guy in and then ran to the corner. He was so wide open that I was scared I'd miss him."

That touchdown was the only score in a 6-0 Iowa win that brought the Hawkeyes a Big Ten championship. Ken Ploen was carried off the field on his teammates' shoulders. To fully understand the impact of Ploen and the 1956 Hawkeye football team, one must consider the previous history of the program. The last 16 years had produced only four winning records. Iowa had never gone to a bowl game, much less the granddaddy of all bowls. "Basically, people thought Iowa would never go to the Rose Bowl Game," said longtime Iowa broadcaster Bob Brooks.

> **Ken Ploen led Iowa in rushing, passing, and scoring in 1956. He is one of only three Hawkeyes to accomplish this feat in a season, joining Aubrey Devine and Nile Kinnick.**

Ploen's final home game came against Notre Dame. Only three years earlier, the No. 1-ranked "Fainting Irish" had infuriated Coach Evashevski. The Hawkeyes held a 14-7 lead late in that 1953 game, and the Irish were deep in Iowa territory with no timeouts remaining. After a Notre Dame player was tackled in bounds, two of his teammates simultaneously faked injuries to stop the clock and allow the Irish to score the tying touchdown with six seconds left.

The 1956 meeting was a different story. Ploen scored two touchdowns, as the Hawkeyes demolished the Fighting Irish, 48-8. "We had cinched the Big Ten," said Ploen. "It was our last game, and it was in Iowa City. We were relaxed and Evy said, 'Go out there and have fun,' so we did. We just went out and kicked their butts. It was a very satisfying win, I'll tell you."

Also that day, a Michigan victory over Ohio State made Iowa's Big Ten championship undisputed. For the first time in 35 years, every team in the Big Ten was looking up at the Hawks. The Iowa Hawkeyes, now ranked third in the nation, were in the Rose Bowl for a rematch with Pacific Coast champion Oregon State.

"The experience of running onto the field at the Rose Bowl is something I'll never forget. Here I was in a stadium filled with thousands upon thousands of people, but yet I felt like I was about 10 years old, back in Clinton, playing a game with my buddies. The emotions, they're hard to explain, but it really was like being a little kid on Christmas morning," Ploen recalled.

In their first encounter, Oregon State held Iowa scoreless through three quarters. This time, with Ploen back in the lineup, it took less than five minutes for the Hawkeyes to score. Using key downfield blocks by Don Dobrino and Jim Gibbons, Ploen sprang for a 49-yard touchdown run on a roll-out, pass-run option to the right. Within seconds, "On Iowa" rang out over the crowd of 97,000. Suddenly, in this most unfamiliar of settings, the Iowa players felt a lot more at home.

Iowa held a seemingly comfortable 21-6 lead at halftime, but the Hawkeye faithful were anything but comfortable. Ploen had suffered a hyperextended left knee and had to be carried off the field in pain just before halftime. Unlike the first encounter with Oregon State, however, he would return for the second half and pick right up where he left off. A fourth-quarter touchdown pass to Gibbons made the final score 35-19. Ken Ploen completed nine of ten passes in the game and became the first Hawkeye to earn Rose Bowl MVP honors.

> **Coach Evashevski played against Nile Kinnick at Michigan in 1939, and he saw similar qualities in his quarterback. "Ploen is a fellow who probably comes closer to being like Nile Kinnick than any I've known since," Evashevski remarked. "He's a fine leader, a clutch player, and an honor student."**

Though much attention was given to the offensive changes in 1956, it was the defense that made the biggest statement in the Rose Bowl season. Led by Frank Gilliam, Alex Karras, and Ken Ploen, Iowa's defense would allow a total of only 84 points by season's end, fewer than nine points per game.

While Ken Ploen's Hawkeye career was over, Iowa's quarterbacking excellence would continue the following fall as he turned the offensive reins over to quarterback Randy Duncan. "We were two different types of quarterbacks," Duncan said. "I was a thrower, and he was a runner. But I learned how to win from him. He was a winner."

Though the NFL showed little interest in Ploen's abilities, one Canadian Football League coach was extremely interested. Coach Bud Grant of the Winnipeg Blue Bombers called Coach Evashevski in early 1957 to discuss the intricacies of Iowa's Wing-T offense. Evy sent Coach Grant tapes from the previous season, and Grant recruited Ploen to Canada.

"I was actually drafted [in the NFL] as a defensive back, not as a quarterback," Ploen said. "That's one of the reasons I think I came to Canada. I had an opportunity with Bud Grant to play offense and quarterback immediately. The starting quarterback had a kidney problem, and he had to sit out 1957, my first year as a pro. So the quarterback spot was wide open. I came up here and competed with Chuck Curtis from Texas Christian and Guy Martin from Colgate. I was able to beat them both out and ended up playing quarterback and a lot of defense here in Canada."

Ploen led the Winnipeg Blue Bombers to four Grey Cup titles in his 11-year professional football career. In 1975, he was inducted into the Canadian Football League Hall of Fame. Today, Ken Ploen still resides near Winnipeg, Canada.

"When I turned 70, I wrote a resignation letter to a radio station up here, and I officially retired," Ploen said. "I am enjoying life right now. I've got a cottage down on the lake. I like to go fishing and hunting there and around the province. I spend as much time as I can with family and friends and just enjoy myself."

Despite making Canada his home, Ploen still has fond memories of his home state. He will be forever remembered by Hawkeye fans as the quarterback who delivered Iowa its first Rose Bowl victory. "As a kid growing up, you dreamed of playing at Iowa and helping them go to the Rose Bowl," Ploen said. "I was fortunate enough to see it come to fruition."

Accolades
• Big Ten MVP (1956)
• First Team All-American (1956)
• Rose Bowl MVP (1957)
• Selected to the all-time University of Iowa football team (1989)
• Inducted into the Canadian Football League Hall of Fame (1975)

No. 11 KEN PLOEN

Year	Rush	Rush Yds	Rush TDs	Pass Att	Compl	Pct	Pass Yds	Pass TDs
1954	15	53	-	9	5	.555	67	2
1955	29	101	1	20	9	.450	132	3
1956	86	487	6	64	33	.515	386	5
Totals	130	641	7	93	47	.505	585	10

How He's Remembered

"Great all-around athlete. Ken played both offense and defense. His ability as a defensive player is never mentioned, but he was just as great defensively as offensively."

Forest Evashevski

"Kenny was an Iowa kid, and he was the quarterback of the first Rose Bowl team. He was the leader both on offense and defense. Because of his all-around passing, running, and general athleticism, I would probably rate him as the best quarterback Iowa's ever had."

Bob Brooks

"Ken Ploen, Ed Podolak, and Tim Dwight are the best Iowa high school athletes in their time that I've seen."

Jim Zabel

"First of all, Ken Ploen was a great, great athlete. His greatest asset was the way he ran the football. No one ever really got a good piece of him. He was elusive."

Randy Duncan

"Ploen was the best all-around player and leader on the '56 team."

Bump Elliott

"My goodness, did I have a great visit with Kenny Ploen when they had the fiftieth anniversary of the '57 Rose Bowl team. Kenny Ploen has gone on to lots of success as a private businessman in Canada after his All-Pro Canadian Football League days were done. To see a guy over seventy years old now and looking as young as he does and as articulate as he is, it really makes you proud as an Iowan to know that these guys have gone through the University of Iowa."

Gary Dolphin

Jersey #11 Honorable Mention

Lester Belding – Football (1918-21)

Lester Belding earned his first Hawkeye football letter at age 17 in 1918. It began a highly decorated football career for this young offensive end from Mason City, Iowa. As only a sophomore, he earned consensus First Team All-American honors. He then became Iowa's first multi-year All-American, earning second and third team honors in 1920 and 1921. Belding was also named All-Big Ten three times. Highlights in his career include a 50-yard touchdown reception against Nebraska in 1919 and three defensive interceptions against Notre Dame in 1921. Belding also ran track at Iowa.

Bob Jeter – Football (1957-59)

Bob Jeter grew up in Weirton, West Virginia, before coming to Iowa to play for Coach Forest Evashevski. Jeter played on Iowa's second Rose Bowl team, starring in arguably the deepest, most talented backfield ever assembled in Iowa City. He led the group in rushing at 7.2 yards per carry, with Willie Fleming just behind at 7.1. Jeter ran for 194 yards on only nine carries versus Cal in the 1959 Rose Bowl, including an 81-yard touchdown. His total yardage and touchdown run were both Rose Bowl records and earned him MVP honors. Jeter earned All-Big Ten honors in 1959 and later had a standout NFL career for Coach Vince Lombardi's Green Bay Packers. Jeter played for the Packer teams that won the 1965 NFL championship and Super Bowls I and II.

#12: GREASED LIGHTNING

"Ronnie Lester is without question the best point guard I've ever seen in Iowa basketball history, and there have been some wonderful point guards. When you think of Dean Oliver, Jeff Horner, and others, it would be hard to rank anyone ahead of those guys. But Ronnie Lester, save for the knee injury, was as jet quick off the first step as anyone I've seen play the game, period, at that position. And I think his quickness is what sets him apart despite his debilitating ACL injury his senior year."

- Gary Dolphin

When Lute Olson took over as Iowa's head basketball coach, he needed a spark to ignite his struggling program. From 1976 to 1980, Olson found that energy in the form of a human lightning bolt named Ronnie Lester. Lester and his teammates jolted Hawkeye hoops back to life with two of the greatest seasons in Iowa history.

Although Ronnie Lester was born on New Year's Day, 1959, in Canton, Mississippi, he grew up on the rough south side of Chicago. He attended Dunbar Vocational High School, where he played on the varsity team as a 5'4" sophomore. By the start of his junior year, Lester had grown eight inches and earned the starting point guard role. However, Lester focused more on passing than scoring. He helped two of his teammates average 20 points per game while leading Dunbar to a 19-5 record.

> As a junior in high school, Ronnie Lester averaged just 10 points per game. As a senior, he exploded for 27 points per game.

Because Lester did not blossom as a scorer until his senior season, he flew under the radar of many college basketball programs. Ronnie selected Iowa over Creighton, Nebraska, and Arizona. Olson later recalled his in-home visit. "[Ronnie] lived in Chicago's Robert Taylor Homes, at one time the largest housing project in the world, but basically an island of poverty, violence, and drugs on the South Side," Olson said. "This building was basically a vertical ghetto. When we went upstairs to his apartment, we had to wait outside as his mother, Nadine, pulled open three or four deadbolts before she could open the door. And this was four o'clock in the afternoon."

Obviously, Iowa would be a major adjustment. "The first year was a big learning experience for me, having never been away from home," Lester said. "I had to adjust to that and a new team and style of play. I just wanted to get better each year, and my second year I knew what to expect and what was expected of me."

Even as a freshman, Lester was the team's second-leading scorer behind senior center Bruce King. Lester and King helped Iowa to a 20-7 record. As a sophomore in 1978, Ronnie Lester emerged as Iowa's leading scorer and team MVP. He led the team in assists and field goal percentage, and he was a First Team All-Big Ten selection. The team took a step back, however, finishing with a losing record despite Lester's outstanding play.

That set the stage for Iowa's 1978-79 season. Flanked by talented underclassmen Kevin Boyle, Steve Waite, Steve Krafcisin, and Vince Brookins, Lester guided the Hawkeyes to a 20-8 record. That record included a 13-5 mark in the Big Ten Conference, which earned Iowa a share of the conference title. Iowa has not won a conference title in basketball since that championship in 1979. Lester again paced the Hawkeyes in scoring, assists, and field goal percentage. In addition to being named Iowa's team MVP and First Team All-Big Ten for the second straight year, Lester was named a First Team All-American in 1979.

However, Iowa was upset by Toledo in the first round of the NCAA Tournament. The Hawkeyes had accomplished everything they could have possibly hoped for in the regular season, but post-season success still eluded them. That would provide the motivation leading into Lester's senior season.

First, Lester played for the 1979 Pan Am Team, coached by Bob Knight. The team won all nine games, averaging 100.8 points per game, and clinched the gold medal over host Puerto Rico by a score of 113-94. "I've always thought that 1979 team was damned near as good as our 1984 Olympic team," Knight said. "I think it was capable of playing any team that ever represented the United States as an amateur team." Lester averaged 10.7 points per game and finished one assist behind Isiah Thomas for the team lead.

Back in Iowa City, expectations were high heading into the 1980 season, as Kenny Arnold and Bobby Hansen bolstered Iowa's defending conference championship team. But everything changed during the finals of a holiday tournament in Dayton, Ohio. "Ronnie Lester...stole a pass and got free on a breakaway," Olson recalled. "One of the Dayton kids chased him, and as Ronnie went up to lay it in, the kid grabbed his left arm and yanked it. Ronnie went flying and landed on his knee. It was diagnosed as a severe sprain, but it was terribly damaging." Lester would sit out the next six games, struggle through three conference games, and then sit out nine more games.

The injury doomed Iowa to just a 9-8 conference record heading into the season finale against Illinois. Iowa was on the NCAA Tournament bubble before that final game. The Hawkeyes announced that they would retire Lester's No. 12 prior to the game. But the campus buzzed with a single question: Would Lester play? The game's other nine starters were announced before Ronnie Lester was introduced to the Field House fans, who greeted him with a thunderous ovation. The Hawkeyes marched to victory behind Lester's 15 points, and the win propelled the team to an NCAA Tournament bid.

> **Despite missing 15 regular season games in 1980, Ronnie Lester was named as a First Team All-American for the second consecutive season.**

Iowa's momentum continued into the NCAA Tournament. Iowa defeated Virginia Commonwealth, N.C. State, Syracuse, and Georgetown in succession to earn the third Final Four berth in school history. But in the national semifinals against Louisville, disaster struck again. Lester, who had ten points on 4-4 shooting from the field and two made free throws, re-injured his knee and was finished for the season. The Hawkeyes fought valiantly without Lester but fell to the eventual national champions, 80-72.

"Many coaches I've talked to say that Iowa with Ronnie Lester, if he's healthy, was destined to win it all," Gary Dolphin said. "They thought Iowa had things going their way after they beat

Georgetown. But they also beat a lot of good teams in that tournament. Of course, Darrell Griffith was healthy and Ronnie Lester was not; that was the difference in the Louisville game, and then UCLA and Louisville met for the championship. But there were a lot of coaches and players who felt Iowa was a better matchup for UCLA in the 1980 Final Four."

The knee injury would also hamper Lester's professional career, though he did win an NBA title with the Los Angeles Lakers in 1985. After his playing career, he joined the Lakers' front office, where he has worked for decades as a scout. Lester would earn enough money in professional basketball to buy his mother a condominium away from the Chicago slums.

When reflecting on Lester's time at Iowa, it is tempting to dwell sadly on that Louisville game and what could have been. However, what could have been should not overshadow what actually was, and the reality was that Ronnie Lester had a magnificent career. He won a Big Ten title, led Iowa to a Final Four berth, and graduated as Iowa's career leader in points, field goals, and assists.

Lester is still fondly regarded for his soft-spoken nature. "He had outstanding athletic ability, but no ego," Krafcisin said. "He was as down to earth as anyone could be. He didn't say much. He just let his basketball style do his talking." Sharm Scheuerman agreed. "Nicest guy that you'd ever meet…Ronnie was just a very unassuming, gosh, outstanding ball player."

On the court, Lester is remembered primarily for his incredible quickness. "Ronnie had a quickness that's hard to describe," Waite noted. "A lot of players are quick, but Ronnie had the ability to stop on a dime. He could change directions without losing anything." Mac McCausland reminisced, "His quickness allowed him to get to the basket and get fouled where other people just couldn't stay with him."

Ronnie Lester was quiet and unassuming away from the basketball court, but aggressive and electrifying on it. Lester's thrilling, energetic play is the reason why Iowa fans still regard him as one of the greatest – and maybe the very greatest – basketball players to ever wear the black and gold.

Accolades
- First Team All-American (1979, 80)
- First Team All-Big Ten (1978, 79)
- Won gold medal with the USA Pan American team (1979)
- Selected to Iowa's All-Century basketball team (2002)
- No. 12 retired by Iowa basketball in his honor

No. 12 RONNIE LESTER

Year	GP	FG-FGA	FG%	FT-FTA	FT%	Reb	Avg	Pts	Avg
1977	27	140-312	44	83-119	70	66	2.4	363	13.4
1978	27	202-423	48	132-177	75	68	2.5	536	19.9
1979	28	194-401	48	136-161	85	63	2.3	524	18.7
1980	17	86-185	47	80-100	80	29	1.7	252	14.8
Totals	99	622-1321	47	431-557	77	226	2.3	1675	16.9

How He's Remembered

"Who do you think is the greatest Iowa men's basketball player of all time? Former point guard Ronnie Lester gets my vote hands down...I'd go out on a limb and say that Lester was as good as Isiah Thomas before Lester's knee was ravaged by injuries."

Pat Harty

"All the players knew Ronnie was the best player on the floor. If we needed a shot, he was the guy who was going to take it. If we needed a basket, he was the guy who made it. Ronnie was the best."

Steve Krafcisin, former Iowa teammate

"If any of you have seen a better guard in the country, then I have to question your intelligence."

Lute Olson

"Ronnie would rather talk about the guys he got to know at Iowa rather than talking about any game or any particular play. What an absolutely delightful gentleman. He's a tremendous administrator, and yet, the first thing he wants to talk about is, 'How's John Streif doing?' He wants to know how some of the old facility guys are doing, and some of the old coaches who have retired. That's Ronnie Lester. He wants to know about the people."

Gary Dolphin

"The quickest guard I've ever seen play for the Hawkeyes. He took over any number of games to win them with that quickness and his very unusual outside shot. He was a fine outside shooter, but his shot was unique. He didn't put any spin on the basketball when he shot it. You could see the seams on the ball when it went through the basket. Players are taught to be good shooters by putting backspin on the ball with the fingers to make it fly true and to draw it down into the basket off the back rim. Somehow, Lester missed out on the lesson as a kid, and in high school nobody changed him. Hawkeye coach Lute Olson also fell in line with that. Since Lester was such a fine shooter without backspin, Olson forbid any of his assistants from changing Lester's shot. Lester was a First Team All-American, proving perhaps that a good shooter can shoot the ball any way he chooses."

Ron Gonder

Jersey #12 Honorable Mention

Gary Snook – Football (1963-65)

Iowa City High graduate Gary Snook lettered three times for Jerry Burns' Hawkeye teams of the 1960s. Gary's best year was as a junior when he threw for over 2,000 yards, which nearly doubled Randy Duncan's previous school record of 1,124 yards. Karl Noonan, a First Team All-American, was the team's primary receiver. Snook's average of 257 yards per game remained a Big Ten record until 1980. Snook set five Big Ten passing records in 1964 and tied two more while earning All-Big Ten honors. He ended his career by throwing for over 1,000 yards his senior year, despite some injuries and a disappointing 1-9 team record.

#13: HUGO EXPRESS

"Rick is kind of a 'Mr. Consistency.' He's worth his weight in gold."

- Hayden Fry

Richard Bass was Coach Hayden Fry's "Rolling Ball of Butcher Knives." Kevin Harmon was the younger Harmon brother. David Hudson was the big, bruising fullback. Rick Bayless was, well, the guy from Hugo.

After lettering twice in high school football and earning All-Conference honors, Bayless decided to walk on to Iowa's football team in 1983. Iowa's rise to prominence and history of walk-on success prompted the Minnesota native to decline offers from smaller schools. It was a choice he would not regret as his career would span the pinnacle of Hayden Fry's success at Iowa.

"Iowa knew about me because [former Hawkeye player] Wally Hilgenberg contacted the staff in Iowa City," Bayless explained. "Hilgenberg and my mother worked together with some clients in a commercial real estate office."

Minnesota had some interest in the in-state prospect for a time, but their interest soon waned. "Halfway through my senior year of high school, Joe Salem, who then was the Minnesota coach, made a lot of changes in his staff, and I didn't hear from them again," Bayless recalled. "I came to Iowa on a recruiting visit and liked it right away."

After sitting out the 1983 season, Bayless played in nine games in 1984. Owen Gill was playing his senior season and Ronnie Harmon had just moved from receiver to running back, so Bayless knew he would be waiting his turn. Like so many walk-ons before and since, he got his start on special teams.

Harmon suffered a broken leg against Wisconsin and was done for the season. Owen Gill moved to running back but was injured in Iowa's last regular season game at Hawaii. This presented Bayless with his first opportunity for significant playing time. He stepped in and rushed 16 times for 96 yards against the Rainbows. He also caught two passes for 42 yards in the 17-6 Iowa win.

"It was a shock; it was like I dreamed it," Bayless said. "It was a weird feeling that I'll never forget. After the game, it seemed so different. I had worked my whole life to prove to myself I could play."

The 6'0", 200-pound freshman finally felt like he belonged. Nevertheless, Harmon recovered from his injury and returned as the clear starter for 1985. Bayless played a key role on special teams again and finished 1985 as Iowa's fourth-leading rusher behind Hudson and the Harmon brothers.

> In 1984, Rick Bayless' first name was mistakenly listed as William in game programs. Therefore, the little-known walk-on was referred to by the public address announcers as William Bayless.

Bayless was still relatively anonymous as his junior season began in 1986. Prior to that year, he had carried the ball just 55 times for 263 yards in two seasons. Iowa opened the season against Iowa State, and, like two years earlier, a Harmon went down with a leg injury. This time, it was the younger brother, Kevin, and Bayless was thrust into the starting role. He would soon prove that he wasn't your ordinary "next man in".

Bayless had a 32-yard touchdown run against the Cyclones and solidified his starting spot in the lineup. He made good on his next opportunity too, rushing for 167 yards against Northern Illinois. The performance included an 87-yard touchdown run in the rain-drenched, 57-3 stomping of the Huskies. Nearly all of his 167 yards (on only eight carries) came in the first half.

Texas El-Paso was the next opponent, and they fared no better than the previous one. Bayless started off with 55 yards on Iowa's first series. For the game, he had 127 yards on 20 carries and scored twice despite not playing in the second half. Meanwhile, Texas El-Paso was held to negative 30 yards rushing.

The Hawks went to 5-0 on the season after hard-fought victories over Michigan State and Wisconsin. The Hawks suffered their first loss of the season at No. 4 Michigan, 20-17. Bayless was held to 70 yards rushing but hauled in four more passes. He was establishing himself as a multi-dimensional player. He would lead the team in both rushing and receptions for the season – a feat only three Hawkeyes previously had achieved.

Iowa got back on track against Northwestern for Homecoming. Bayless led the charge with 33 rushes for 183 yards. "Bayless, he of sure hand and determined feet, was the real hero for Iowa's offense. He carried 33 times and earned high marks from Fry. The 183-yard output was the fourth-highest in the Big Ten this season," wrote Al Hall of *The Cedar Rapids Gazette*.

After losses to Ohio State and Illinois, Iowa finished the 1986 regular season with wins against Purdue and Minnesota. Bayless ran for 121 yards against Purdue and hauled in a 31-yard touchdown reception. Against Minnesota, Bayless became the third Iowa player to gain 1,000 yards in a season. After a successful season, Iowa was invited to San Diego and the Holiday Bowl. The Holiday Bowl is known for having close games and dramatic finishes; the 1986 game did not disappoint. The Hawkeyes were playing San Diego State on their home field.

Mark Dukes of *The Cedar Rapids Gazette* described Iowa's first score against the Aztecs. "[Bayless] scored his 11th touchdown of year as he shrugged off a tackle at the four and bulled into the end zone," Dukes wrote. Bayless ended up with 110 yards on 19 rushes. And, for the second consecutive game, Rob Houghtlin ended the game with a field goal in the 39-38 Iowa victory.

Rick Bayless had just completed one of the most decorated seasons an Iowa running back had experienced to date. He was named team MVP, and he was an All-Big Ten selection and an

Honorable Mention All-American. He ran for 110 yards or more on the ground five times that season, with another 99 yards against Ohio State.

> **Rick Bayless handled the ball 246 times in 1986 with only one fumble. "You'd have to hit him over the head with a sledgehammer to have him drop the ball," Fry said of Bayless.**

A season like 1986 would seemingly make Bayless a shoo-in for the starting spot the next season. But Iowa's program had risen to where they had a stable full of tailbacks vying for the position each year. This was a good thing, since the injury bug seemed to bite the team frequently. 1987 would be no exception, and this time it was Bayless who would miss significant playing time.

After an injury in practice, Bayless lost his starting position for the Kickoff Classic against Tennessee. Due mostly to ongoing injuries, he was never able to regain his place in the lineup. He ended the season having played in only seven of 13 games and never broke 44 yards rushing. While it was a disappointing senior season for the running back from Hugo, Minnesota, Rick Bayless accomplished things at Iowa that very few running backs have.

"I didn't want to look back and say, 'Could I have done it?'" Bayless explained on why he took a chance at Iowa. "Most of my options were smaller schools. I just felt that I had to give Division I ball a try because I wouldn't be happy not knowing whether I could have done it or not."

From both a team and personal perspective, he had indeed "done it" as a Hawkeye. His teams went to four consecutive bowl games including the 1986 Rose Bowl. So many young boys playing catch in their back yards can only dream of scoring an 87-yard touchdown in Kinnick Stadium or being named Honorable Mention All-American.

What Rick Bayless lacked in pizzazz, he made up for in consistency. He followed the same journey that most walk-ons take. He worked hard in practice, played hard on special teams, and made sure that he was ready if called upon. It is a path that walk-ons such as Dallas Clark, Sean Considine, and Bruce Nelson have also followed on their way to their own success. Just like the guy from Hugo, each of these walk-ons took a chance and, when given an opportunity, made the best of it.

Accolades
• Honorable Mention All-American (1986)
• All-Big Ten (1986)
• Third player in school history to rush for more than 1,000 yards in a season
• Fourth player in school history to lead team in rushing and receiving in the same season

No. 13 RICK BAYLESS								
Year	Rush	Yds	Avg	TDs	Rec	Yds	Avg	TDs
1984	27	140	5.2	0	5	66	13.2	0
1985	28	123	4.4	2	1	12	12.0	0
1986	216	1,150	5.3	10	30	209	7.0	1
1987	46	148	3.2	1	3	17	5.7	0
Totals	317	1,561	4.9	13	39	304	7.8	1

How He's Remembered

"For two years he's been as fine a specialty team player as we've had. He's done everything we've asked of him."

Hayden Fry (1986)

"Rick Bayless probably did the most with the least of any running back I can remember in the Hayden Fry era. Rick wasn't big; Rick wasn't fast; he really wasn't even quick. But he was tough, tougher than leg leather. He'd take the hit and get up and get back and take another hit, and he'd pound away. He was a great third-down back, because he'd get you that tough yard."

Frosty Mitchell

"Bayless is no different than any other successful athlete; he has honed his natural ability with hard work. But perhaps more so than others, he is hard-driven by a revved-up internal engine. It gives him an edge."

Brian Chapman, *The Des Moines Register*

"What's nice about Bayless is we may all block for a certain play and the hole may not be where it's supposed to be, but he'll find a way to break in the line and get yards out of it. That's what he does best."

Dave Croston, former Iowa teammate

"Bayless came to Iowa without a football scholarship...he climaxed by being named the team's most valuable player [in 1986]. That's storybook stuff, an accomplishment that keeps alive the spirit of every kid in the Hugo, Minnesotas of the world that there's still a place in college football for someone willing to work."

Ron Maly

#14: IOWA'S COLOR OF FALL

"Nobody played the game with greater heart than Ed Podolak. Not only was he tremendously instinctive and smart as a multi-position player, but, as many coaches will tell you, in order to succeed at football you've got to have great heart. And Podolak has it to this day. You can hear it in his broadcasts. You certainly saw it with Iowa when he made the position switch from quarterback to tailback. How many guys at a Big Ten university then or today, can switch from quarterback to tailback and become All-Big Ten and put up All-American-type numbers?"

- Gary Dolphin

In the early years of Iowa football, versatility was defined by people such as Aubrey Devine and Nile Kinnick. Back then, players typically played both offense and defense; by the nature of the game, you had to be skilled at multiple positions. Over time, the game has become more specialized. Nevertheless, you do have recent examples of great versatility; Hawkeyes such as Ronnie Harmon and Tim Dwight come to mind. In the 1960s, one name came to define versatility for the Iowa football program – Ed Podolak.

Ed, the son of Joe and Dorothy Podolak, grew up in the small town of Atlantic in southwest Iowa. The 6'1", 200-pound quarterback was a Second Team All-State selection in 1964 as a senior. Podolak was recruited to the University of Iowa by Coach Jerry Burns. "I spent a whole year recruiting [Podolak], and then I finally got him down here. And then they said, 'Well, we'll take Eddie and get rid of you,'" Burns recalled with a laugh.

Podolak began his sophomore season under new coach Ray Nagel. Nagel preferred a dual-threat quarterback that could either run or pass; this suited Podolak's skills perfectly. Before the 1966 season-opening game against Arizona, Nagel could not decide between Podolak and junior quarterback Chuck Roland. The coach decided to flip a coin to determine who would start. It came up heads, and Podolak started the game. He threw for a touchdown and ran for two more before Nagel substituted for him with a 21-0 lead. The Hawkeyes won easily.

That would be the only easy part of Podolak's sophomore season. The Hawks fell into a four-game tailspin that included an ugly 15-quarter scoring drought. Podolak snapped the scoreless streak by throwing for a touchdown, running for a two-point conversion, and breaking free for an 87-yard touchdown against Northwestern. However, the Hawks still lost to the Wildcats for their 16th consecutive Big Ten defeat. It was one game short of the conference record, behind Northwestern's 17 straight conference losses from 1913-1915.

Iowa's next game was against the Indiana Hoosiers, and the Hawkeyes battled hard to stay out of the record books. The game was close from start to finish, and with 1:29 left in the game, Indiana scored a touchdown to take a 19-17 lead. Just as it appeared that the Hawkeyes were going to set a conference mark for futility, Podolak led Iowa on a 52-yard drive down the field. The Hawkeyes kicked a field goal with 39 seconds left and held on for a 20-19 win.

> **In 1966, Ed Podolak finished second in the Big Ten in total offense behind Bob Griese.**

The Hawkeyes' struggles continued in Podolak's junior season. In the season opener against Texas Christian, Podolak completed seven of ten passes for 91 yards and a touchdown and added 96 yards and a touchdown rushing in a 24-9 victory. It was Iowa's only win of the year, as the Hawkeyes finished 1-8-1. "It was frustrating to keep getting beat, because I'd played for high school teams that never lost," Podolak said. "I had expected to be part of a healthy, winning program, but the wheels came off. Those first two years were a struggle."

Individually, Podolak was establishing himself as a dynamic playmaker at the quarterback position. While he again threw for over 1,000 yards on the season, he threw more touchdowns, cut his interceptions in half, and raised his completion percentage from 40 percent to 49 percent.

The 1968 season started off with Iowa's biggest win in years. Eighth-ranked Oregon State fell to the Hawkeyes, 21-20. Ed Podolak ran for two touchdowns before leaving the game with a concussion. Reserve quarterback Larry Lawrence then took over and helped lead Iowa to the upset. After the big win, Iowa fans celebrated and tore down the goal posts.

Podolak suffered a second concussion in a loss the following week against Texas Christian. "I spent four or five days in a Texas hospital, and that was probably my worst injury as a player," Podolak recalled. He missed the following game against Notre Dame and was not himself in his first week back against Indiana, fumbling twice early in a loss to the Hoosiers. After three straight losses, the 1968 season was beginning to look similar to the previous two years – follow a season-opening win with a long losing skid. However, this team would prove to be very different.

In both his junior and senior seasons, Podolak missed time due to injuries. Larry Lawrence had proven to be an able replacement for Podolak. In an effort to get the best players on the field and shore up a depleted running back corps, Nagel made a big change. He put both Lawrence and Podolak in the starting lineup against Wisconsin – Lawrence at quarterback and Podolak at tailback. As a tailback, Podolak still presented a run-pass option – sometimes he threw, sometimes he made the defense think he was going to throw to freeze the defenders.

Iowa pummeled Wisconsin, 41-0, in their first game with Podolak at tailback. It was only Iowa's second win in its last 28 Big Ten games. It was the most points Iowa had scored since 1961, and it was Iowa's first shutout in 70 games. "Podolak was a good quarterback, and he's a magnificent tailback," noted Maury White of *The Des Moines Register*. Wisconsin head coach John Coatta said, "They ran some traps that messed us up and we never recovered. That Podolak was especially effective."

Iowa rushed for 319 yards and brought home Floyd of Rosedale two weeks later, as they beat Minnesota for the first time in five years, 35-28. But the offense truly hit its peak the following week against Northwestern. Two years earlier, Podolak watched Michigan State's Clinton Jones gain 268 yards against the Hawkeyes to set a single-game Big Ten rushing record. Podolak topped that mark as a senior by running wild for a Big Ten-record 286 yards on only 17 carries in a 68-34 beating of Northwestern. He scored two touchdowns and also completed a 34-yard pass before leaving the game midway through the fourth quarter with an injury.

"Podolak sat in pain, an impromptu sling supporting his right arm, after putting the final flourish on the greatest rushing day any back ever had in a Big Ten game," wrote Maury White. It would only remain the Big Ten's greatest rushing day for one week, however. Michigan's Ron Johnson broke the record seven days later against Wisconsin. Iowa closed out 1968 with a valiant 33-27 loss to No. 1-ranked Ohio State and a win over Illinois.

Prior to the 1968 season, Iowa had finished last in the Big Ten four years in a row and had just a 3-27-2 record in their last 32 conference games. Iowa's 4-3 mark in Big Ten play in 1968 was the school's first winning record in the Big Ten since 1960. It was an encouraging end to Iowa's season and Podolak's career.

Iowa's offense in 1968 rewrote the conference record books. The Hawkeyes scored 256 points in Big Ten play for an average of 36.6 points per game. Both were Big Ten records. Iowa's 482 yards per game in conference play also set a Big Ten record. Podolak's 937 rushing yards set a school season record, while his average of 6.1 yards per carry ranked sixth in the nation in rushing average.

> **In 1968, Ed Podolak placed third in the Big Ten MVP voting and 12th in the Heisman Trophy balloting.**

Podolak moved on from Iowa to star for the Kansas City Chiefs. His thirst for team success as a Hawkeye was quenched his rookie season; he played in Super Bowl IV, where his Chiefs defeated the Minnesota Vikings. Two years later, he had 350 all-purpose yards in a playoff loss to the Miami Dolphins. It is still the NFL record for all-purpose yards in a playoff game. After a nine-year career, he left Kansas City as the franchise's career rushing leader, and he was named to the Chiefs' Hall of Fame in 1989.

Throughout his career, Podolak was a strong and agile runner. He wasn't particularly elusive, and he didn't have tremendous speed. However, one thing that separated him from many ball carriers was his ability to follow his blockers and see the field well. He had great vision of the defense and was a very smart football player. It shows to this day.

Podolak is a Hawkeye through and through. He and his wife Vicki have two daughters, the youngest of which played for Lisa Bluder's Hawkeye basketball program. Since 1982, Ed has served as the color commentator for Iowa football games. His experience and ability to analyze the game has made him a favorite among Iowa fans. He has an uncanny ability to see the whole field and not focus on just one portion of the action. He truly does color the picture as Gary Dolphin describes the action.

"One unique thing you should know about Ed Podolak and I is he has never, ever used a pair of binoculars and I have never, ever been without a pair," Gary Dolphin explained. "I asked him a year or two in, 'Eddie, I know you have good eyesight, but how can you not use binoculars?' He said, 'Because I want to see the defense.' And that's so true of any great offensive player, he's looking over that line of scrimmage, he wants to see the defense and how they're aligned. People say, 'That Eddie is so good at analyzing plays.' I said, 'Because he sees the whole field.' It's as simple as I tell you what happened and he tells you why it happened. You've got to get lucky once in a while, and I've gotten lucky with Eddie and Bobby."

Ed Podolak had exceptional vision, heart, and toughness. He possessed athletic versatility, the mind and arm of a quarterback, and the legs of a running back. As a broadcaster, he wears his black and gold heart on his sleeve. Put it all together, and there is no doubt that Podolak is truly a Hawkeye great.

Accolades
- All-Big Ten (1968)
- Team captain and MVP (1968)
- Broke school record for total offense in a career
- Inducted into the State of Iowa Hall of Fame (1986)
- Inducted into the Kansas City Chiefs Hall of Fame (1989)

No. 14 ED PODOLAK

Year	Att	Compl	Pct	Yds	Int	TDs
1966	191	77	40.3	1,041	18	3
1967	162	79	48.7	1,014	9	5
1968	45	16	35.6	261		-
Totals	398	172	42.3	2,316		8

No. 14 ED PODOLAK

Year	Rush	Yds	Avg	TDs
1966	141	450	3.2	3
1967	112	323	2.9	3
1968	154	937	6.1	8
Totals	407	1,710	4.2	14

How He's Remembered

"Here's Hartlieb going out, he looks, he throws – it is – complete! AND IT'S AN IOWA TOUCHDOWN! IT'S AN IOWA TOUCHDOWN! IT'S AN IOWA TOUCHDOWN! Marv Cook! I can't believe it! Marv Cook got in the open at the five, Hartlieb passes to him, Ed Podolak is hugging and kissing me!"
Jim Zabel's radio call during the Iowa-Ohio State game in 1987

"We admire the sportsmanlike qualities of Ed Podolak... Win, lose, or draw, he's always stood up with dignity and answered questions honestly, although never to the point of criticizing the coaches or shifting the blame to teammates. Matter of fact, if we were playing college football today, Ed Podolak is the kind of teammate we'd appreciate having. We'd block a little harder for him or stretch a little farther for his passes or play defense a little tougher, because we could be sure he'd call attention to this in answering questions by the press after games."
Gus Schrader

"Podolak was great, too. He did everything. He was a tremendous all-around player. He was one of the best. In fact, he still holds the Iowa record for rushing in a Big Ten game. He didn't even play most of the last quarter of that game, and he still piled up all those yards. He's still broadcasting, of course, and most fans are familiar with him from that standpoint, but he was an exceptional player."

Buck Turnbull

"I remember being scared to death before my first Iowa football game [as a broadcaster]. Iowa and Kansas State were playing at the Eddie Robinson Classic down at Arrowhead Stadium. The night before that game, Ed Podolak, Gary Dolphin, and I went to this steakhouse in downtown Kansas City – a steakhouse that I believe Eddie had frequented quite a bit when he played for the Chiefs.

In the middle of dinner, Ed says, 'Okay, it's time for a rite of initiation.' He looked over at me and said, 'Here's what we did in the NFL. Whenever a rookie came on board, they had to stand up and sing their school fight song.' This is a nice restaurant, cloth tablecloths, candles lit and everything. So he said, 'Get up. Sing your alma mater's fight song.' I looked at him and said, 'You know, Eddie, that's a problem. I went to school at St. Ambrose and we don't have a fight song.'

'You don't have a fight song!? Can you even call that a school? Well then, get up and sing the Iowa Fight Song.' I probably ruined at least ten dinners that night, because I am tone deaf and a terrible singer. But I got up and sang the Iowa Fight Song right in the middle of a restaurant. I sat back down and oh gosh, everyone had a great laugh."

Mark Allen

Jersey #14 Honorable Mention

Chris Kingsbury – Basketball (1994-96)

Chris Kingsbury came to Iowa as a coveted McDonald's All-American out of Hamilton, Ohio. He is mostly remembered by Iowa fans for one thing – deep three-pointers. The burly 6'5" shooting guard was capable of shooting up to 30 feet from the basket with ease. Kingsbury had the shooting range of perhaps no other player in Iowa basketball history. Amazingly, 226 of his 333 career field goals at Iowa were three-pointers. This ranks him second to only Jeff Horner in career three-pointers. His best year at Iowa was as a sophomore in 1995, when he averaged 16.8 points per game. He set an Iowa record with 117 three-pointers that year and made nine three-pointers in a single game not once but twice (against Drake and Long Island). Kingsbury was a Second Team All-Big Ten selection in 1995.

#15: NO HELMET REQUIRED

"No All-America team will be complete unless it includes Duke Slater. No better tackle ever trod a western gridiron."

- Knute Rockne

It takes a special person to earn the nickname "Duke." Today, that nickname is most popularly associated with movie star and Iowa native John Wayne. Wayne's characters exhibited toughness, fairness, and a strong work ethic. As a result, the nickname "Duke" often evokes images of those same qualities. Long before Marion Morrison made a motion picture as John Wayne, a young black man named Fred Slater had become an Iowa legend in real life by displaying toughness, fairness, and a commitment to hard work.

Frederick Wayman Slater was born December 9, 1898, one of six children born to Reverend George and Letha Slater of Normal, Illinois. Young Fred had a difficult childhood. George Slater was a Methodist minister, and the Slaters moved from town to town, going wherever the ministry led them. The Slater family was extremely poor, and Fred learned the game of football by playing with the neighborhood boys on the streets and vacant lots. At age 11, Fred Slater had to deal with the death of his mother, Letha.

> **Like John Wayne, Fred Slater was given the nickname "Duke" as a boy when the name of a beloved pet dog was transferred to him. It stuck with him the rest of his life.**

When Duke was 13 years old, the family moved to the Hawkeye State after George Slater was named as the pastor of a Methodist church in Clinton, Iowa. Reverend Slater thought football was too dangerous a sport for Duke, and he forbade his son to play for the high school team. However, Duke went on a hunger strike for several days until his father acquiesced. His father had only one condition: Duke must take great care not to get hurt. As a result, for his entire career, Duke was always careful to never complain about or let anyone see his injuries.

Every high school player was expected to provide their own shoes and helmet. However, the Slaters were so poor that George Slater could only afford to buy Duke one or the other. Duke Slater decided that he needed shoes more, so he played every game at Clinton High School without a helmet. Meanwhile, his feet were so big, his shoes had to be special ordered from Chicago. Throughout his career, spectators would marvel at the size of Slater's feet.

Slater led Clinton to the mythical Iowa high school state championship game on Thanksgiving in 1914. The title game against West Des Moines High ended in a 13-13 tie. West Des Moines was led by Aubrey and Glenn Devine, Slater's teammates at Iowa.

Aubrey recalled, "We were on Clinton's 10-yard line with a few seconds to go. I tried to forward pass but never was able to get rid of the ball as a big boy wrapped his arms around me and smothered me to the ground. That was my first taste, so to speak, of Duke Slater. In later years he was on my side, which made the going much easier."

Duke Slater wanted to attend college, and he could not afford out-of-state tuition, so he enrolled at the University of Iowa in 1918. At that time, eligibility rules had been suspended due to World War I, so Slater was able to play and letter for the football team as a freshman. He became a starter at the tackle position for the Hawkeyes as a freshman and was selected to the All-State team at the end of the year by *The Des Moines Register*.

As a sophomore in 1919, Slater was a unanimous All-Big Ten selection and a Second Team All-American. He led Iowa to the brink of the conference title, as Iowa posted a 5-2 record, with the two losses coming by a combined five points. Sportswriter Walter Eckersall saw Slater in action that season and reported, "Slater is so powerful that one man cannot handle him and opposing elevens have found it necessary to send two men against him every time a play was sent off his side of the line."

The 1920 season was supposed to be Slater's last at Iowa. As a junior, Duke was again a unanimous First Team All-Conference selection, but he was overlooked for All-American honors. Iowa again finished the year with a 5-2 record.

Duke Slater had used up his three seasons of eligibility with the 1920 campaign. However, late in the year, the Big Ten ruled that any player who had played as a freshman in 1918 would be granted a fourth year of eligibility by the league. Slater had one more college season to play.

In his senior year in 1921, the first major test of the season was against Notre Dame, which had not lost a game since 1918. Duke helped Iowa defeat the Irish, 10-7, and end Notre Dame's 20-game unbeaten streak.

> **Iowa photographer Fred Kent snapped one of the most famous pictures in Iowa football history during the 1921 Notre Dame game, capturing a helmetless Duke Slater clearing a hole for teammate Gordon Locke by blocking three Notre Dame defenders.**

Notre Dame coach Knute Rockne declared, "This fellow Slater just about beat my team single-handed in the only contest we lost. Realizing the great strength of Slater, and the fact that he knew how to use that strength to intelligent advantage, I had four of my players massed around Slater throughout the game. Occasionally, my boys would stop the big tackle, but those times were the exception. Usually, he made such holes in my strong line that fullback Locke would go through for long gains, often standing straight up as he advanced with the ball."

Colleges provided helmets for their players, but players were not required to wear them. Iowa offered Slater a helmet, but he was so used to playing without one in high school that he played helmetless until his senior year. However, the hitting in that Notre Dame game was so intense that later in the game, Duke finally donned a helmet. He would sporadically wear a helmet from that game forward until the last game of the season against Northwestern.

In Slater's final game for the Hawkeyes, he played helmetless one last time, leading Iowa to a 14-0 victory over the Northwestern Wildcats. The win secured a perfect 7-0 record for the Hawkeyes and Iowa's first Big Ten title in 21 years. Iowa had a 23-6-1 record in Duke's four seasons. Slater was named All-Big Ten for the third straight season in 1921 and was a First Team All-American, making him the first black All-American at Iowa. Popular magazine *Leslie's Weekly* named Duke Slater as their college football player of the year for 1921.

Duke Slater earned four letters in football and three letters in track, where he threw the shot put and the discus. He also participated in intramural wrestling and even tried his hand at boxing. Slater worked his way through college with no financial assistance, peeling potatoes in the basement of a local hotel during the year and shoveling coal during the summers. He earned his degree before signing a contract to play with the NFL's Rock Island Independents in 1922.

Slater had a ten-year career in the NFL, the longest career of any black player prior to World War II. He played for the Independents until the team folded in 1926, when his rights were acquired by the Chicago Cardinals. When he joined the Cardinals in 1926, he became the first African-American player to play for a current NFL franchise. Duke Slater played from 1926 to 1931 with the Chicago Cardinals, and he was an All-Pro selection in seven of his ten professional seasons. In two of those years (1927 and 1929), he was the only black player in the NFL.

As great as he was, Slater is probably as well-remembered for how he played the game as he is for how well he played the game. A consummate gentleman, Duke faced racial prejudice with dignity. An *Associated Press* report in 1934 stated, "Duke was the idol not only of those who knew and respected ability, but who had a weakness as well for sportsmanship, good nature, and manliness, regardless of race or color. He never lost his temper, never lost the grin that continually split his huge face, and never was more than an arm's length, either, from the man with the ball."

During Duke's NFL off-seasons, he returned to Iowa to attend law school, earning his degree in 1928. He then practiced law in Chicago while playing for the Cardinals. After one year as a high school coach and athletic director in Oklahoma City, Slater returned to Chicago in 1933 as an attorney. He coached numerous African-American all-star squads throughout the 1930s before being elected as a Municipal Court judge in Cook County, Illinois, in 1948.

Duke's life became an example of how to overcome a poor background, racial discrimination, and other adversity to achieve remarkable success. Slater credited football for aiding his personal and professional development. "Football is a rugged, demanding sport," Slater said, "and it teaches you to put every effort forth. The finest thing about playing is that you retain a lot of the give and take the rest of your life."

Tough, fair, and hardworking, Duke Slater was as outstanding a football player and human being as the University of Iowa has ever produced.

Accolades
- First Team All-American (1921); Second Team All-American (1919)
- All-Big Ten (1919, 20, 21)
- Selected to the all-time University of Iowa football team (1989)
- Inducted into the College Football Hall of Fame (1951)
- Slater Residence Hall in Iowa City is named in his honor

How He's Remembered

"Slater is one of the greatest, if not the greatest, tackle I have ever seen in action. No All-America team would be complete without him."

Howard Jones

"Iowa never failed to score when it got close to its opponent's goal line when Slater was playing, and I have yet to see his equal."

Aubrey Devine

"Duke Slater was the best tackle I ever played against. I tried to block him throughout my college career but never once did I impede his progress to the ball carrier."

Fritz Crisler

"Every line coach dreams of walking onto the field some afternoon and finding another Duke Slater out there ready to go to work. I've played against and coached a lot of good linemen, but that Slater topped them all."

Burt Ingwersen

Jersey #15 Honorable Mention

Willie Fleming – Football (1958)
Willie Fleming's Iowa career can be summarized as short but spectacular. In 1958, he was part of what was arguably Iowa's most talented backfield ever. He played right halfback; Bob Jeter played left halfback; and Randy Duncan led them at quarterback. Fleming averaged a tremendous 7.1 yards per carry and set a modern school record for touchdowns in a season with 11. That total includes two touchdowns in the 38-12 Rose Bowl win over California. He returned kickoffs with a 43-yard average, returned punts with a 28-yard average, and also played defense that season. The Iowa team of 1958 finished the year ranked second in the nation. Fleming failed to remain eligible for his junior year, so his career at Iowa was over after one season. He then had a terrific career in the Canadian Football League and was inducted into the Canadian Football Hall of Fame in 1982.

"Willie Fleming, without a doubt, was the greatest running back I've ever coached. I think had Willie remained at Iowa, he would have gone down as one of the greatest halfbacks who ever played. He could do everything. For a man who was 5'9", he could stand under a basket and dunk a basketball, he had so much spring. He had tremendous explosion. He was a fine defensive player with tremendous quickness. He was one of the few halfbacks on defense who could make a mistake and recover fast enough to turn it into an interception on a pass play. He had all the assets a halfback needs and a real fine attitude. Willie's handicap was only playing one season."

Forest Evashevski

Don Nelson – Basketball (1960-62)

Don Nelson came to Iowa from Rock Island, Illinois. By the time he left Iowa, he owned seven school records. Nelson played three years for the Hawkeyes and left as Iowa's all-time leading scorer with a career average of 21.2 points per game in addition to 10.9 rebounds per game. In 1961, four of the five starters on Iowa's basketball team were ruled ineligible after the first semester. Nelson, the lone remaining starter, still managed to lead Iowa to a second-place finish in the Big Ten and a No. 8 national ranking. In the process, he set Iowa's season scoring record. He was named team MVP three times, All-Big Ten twice, and All-American twice. He led the team in points and rebounds each year he played and has the fourth-highest career scoring average in Iowa history.

Nelson went on to play in the NBA for 14 seasons, mostly with the Boston Celtics. He helped the Celtics win five NBA championships and became known as one of the greatest "sixth men" of all-time. The Celtics have retired his No. 19 jersey. In 1976, Nelson began a long NBA coaching career. He coached "Dream Team II" to a gold medal in the 1994 FIBA World Championship. On April 7, 2010, Don Nelson set the record for most coaching wins in NBA history with his 1,333rd career victory.

"Nelson was probably one of the toughest players I've ever seen. He had nice touch, but we had to use him inside under the basket. He would get clobbered, but he was a tough, solid, strong player."

Sharm Scheuerman

Jimmy Rodgers – Basketball (1963-65)

Originally from East Levden High School in Franklin Park, Illinois, Jimmy Rodgers played guard for Sharm Scheuerman and Ralph Miller-coached teams in the early 1960s. In his first game as a Hawkeye, the 6'3", 185-pound guard scored 18 points in a win over Evansville. Though he never led Iowa in scoring, he averaged over 10 points per game each of his three years. His memorable games include an 87-82 win over John Wooden's No. 1-ranked UCLA team his senior year. This immediately followed a win over No. 5-ranked Indiana that same season. Rodgers would go on to coach in the NBA. He was the head coach of the Boston Celtics and Minnesota Timberwolves, and he won six NBA championships as an assistant coach with the Celtics and Chicago Bulls. He is the father of former Iowa quarterback Matt Rodgers, who led Iowa to the 1991 Rose Bowl.

#16: GO LONG

*"Chuck is my greatest Iowa player in my time in all ways –
as a player, as a person, as a leader, just in every way."*
                                                    - Ron Gonder

There is no way Chuck Long's parents could have known on
February 18, 1963, that their newborn son was a future
quarterback. Still, it must be more than just a coincidence that
they blessed him with the perfect quarterback name. Whatever
the case, as Iowa's quarterback from 1981 to 1985, Chuck Long
made his perfect name a household one.

Chuck Long was an overlooked name coming out of high school. He earned seven letters at
Wheaton North High School in football, basketball, and baseball. He was elected captain of
his football and baseball teams, and as a high school quarterback, he was selected to the All-
State championship squad when he led Wheaton to an Illinois state title in 1979. Long also
garnered All-State recognition in football as a senior in 1980. Due to his team's strong running
attack, however, he only threw five or six passes a game his senior season, which resulted in
few scholarship offers.

> **Despite his paltry passing statistics, Chuck Long caught the attention
> of Iowa coach Hayden Fry. "To this day, I ask Hayden, 'How did you
> ever find me?'" Long has said. "He still won't tell me."**

In 1981, a Big Ten rule prohibited redshirting freshmen. As a result, several conference
coaches decided to play freshmen and redshirt them as sophomores. Long completed one pass
against Northwestern and rushed for 11 yards at the end of the 1982 Rose Bowl as a redshirt
freshman. "Then, in my second year, they decided the rule wasn't good and got rid of it,"
Long said. "Some of my classmates got redshirted as sophomores as a result of that. I didn't.
I earned a starting job, so the NCAA in my senior year came back and said, 'Hey, we screwed
you out of a year.' They said I could have an extra year, so I was actually a senior twice."
That loophole would allow Long to become the only known player in college football history
to play in five bowl games.

Prior to the 1982 season, Fry made waves when he declared that Long, then a complete
unknown, was "destined for greatness." Although Long started the season opener against
Nebraska, he was benched following a 42-7 loss. He was reinserted into the starting lineup for
Iowa's third game that year, however, and he led the Hawkeyes to a 17-14 victory over
Arizona. That cemented a starting spot on the team, and the rest is history.

In the 1982 Peach Bowl against Tennessee, Long set Peach Bowl records for passing yards and
total offense as he led Iowa to its first bowl victory since 1959. By the end of his sophomore
season in 1983, he owned Iowa's season and career records for yards passing, touchdown
passes, and total offense. He finished the 1983 season second in the nation in passing behind
Steve Young. Long earned his first All-Big Ten selection and led Iowa to the Gator Bowl as a
sophomore.

Chuck Long would attract national attention in 1984 when he broke an NCAA record for consecutive completions with 22 straight against Indiana. "I didn't even know I had that many in a row until someone told me after the game," Long said. What the fans and Hoosier players may not have known was that Long had spent the previous few days battling a sore elbow.

"I caught the flu Thursday and it went down to my right elbow because that was the weakest part of my body with all the passes I'd been throwing," Long said. "My elbow swelled like a balloon. I got treatment all day Friday, then Saturday morning I woke up with a big elbow again. The doctor gave me an antibiotic, but it still hurt. I asked the trainer if I had any serious chances of hurting my arm, and he said only if I landed on it a lot. I said I was willing to take the chance."

Long finished the 1984 campaign in impressive fashion. Ignoring wind and rain, he helped the Hawkeyes score 55 points against Texas in the Freedom Bowl, which were the most points that had been scored against the Longhorns in 80 years. Long completed 29 of 39 passes for 461 yards and six touchdowns. His six passing scores set a new all-time bowl game record. He was named All-Big Ten, was a finalist for the Davey O'Brien Award, and finished seventh in the Heisman Trophy balloting. Hawkeye fans were understandably nervous that Chuck Long might bolt for the NFL after such an impressive showing.

> When Chuck Long announced at a press conference that he would remain at Iowa for his senior season, Hayden Fry joked, "It was the greatest recruiting job I ever did."

His return sent expectations for Iowa's 1985 season through the roof. On October 1, 1985, Iowa was ranked No. 1 in the AP poll for the first time since 1961. In Iowa's first game as the nation's top-ranked team, they faced a tough Michigan State squad. The Spartans led, 31-28, in the final moments. "Long completed pass after critical pass until we reached the Spartan one-yard line with less than a minute remaining," Fry recalled. "We called a play named 'Fake 47 sucker pass', in which Long faked the handoff to Harmon then bootlegged right with the option to run or pass. [Mike] Flagg, at tight end, faked a block then released into the end zone to catch the ball. But because the Michigan State cornerback came down so hard on the fake to Harmon, there was no defender between Long and the goal line. All he had to do was stroll into the end zone."

Chuck Long held the ball high above his head as he crossed the goal line to give Iowa a 35-31 victory. When his name is mentioned to Iowa fans, that image of Long striding into the end zone may be the first picture that comes to mind. "In an important, pressure-packed game that we had to win to stay number one, Long gave the capacity crowd and a national television audience a spectacular performance," Fry noted. "He completed 30 of 39 passes for 380 yards and four touchdowns and scored the winning touchdown himself."

Long later led Iowa to a win over No. 2 Michigan, as Iowa would go on to claim the Big Ten title outright. He became the fourth quarterback to lead Iowa to an outright Big Ten title, joining Aubrey Devine, Ken Ploen, and Randy Duncan. Long finished the season ranked in the top ten in the nation in passing for the third straight season. Although he finished second in what was then the closest Heisman Trophy race in history, he was named Big Ten Player of the Year and a unanimous First Team All-American. He also won the Maxwell Award and the Davey O'Brien Award as a senior. When Chuck Long graduated, he owned every single school passing record except one, passes attempted in a game.

After spending eight of his nine seasons in the NFL with the Detroit Lions, Long successfully transitioned from player to coach. He was an Iowa assistant coach for five seasons under both Hayden Fry and Kirk Ferentz before leaving for Oklahoma. He won a BCS national championship as an offensive coordinator at Oklahoma under his former Hawkeye teammate, Bob Stoops. Long later joined a long line of former Fry assistants to become a head coach when he spent three seasons as the head football coach at San Diego State University from 2006 to 2008.

Chuck Long had both one of the greatest names and one of the greatest careers of any quarterback in college football history. Was that simply destiny or chance? Either way, one thing is certain – Chuck Long is a name that Iowa Hawkeye fans will never forget.

No. 16 CHUCK LONG						
Year	Yds	Att	Compl	Pct.	TDs	Int
1981	14	1	1	100.0	0	0
1982	1,678	227	148	65.2	11	11
1983	2,601	265	157	59.2	14	12
1984	2,871	322	216	67.1	22	13
1985	3,297	388	260	67.0	27	16
Totals	10,461	1,203	782	65.0	74	52

Accolades
• Unanimous First Team All-American (1985)
• First player in Big Ten history to surpass 10,000 passing yards
• Only player in college football history to play in five bowl games
• Selected to the all-time University of Iowa football team (1989)
• Inducted into the College Football Hall of Fame (1999)

How He's Remembered

"Chuck Long is arguably the greatest quarterback ever to play at Iowa...Long could read defenses unlike anybody I had seen at Iowa to that point...he had that sixth sense – he knew what a defense was going to do as soon as he broke the huddle."

Gary Dolphin

"Chuck Long is just a marvelous person. Off the field, he was just a teddy bear, but boy, when he strapped up that chin strap and stepped across the line, it was a new world. He never got angry at other players in the huddle; players marveled at it. Tackles would miss a block and Chuck would get teakettled, and he'd slap 'em on the rear and say, 'Get 'em next time,' where most quarterbacks would have been giving them a speech. He was absolutely unflappable in a competitive situation. He was just so good at that as well as being a great forward passer and just an absolutely great individual as a person."

Frosty Mitchell

"Chuck was my mentor in a lot of ways. He helped me with my decision making. He was supportive as I tried to get better, and he was a guy who taught me how to use my head in the passing game. We outsmarted a lot of opponents because we made great decisions while being in the pocket."

Chuck Hartlieb

"He was a good student, an excellent character, and a good leader. There was an aura about him to be successful."

Bill Snyder

"Since 1981, there have been nine teams win the Big Ten title. The team that broke the ice was Iowa...History changed, and a lot of that was Coach Fry, and a lot of that was Chuck Long."

Kirk Ferentz

Jersey #16 Honorable Mention

Paul Krause – Football (1961-63)

Originally from Flint, Michigan, Paul Krause played football under head coach Jerry Burns. Krause played a number of positions, including halfback, flanker, defensive back, and punt returner. He returned a punt 82 yards for a touchdown as a junior in a 1962 win over his home-state Michigan Wolverines. Krause led the Hawkeyes in receiving as a junior and in scoring as a senior, but he enjoyed his greatest success as a tall and rangy 6'3", 170-pound defensive back. The 1963 Iowa team captain blossomed in the NFL, playing in four Super Bowls as a member of the Minnesota Vikings. Krause still holds the NFL record for career interceptions with 81; he broke the record of 79 interceptions that had been held by fellow Hawkeye Emlen Tunnell. In 1998, Krause joined Tunnell as the second Hawkeye to be inducted into the Pro Football Hall of Fame.

Deven Harberts – Football (1986-88)

Coach Hayden Fry recruited wide receiver Deven Harberts to the Hawkeyes from tiny Walnut, Iowa. Harberts lettered in his final two seasons with the Iowa football team, and his senior year in 1988 was one to remember. He caught 11 passes for 233 yards against Indiana that season, a performance that stands as the second-most receiving yards in school history. Harberts had 880 yards receiving in 1988, which ranks eighth all-time. He was an All-Big Ten selection as a senior, and he ended his career in fine fashion, with two touchdown catches in the Peach Bowl against N.C. State.

#17: MURRAY THE MAGICIAN

"Iowa basketball today really started with the foundation that Murray brought to the game. He became a state hero much the same way as Kinnick did in football, and he was somethin' else as a player."

- Bob Brooks, sports announcer and former Iowa classmate of Wier

He has been described as a contortionist, mystifying, and unconventional with the ball. Whichever label may apply, Murray Wier was undoubtedly one of the finest Iowa basketball players ever. Wier played for Iowa in the late 1940s with other stars such as Dick Ives and Herb Wilkinson. The fiery little red-headed forward would be Big Ten MVP and First Team All-American for Coach Pops Harrison before his career ended.

It was in the little town of Grandview, Iowa, where Murray Wier began playing ball. His flair for the dramatic developed early.

"I grew up with two older brothers and, of course, they were a lot bigger than me. So we'd play in the back yard, and I'd kind of have to heave the ball to get it over their heads. It's just something that kind of stuck with me," Wier recalled. "I had what you'd call crazy shots, but for me, it was sort of natural."

Prior to his senior year of high school, James and Ruth Wier moved to nearby Muscatine, presenting Murray an opportunity to play basketball at a larger school. He made good on the opportunity; Murray was named team captain and First Team All-State. In his first game as a Muskie, Wier scored 15 points in an upset win over arch-rival Davenport.

Despite Wier's diminutive stature, his basketball heroics began to garner the attention of collegiate programs, primarily the University of Iowa. "Pops Harrison, the coach, came to our house twice. It was a big thrill; here was the University of Iowa coach coming to see me, and I was just overwhelmed," Wier said. "I always followed Iowa sports on the radio when I was growing up. I always thought it would be great to be a player there, and then I was going to get an opportunity to do it. It was a great honor."

"I was also recruited somewhat by Iowa State and Drake," Wier continued. "Once I had a chance to go to Iowa, I wouldn't have gone anywhere else. Not that there was anything wrong with the others by any means, but I always wanted to be a Hawkeye."

Wier played the role of "sixth man" during his freshman year at Iowa. Led by Dick Ives and the Wilkinson brothers (Herb and Clayton), the 1945 team was no ordinary team. These Hawkeyes finished as the Big Ten champions with a 17-1 overall record. This record still stands as the highest season winning percentage by an Iowa team. Oddly enough, the Hawks did not play in the post-season in 1945. In fact, Murray Wier never played a post-season game in his four years at Iowa.

"Pops, as good of a guy as he was, somehow he didn't want any part of it," Wier said. "When I was a freshman, we won the Big Ten, and he turned the NCAA bid down.

"And when I was a sophomore, he turned the NIT bid down. We were down to two games with Ohio State. They had two road games, and we were at home one and on the road one. I think he figured the worst that could happen is we'd end up in a tie and, since they'd gone the year before, we'd get the bid. Well, lo and behold, they won 'em both and we lost 'em both, so we didn't get to go anywhere. When I was a senior, we should have gotten a NIT bid because we finished second. We got beat at Michigan for the Big Ten title. I think they got tired of asking Iowa, so we didn't get any bid. We were just out in the cold."

> **At 5'8", Murray Wier is the shortest single-season scoring leader in Division I NCAA basketball history.**

Despite not seeing eye-to-eye on post-season opportunities, Wier still holds his former coach in high regard. "Well, I've said this many, many times; other than my own father, he was the most important man in my life," Wier said. "I mean, you think, 'Okay, he's a coach; he's coaching ya and you come out and ya play.' But there's so much more to it than that, the things that he did for you off the floor. I can't say enough good things about him. Just a great guy."

As his years at Iowa progressed, Wier became more and more the focal point of Iowa's offense. He soon became a Field House favorite with his acrobatic exploits.

"The biggest thrill I got in a particular game," Murray said, "was when I was a sophomore. We were playing Minnesota in a Big Ten game in Iowa City, and they had a great team. Guys had come back from the service for 'em, and they were undefeated in the Big Ten at the time. They were ahead of us the whole ballgame, six, seven, eight points; and we had a rally in the last waning moments of the game. With three seconds to go, I had the ball; and I, it wasn't really a shot, I just threw the ball because there wasn't any time, and it went in. And, by God, I'll never forget it. We beat them in overtime."

His career culminated as a senior in 1948 as the Hawkeyes finished 15-4. Murray Wier produced arguably the most successful season ever by an Iowa basketball player. He broke the Big Ten season scoring record and was named Big Ten MVP. He was a consensus First Team All-American. He also became the only Iowa basketball player to lead the nation in scoring (21 points per game) in a given season.

After his playing days at Iowa, Wier moved on to a brief professional career. He was drafted by the Fort Wayne (now Detroit) Pistons in the 1948 BAA draft (the BAA was renamed the NBA a few years later). He played two years for the Tri-City Blackhawks, coached then by future legend Red Auerbach. The Blackhawks were based in what is now known as the Quad Cities; the franchise would later move to Atlanta and become the Atlanta Hawks. Wier's third and final year of professional ball was spent with the Waterloo Hawks of the National Professional Basketball League.

When his playing career ended, Wier remained in Waterloo to serve as athletic director at Waterloo East High School for 34 years. He also coached boys basketball for 24 years and tennis for 10 years. His basketball team won a state championship in 1974, and he compiled a 374-140 career coaching record.

In 2002, Wier was named to the University of Iowa's All-Century Team. He joined 12 other members in Carver-Hawkeye Arena to commemorate 100 years of Iowa basketball. A lot has changed in Iowa basketball since Wier's playing days in Iowa City. Among these changes was the move from the historic Field House to Carver-Hawkeye Arena in 1983.

"It had a personality," Wier said of the Field House. "Of course I'm prejudiced; I always liked the Field House better than Carver because the Field House had that tremendous noise. There was something special about it. It was uncomfortable for people who were sitting in the upper deck because they're in metal bleachers, but it was also uncomfortable for the visiting team. Carver-Hawkeye is such a nice place that a guy could go to sleep watching a game. You didn't go to sleep in the Field House. There was enough noise it'd drive you nuts, ain't nobody that's going to go to sleep."

> **Though not retired, Murray Wier's No. 17 jersey may never be worn again by an Iowa basketball player. Currently, numbers with digits greater than five are not used to avoid confusion when referees signal to the scorer's table.**

Today, Murray Wier spends his retirement years in Georgetown, Texas. He stays active by playing tennis regularly.

"Oh yeah, I'm still playing," Wier said. "I always liked the game and never got really much of a chance to play until later in my life, but I've picked it up. It's a great game; it's got a lot of basketball [skills] to it – hand-eye coordination, footwork, quickness. It's very competitive; there are a lot of connections. Oh yeah, I still love to play."

Accolades
- First Team All-American and Big Ten MVP (1948)
- Left school as Iowa's all-time leading career scorer
- Broke Big Ten record for career points in conference games
- Only basketball player in Iowa history to lead the NCAA in scoring average
- Selected to Iowa's All-Century basketball team (2002)

No. 17 MURRAY WIER							
Year	GP	FG-FGA	FG%	FT-FTA	FT%	Pts	Avg
1945	17	58	-	18-33	55	134	7.8
1946	18	57	-	39-62	63	153	8.4
1947	18	105-348	30	62-93	67	272	15.1
1948	19	152-429	35	95-136	70	399	21.0
Totals	72	372	-	214-324	66	958	13.3

How He's Remembered

"He was unguardable. He'd fire 'em off his ear or up from an ankle with equal abandon, even hoisting in baskets from midair in the midst of a dive. He didn't shoot baskets. He threw 'em in while racing, whirling, and engaging in some other means of rapid transit."

Bert McGrane

"One of the most unusual players ever at Iowa...great ball-hawk and dribbler...his one-handed shots from crazy angles when closely guarded are positively uncanny at times...probably the hardest man to guard in the league."

1947 University of Iowa Release to Writers and Broadcasters

"With Murray, there have been two things that stick out most. He is an extremely competitive person. Anybody that's ever been around him knows he's very short and direct in verbal discussion, as well as getting his point across, and that's the way he played the game. He was very aggressive in attacking the basket. He was one of those people who used a hook shot because he was only about 5'8" or 5'9". When he'd drive to the basket, he'd throw it high off the glass left-handed or right-handed. The other thing that was most memorable about him is he's only one of three Iowa players that have led the country in a particular category. He led the country in scoring. Kent, my son, led it in three-point shooting percentage, and then Reggie Evans led it in rebounding. Murray is the most competitive and one of the really elite players to play at Iowa."

Mac McCausland

"Murray Wier was one of the most unique players I've ever seen. He could come down going toward the basket and shoot a hook shot. Now, this is going to sound funny to a lot of people, because they can't fathom that. But he could. He was one of the most exciting players I've ever seen. He had a unique way of getting his shot off. He was only, what, 5'8"? But he could get his shot off against anybody. He could drive toward the basket, it wasn't a sideways hook, it was coming toward the basket and he could hook it up. Don't ask me how he did it, but he was unique."

Sharm Scheuerman

"He was a little devil. He got in everybody's hair. He made some terrific shots that you would think were impossible, but he made them. He'd get underneath the basket and flip it up one way or another."

Jack Dittmer

"When I was in junior high or high school, I would always listen to the Iowa games. I saw him at our All-Century team meeting, and it was nice visiting with him. I said to him, 'Gee, way back then Murray, 21 points [per game as a senior], that's great! You were a shooter.' He looked at me and winked and said, 'Bill, they never did tell you that I shot 33 times a game.' He was very feisty on the floor. I think he still is."

Bill Seaberg

Jersey #17 Honorable Mention

Willis Glassgow – Football (1927-29)

Willis Glassgow was an All-State quarterback in high school in Shenandoah, Iowa. After one year at the University of Nebraska, Glassgow transferred to Iowa, where he became a two-time All-American halfback and Iowa's first Big Ten MVP. In his first game as a Hawkeye against Monmouth in 1927, he ran for three touchdowns and kicked two extra points in the second quarter alone. Glassgow was an accomplished punter and kicker, and he lettered on Iowa's 1927 Big Ten championship baseball team. In his senior season in 1929, Iowa (Kinnick) Stadium opened, and Glassgow was the first player to score in the new facility on a 30-yard touchdown run. Upon graduation from Iowa Law School, he signed with the St. Louis Cardinals in baseball. He also played two seasons in the NFL before returning to Iowa to practice law. In 1989, he was selected to the all-time University of Iowa football team.

"I think Bill's greatest attribute as a ball carrier was the fact that you could never run him out of bounds. When tacklers would corner him against the sidelines, he'd cut back, put his head down and let them have it. I'll never forget one game at Minnesota. He ran into a tackler so hard, the poor Minnesota fellow got up and lined up in our backfield on the next play."

Burt Ingwersen

#18: FIELDS OF GREEN

"The thing I admired most, besides the tremendous player that he was, I thought he was one of the great ambassadors that Iowa football has ever had off the field. I don't know that I respected a player from an opponent's team more than I had Chad Greenway at the time."

- Dan McCarney

Highway 34 through Davison County, South Dakota, isn't exactly on every coach's recruiting destination checklist. In college football, it helps to have people "on the ground" to scout the nation. In fall 2000, Coach Kirk Ferentz had the right connections on the recruiting trail. Jon LaFleur resided in South Dakota and contacted Iowa's staff about a prospect that had caught his eye. LaFleur, a former Iowa player in the 1990s, observed the Mount Vernon Knights win the nine-man state championship. The Knights were led by a quarterback/free safety named Chad Greenway. LaFleur was impressed with his athleticism and versatility on the field and decided to make sure Iowa was aware of him.

"In our offense we ran a lot of option, so it was nice to have your best athlete play quarterback," explained Myron Steffen, Greenway's high school coach. "As far as free safety, we had some pretty good kids and played a 4-2, but it was nice that Chad came up and played the run like a linebacker. It was nice to have that 6'4" kid back there with a little speed when they did throw deep on you. That's why I played him at free safety. He also was a good tackler."

Chad credited his background growing up on a farm for teaching him the merits of hard work. "Growing up on a farm was an excellent experience - the work ethic and just learning from my dad how to do things the right way," Greenway recalled. "The biggest thing you take from a farm is work ethic. I know people hear that you work on a farm, but you really do work on a farm."

Greenway had received some interest from in-state schools but had not received a scholarship offer from a larger Division I-A school. He eventually took an official visit to Iowa. The Hawkeyes were struggling that season and brought a 2-8 record into the Northwestern game. The Wildcats were two games away from the Rose Bowl, but they left with their third loss of the season. Chad entered a jubilant locker room and met Coach Ferentz for the first time.

"The energy in his face – you could just tell that guy loved football," Ferentz later recalled. "I told my staff, 'I sure hope we love the tape [of Greenway playing].'"

Apparently, they did. Chad became part of a solid recruiting class Iowa signed in February of 2001. Chad was given a two-star out of five rating by most recruiting prognosticators. He was one of the lesser-known recruits of the class and came with little fanfare.

Once fall camp started in 2001, it became evident the question was not whether he would eventually play, but where. Iowa assistant coach Bret Bielema eventually tried Greenway at weakside linebacker in practice. There, he found a home on the field for the rest of his career. "When they recruited me, it was as an athlete," Greenway said. "No one really knows what that means. But now I've found my niche."

"I always thought he could play SAM, MIKE or WILL [linebacker] in college football [and possibly] defensive end," said former Iowa State head coach Dan McCarney. "He probably could have played safety the way he could run. He's one of those guys that I could pick out five, six, or seven positions on defense, and I think he could go be an all-star at those positions."

Chad was redshirted his first year at Iowa. He suffered a torn ACL the following spring that required reconstructive surgery and sidelined him for the first four games of 2002. He first made his presence felt with seven tackles in a win over Purdue. Greenway spent the rest of the year playing mostly spot duty on defense and special teams. Iowa completed an unblemished 8-0 Big Ten schedule and shared the conference championship with BCS national champion Ohio State.

The 2003 season brought about a changing of the guard in Iowa's linebacking corps. Greenway, now a sophomore, replaced Kevin Worthy at weakside linebacker. Abdul Hodge replaced All-Big Ten inside linebacker Fred Barr. This pair of sophomore linebackers would arguably become Iowa's finest to play together for three years. For all time, they will be linked together by admiring Hawkeye fans.

"I met Abdul a couple of times, and I know Chad and him were good friends," said Steffen. "They came from totally different backgrounds. I believe Abdul came from Fort Lauderdale, a big-city guy, and Chad was a farm boy. I know they enjoyed each other's company. They enjoyed competing with and against each other. I know they're still great friends to this day. Abdul was at Chad's wedding this summer. It's a good story."

> **Chad Greenway ranks fifth in school history with 416 career tackles.**
> **Former teammate Abdul Hodge ranks third with 453.**

Greenway had a fine season as a sophomore, recording 17 tackles in a game against Iowa State and matching that feat against Arizona State. Iowa finished the year with ten wins and an Outback Bowl victory. The Hawks opened the following season with a throwback game against Kent State. Dressed in a replica jersey of the Ironmen, Greenway dominated the game, making ten tackles and two interceptions and finishing his second pick with a soaring leap for a touchdown.

That was only the beginning of a magical junior season for Greenway, as Iowa made an improbable run at a Big Ten title. The Hawkeyes' final road game of the season was in Minneapolis against the Gophers, and the Hawks were clinging to a two-point lead with a minute left. Minnesota had gashed Iowa all game with their running attack, and they moved into position to attempt a game-winning field goal. On second down and eight from the Iowa

31-yard line, Greenway sliced through the line and drilled Gopher back Marion Barber III for a four-yard loss. The tackle with 56 seconds left in the game killed the Minnesota drive and forced the Gophers to attempt an errant 51-yard field goal. Iowa escaped with a two-point victory. The following week, Greenway had ten tackles, a sack, and a forced fumble, as Iowa defeated Wisconsin to clinch their 11th Big Ten title.

As a senior in 2005, Greenway played sparingly in the opening game, a 56-0 victory over Ball State. He then recorded double-digit tackles in each of the next ten games, leading Iowa to a
7-4 record and their fourth straight January bowl game. While losses to Michigan and Northwestern by a combined four points cost Greenway the third Big Ten title of his career, he was named a Second Team All-American as a senior.

From Greenway's freshman year through his senior year, Iowa football attained great success. For three consecutive years, they ended the season ranked eighth in the nation. Thirty-eight wins in four seasons was unprecedented in Iowa's football program. Chad Greenway played a huge role in the success of that great Iowa run. The combination of Greenway and Hodge was an imposing challenge for any opposing offense.

> **Chad Greenway became the first Iowa linebacker to be selected in the first round of the NFL Draft.**

Chad was drafted as the 17th overall pick in the 2006 NFL Draft by the Minnesota Vikings. He missed his entire rookie season with a torn ACL, but he came back strong in 2007, leading the Vikings with six takeaways. The following season, Greenway led the team with 150 tackles. He led the team in tackles in 2009 with 127 and led all NFL linebackers with six takeaways while helping guide the Vikings to the NFC championship game. As a modern-day "Purple People Eater", Chad wears No. 52 with the Vikings in honor of his former Iowa teammate, Abdul Hodge.

While at Iowa, few players were as visibly excited to play on Saturdays as Chad Greenway. He was a high-energy player from kickoff to the final gun. He was a huge asset for Hawkeye football, and it all started with an observant eye in South Dakota. Here's to Jon LaFleur!

Accolades
- Second Team All-American (2005)
- All-Big Ten (2004, 05)
- Team captain and MVP (2005)
- Ranks fifth in school history in career tackles

No. 18 CHAD GREENWAY								
Year	Solo	Asst	Total	TFL	Sacks	Int-Yds	Forced Fumbles	Blocks
2002	8	7	15	0/0	0/0	0/0	0	0
2003	78	54	132	13/26	2/7	0/0	1	1
2004	71	42	113	8/23	3/6	3/54	1	1
2005	95	61	156	10/25	2/6	1/16	0	0
Totals	252	164	416	31/74	7/19	4/70	2	2

How He's Remembered

"Chad is a high-energy player that loves the game and the competition involved. As a result, he made everyone around him better."

Kirk Ferentz

"Most overrated player in the Big Ten: Chad Greenway."

2004 *Sporting News* College Football Preview

"There probably is no better linebacking pair in the nation than Chad Greenway and Abdul Hodge. Greenway is bigger and better equipped to take on massive blockers. Plus, he has underrated speed that makes him effective in back-side pursuit."

2005 *Sporting News* College Football Preview

"Chad Greenway is one of my all-time favorite players for a lot of reasons. I don't know if I've ever seen a more instinctive linebacker, and I've seen some great ones at Iowa. We have been blessed with some unbelievable linebackers...but you'd be hard pressed to find a combination or a package of skills like Chad Greenway. First off, he's tall and rangy, he's big at 250 pounds, and yet he hasn't lost any speed. He could still run with wide receivers and tight ends, and that's what made him so endearing to the Minnesota Vikings when they drafted him. He's just the total package with speed, size, tenacity, but also a very smart player, very instinctive...How he grew, not only on the field but off the field in front of the cameras and microphones, I really think is one of the better stories of Iowa football in recent memory."

Gary Dolphin

"He's clearly one of the best linebackers I've ever coached against. You were always aware of where Chad Greenway was."

Dan McCarney

Jersey #18 Honorable Mention

Lowell Otte – Football (1922-24)

Lowell Otte was a talented student-athlete that came to Iowa City from Sidney High School. He was a reserve end as a sophomore on Coach Howard Jones' Big Ten championship team in 1922. Otte earned a starting spot as a junior and was chosen as an All-Big Ten selection in each of his final two seasons. He was a talented, fast end who also lettered in track in 1924. Otte was invited to the first ever East-West Shrine game in 1925, but he had to decline due to an injury he sustained in his final game as a Hawkeye, a 9-2 victory over Michigan. Otte was also a terrific student; he was elected senior class president and was a finalist for the Rhodes Scholarship. He played two seasons of professional football with the New York Yankees of the AFL in 1926 and the Buffalo Bisons of the NFL in 1927.

Dennis Mosley – Football (1976-79)

A native of Youngstown, Ohio, Dennis Mosley earned All-State honors in football and was a state champion in three high school track events. He would also compete in track at the University of Iowa. Mosley played his first three years for Coach Bob Commings. In Mosley's sophomore year of 1977, he scored on runs of 74 and 77 yards against Indiana and Iowa State respectively. In his junior season, he missed three games with a rib injury which limited him to 292 yards on the ground. First-year coach Hayden Fry proclaimed in 1979 that Mosley would become Iowa's first 1,000-yard rusher. The 5'11", 179-pound senior responded with 1,267 rushing yards. Mosley's senior season highlights include a three-touchdown, 229-yard performance against Iowa State. He placed ninth in the nation in rushing and fifth in scoring as a senior in 1979. Mosley was the first Hawkeye to lead the Big Ten in rushing since Bob Jeter in 1959, and his career total of 2,133 rushing yards was an Iowa record at the time. He currently stands in ninth place on Iowa's all-time rushing list.

"He was a kid that you just loved coaching and loved being around. Dennis always had a smile on his face. He was a tremendous athlete, but there was no doubt Hayden Fry's offensive system brought out the best in Mosley. He bought into it after playing in the Wing-T offense under Commings. It was a completely different style, but he was one of the real early sparks to draw interest and excitement to the offense Coach Fry was going to bring to the University of Iowa. And he obviously flourished, rushing for over 1,000 yards his senior year."

Dan McCarney

#19: A HAWKEYE HIGHLIGHT REEL

"[Ferguson] is not just a sprinter. He's what we like to call a heavy-duty halfback...Remember some of Fergie's long runs? He stiff-armed or shook off tacklers like a runaway army half-track. He's one of the most vital cogs in the Hawkeye machine."

- Gus Schrader

Nothing excites a crowd quite like seeing one of their players running seventy, eighty, or even ninety yards for a touchdown. Larry Ferguson was one of the most exciting runners to wear an Iowa uniform, and he was a key member of the Iowa football team from 1959-1962.

Larry Ferguson arrived on the Iowa campus from Madison, Illinois. He had offers from several Big Ten schools, but he chose to play for Coach Forest Evashevski. As a sophomore fullback in 1959, Ferguson tallied only nine carries as seniors Bob Jeter and Ray Jauch carried the offense. Yet Ferguson's 5.5 yards per carry average would be a sign of things to come.

With the losses of Jeter and Jauch the following season, Evy moved Ferguson to the halfback position, while junior Wilburn Hollis manned the quarterback position. The 1960 season was Coach Evashevski's last on the sidelines. The team wanted to send Evy out on a high note, but to do that, the Hawkeyes would need to overcome the most murderous schedule Iowa had ever faced.

The Hawks faced tenth-ranked Oregon State in the season opener, and Iowa led just 16-12 with eight minutes to play in the game. OSU had backed Iowa up to their own 15-yard line before Ferguson made his presence felt. He stiff-armed a player at the line of scrimmage, broke a tackle at the Iowa 40-yard line, got hit at the Oregon State five-yard line, and dove into the end zone. The 85-yard touchdown run was Iowa's longest touchdown play in six years and sealed the upset for the Hawkeyes.

For an encore, Ferguson returned an interception 70 yards for a touchdown the following week to help Iowa pound sixth-ranked Northwestern, 42-0. He also had a 58-yard touchdown run called back by a holding call. "I would like to say that Iowa's backs are just better than outstanding. Larry Ferguson is one of the best left halfbacks I've seen," Northwestern coach Ara Parseghian said.

Ferguson scored a touchdown the following week to help Iowa knock off No. 13-ranked Michigan State in East Lansing before the Hawkeyes returned home to play No. 12-ranked Wisconsin. Although Ferguson scored a touchdown for the fourth straight game, the Badgers and the Hawks were knotted up at 21 with just over a minute to play. The Badgers were forced to punt, and Ferguson broke several tackles to return the punt 51 yards to the Wisconsin

29-yard line. Hollis appeared to throw a game-winning touchdown pass to Ferguson, but it was negated by a penalty. Still, Hollis soon threw a second game-winning touchdown pass in the final minute to win, 28-21.

With wins over four straight ranked opponents, the Hawkeyes were awarded the consensus No. 1 ranking in the nation for the first time in school history. Ferguson was finally held out of the end zone by No. 10 Purdue, but Iowa got the win in their first week at No. 1. The Hawkeyes then went out of conference to play No. 15-ranked Kansas. Ferguson scored another touchdown to lead Iowa to a 21-7 win.

Many Iowa fans fondly remember when No. 1 Iowa defeated No. 2 Michigan, 12-10, in 1985. Twenty-five years earlier, No. 1 Iowa squared off with No. 2 Minnesota in a game of national importance. Second-ranked Minnesota was also undefeated, but they had not played anything resembling the difficult schedule the Hawkeyes had faced. Ferguson was clearly Iowa's most effective weapon against the Gophers, with runs of 21, 11, 16, and 19 yards. But three fumbles in Minnesota territory – none by Ferguson – gave the Gophers easy touchdowns and led to a 27-10 defeat.

> **Every one of Iowa's nine opponents in 1960 spent at least one week in the top 12 of the national rankings.**

The Hawkeyes returned home for Evy's final Big Ten game against third-ranked Ohio State. In an emotional game, Iowa pounced all over the Buckeyes, taking a 28-12 lead into the fourth quarter. The Hawkeyes were pinned deep on their own nine-yard line when Ferguson took the ball. He burst out to midfield before being pushed toward the right sideline by the Buckeyes' Bill Wentz. Ferguson tight-roped the sideline, fought off Wentz, separated from the defender, and scored on a 91-yard touchdown run. "I had the angle on him and thought sure I'd get him," Wentz said. "But the guy turned on another jet and pulled away from me."

Coupled with Minnesota's loss to Purdue, the win over Ohio State gave Evy his third Big Ten title, a school record. The national television audience that watched Iowa dismantle the Buckeyes had to be impressed. Frank Finch of *The Los Angeles Times* wrote, "We thought we had seen the ultimate in college team speed when Evy turned Willie Fleming and Bob Jeter loose in the Rose Bowl in 1959, but the Hawkeye race horses that ran away and hid from the lumbering Ohio Staters must constitute the swiftest stable of backs ever to break from the starting gate. Larry Ferguson's burst of speed at the one perilous point of his 91-yard touchdown gallop almost blew out our TV tube."

Iowa's 1960 schedule concluded with a game against unranked Notre Dame. It was Iowa's first and only unranked foe of the year. Ferguson gained 94 yards to lead all rushers, and the Hawkeyes blanked Notre Dame, 28-0. Iowa narrowly finished behind the Gophers in both major polls. Today, that might have gained them a spot in the BCS National Championship Game. Back then, it didn't even garner them a bowl game.

Hollis recently stated, "We were all very, very motivated to win. We never, ever thought about losing. We never went into a game thinking we wouldn't win, and that was kind of Larry's philosophy. He always wanted to be the best at his position. He was very fast. He was a smart football player and very confident. I think that is what probably made him successful. He was just a really, really tough competitor."

Over the past decade, Evashevski had clearly elevated Iowa's football program to a level never seen before. He turned the program over to Coach Jerry Burns, and expectations were sky-high. The Hawkeyes began the 1961 season with the No. 1 ranking in the nation. With Ferguson and Hollis ready for their senior seasons, Iowa was considered a legitimate Big Ten and national title contender. But disappointment awaited Ferguson and the Hawkeyes.

> **Larry Ferguson was a First Team All-American in 1960.**
> **His season average of 7.4 yards per rush remains**
> **unmatched by any Iowa running back.**

Iowa opened the 1961 season against California. On his third carry of the game, Ferguson suffered a knee injury. "No doubt Iowa's offense, as well as its defense, suffered when All-American halfback Larry Ferguson sprained his left knee midway in the first quarter," wrote Tony Cordaro of *The Des Moines Register*. "Ferguson, who picked up 35 yards in three carries before he left the game, was not believed to be seriously injured."

Though not apparent at first, it was a very serious injury. Torn ligaments ended Ferguson's 1961 season as soon as it started. Torn ligament injuries were much more serious in the 1960s than they are with today's advanced medical practices. The recovery time was longer, and the chances of the player regaining form were not as good. As if that weren't bad enough, Hollis was lost for the season with a wrist fracture in the very next game.

"We started out No. 1 in the nation," recalled Hollis. "In the first game, Ferguson busts up a knee. Then in the second game, I got hurt. One of our really good tight ends got hurt, and one of our tackles got hurt. So Jerry Burns starts out with a team rated No. 1 in the nation, and within the first few games he lost four of his key players."

The Hawkeyes staggered to a disappointing 5-4 record in 1961. Since Ferguson had only played in one game, he was granted a medical redshirt and allowed to return for a senior season in 1962. Hollis, however, had been injured in the second game, so his appeal was denied, ending his career.

As a senior in 1962, Ferguson again led the Hawkeyes in rushing with 547 yards on 113 carries. Ferguson was an All-Big Ten selection, and he was named team captain and MVP. While Ferguson lacked some of the breakaway speed he had displayed as a junior, he still showed flashes of his old explosiveness, like when he caught an 80-yard pass for a touchdown against Wisconsin.

Against Purdue the following week, Ferguson played with a painful hip injury. He had 56 yards rushing and 34 yards receiving, in addition to a 40-yard return of a blocked field goal. Ferguson also had a touchdown called back due to a penalty in the loss to the Boilermakers. "He's the best in the country. I don't care what you say – not another kid in the country could have played the second half with that injury," Coach Burns declared.

Still, the loss dropped the Hawks to a 2-3 record, so Ferguson called a players-only meeting. The Hawkeyes responded by stunning Ohio State, 28-14. "Their captain sparked them," Ohio State coach Woody Hayes acknowledged. Ferguson sparked Iowa again two weeks later with one last great performance. In his final home game, he was awarded the game ball after he rushed for 153 yards and a touchdown to help Iowa upset Michigan. The Hawkeyes defeated both Michigan and Ohio State in the same season for the first time; it has not happened again since.

Ferguson amassed 1,297 yards on 215 carries over his career. His career average of 6.03 yards per carry remains a school record, which is even more impressive considering the severity of his knee injury. He represented Iowa one final time in the 1963 College All-Star Game. Ferguson's All-Stars beat the NFL champion Green Bay Packers; it was the last time the All-Stars defeated the NFL champions before the game was discontinued after 1976.

Although Ferguson was drafted in the fourth round by the NFL's Detroit Lions, he never regained his form after the knee injury. He retired after just one professional season.

As a Hawkeye, Larry Ferguson displayed a flair for the dramatic. He was known for his long runs and pass receptions. Had he not been injured in 1961, he may have been considered Iowa's premier runner of that era. That's saying something, considering the talented backs the Hawkeyes had in those days. As it was, Ferguson provided several highlight plays for one of the greatest teams in school history.

Accolades
• First Team All-American (1960)
• All-Big Ten (1960, 62)
• Team captain and MVP (1962)
• Selected for the College All-Star Game (1963)

No. 19 LARRY FERGUSON

Year	Att	Yds	Avg	TDs
1959	9	50	5.5	1
1960	90	665	7.4	6
1961	3	35	11.7	0
1962	113	547	4.8	3
Totals	215	1,297	6.0	10

How He's Remembered

"Ferguson's 91-yard run stands as one of the great scrimmage advances in Big Ten history."
                              The Des Moines Register (Nov 13, 1960)

"One of the best 'heavy-duty' halfbacks Iowa has ever had."

                              Gus Schrader

"Fergie is the best halfback in the United States in my opinion."

                              Jerry Burns

"That Ferguson is as good a runner as there is in the country. He can play on anyone's team."

                                                              Joe Kuharich, former Notre Dame coach

"Despite his hard-luck career, Ferguson still left school as Iowa's No. 3 all-time rushing leader with 1,297 yards on 215 carries. But it's unfortunate to consider what could have been for this speedster who showed he could out-run defenders but not bad luck."

                                    Mike Finn & Chad Leistikow, *Hawkeye Legends, Lists & Lore*

Jersey #19 Honorable Mention

Karl Noonan – Football (1963-65)

Karl Noonan was a First Team All-State end at Davenport Assumption who chose the Hawkeyes over Notre Dame. He played sparingly on defense his sophomore year in 1963. The following year, he switched to receiver and became one half of a lethal passing attack. With Gary Snook at quarterback, Noonan caught 59 passes for 933 yards. This shattered school records in both categories, and both records stood until 1980. He is still the only Hawkeye to average over 100 yards per game receiving over an entire season. Noonan ranked third in the nation in receiving and was named team MVP, All-Big Ten, and First Team All-American in 1964. Entering his final year, Noonan was named 1965 team captain. He again led the team in receiving but earned less recognition than the year before, partly due to the team's 1-9 record. He played six seasons for the Miami Dolphins and made the 1968 Pro Bowl.

Keith Chappelle – Football (1979-80)

Keith Chappelle came to Iowa as a coveted receiver from California's Glendale Junior College with quarterback Gordy Bohannon. In 1980, he finished second in the nation in receiving, hauling in 64 passes for 1,037 yards and six touchdowns. All were Iowa records. He was named team MVP and earned Second Team All-Big Ten honors as a senior. His career highlights include a 191-yard, two-touchdown performance against Illinois. Chappelle concluded his career with 11 receptions for 143 yards in the 1980 Japan Bowl.

#20: DEAN-O

"I think when Dean Oliver left Iowa, fans really then understood what he meant to the team. He was kind of the glue that held them together."

- Pat Harty

Aplington-Parkersburg produces football linemen, Iowa City produces Hilgenbergs, and Mason City produces point guards.

The first great Mason City point guard of recent years was Dean Oliver, who starred at Iowa from 1997-2001. He committed to play for Iowa as a sophomore in high school, the same year as fellow Iowan Ricky Davis. In fact, they did it at the same time.

"Not many high school sophomores call news conferences, but that's what Dean Oliver and Ricky Davis did Wednesday," wrote Rick Brown of *The Des Moines Register* on November 17, 1994. "Oliver, of Mason City, and Davis, of Davenport North, said Wednesday they will accept scholarship offers from the University of Iowa basketball program even though they have three seasons of high school eligibility remaining."

At the time, it was the earliest a high school athlete had ever committed to play basketball for the University; the late Chris Street had previously held that distinction. Years later, Jeff Horner would commit to Iowa as a freshman. Horner was another Mason City point guard who idolized Oliver growing up.

"I think Dean was a big influence on Jeff Horner," said Pat Harty of the *Iowa City Press-Citizen*. "Dean kind of came at a time right after Fred Hoiberg. I think he kind of symbolized the improvement of high school basketball in Iowa over the last ten to fifteen years."

Before Oliver's days in Mason City were over, the left-handed point guard led the Mohawks to consecutive state championships and a 35-game winning streak. He and future Hawkeye Kyle Galloway each scored 38 points as opponents in the championship final; Oliver played for Mason City, and Galloway played for Sioux City West.

> **Dean Oliver had a career-high 12 assists against Chicago State as a freshman in 1997.**

Oliver began his Iowa experience in 1997 under the tutelage of Dr. Tom Davis. Andre Woolridge led the previous year's team to a second place finish in the Big Ten, and now it was Oliver's turn to step in at point guard. Trying to replace Andre's 20 points per game average was unrealistic for a freshman, but fans hoped Oliver could be a solid point guard to complement senior Ryan Bowen and freshman Ricky Davis. Dean started 30 of the team's 31 games and set a school record for assists by a freshman with 131.

Iowa finished 20-11 that year falling just short of an NCAA Tournament bid. They lost to Georgia in the first round of the NIT. Most notably, it was announced that Coach Davis would be stepping down after the 1998-99 season. It was a controversial move made mostly to stop a decline in ticket sales and a feeling that the program had stagnated.

Davis had a very deep team in his final season as Iowa's coach. Jess Settles was granted a sixth year of eligibility and joined Oliver, Kent McCausland, J.R. Koch, and Jason Bauer in the starting lineup. Guy Rucker, Joey Range, Jake Jaacks, Duez Henderson, and Sam Okey also provided minutes. It was a bittersweet season; while it was Davis' last year at Iowa, he went out in style. Iowa finished third in the Big Ten with perhaps the most memorable game of the season being an 85-81 win at Kansas. Iowa trailed by 18 points with 13 minutes left before rallying to end the Jayhawks' 62-game home winning streak.

The Hawkeyes advanced to the Sweet Sixteen before losing to the eventual national champion Connecticut Huskies. Sophomore Dean Oliver had a solid tournament by scoring 15 points against Alabama-Birmingham and 17 in an upset win over Arkansas. He led the team in points, assists, and steals.

Exit Tom Davis, enter the Steve Alford regime. While many changes accompanied the coaching transition, Dean Oliver provided a stabilizing presence. Though Iowa finished the 2000 season with a 14-16 record, Oliver led the team in scoring with 13.6 points per game and was a Third Team All-Big Ten selection for the second straight season.

Unbeknownst to many, basketball wasn't the biggest challenge for Dean Oliver at the time. His personal life was turned upside down his freshman year when his father was accused of participating in an interstate drug ring. Dean found out about the situation from a reporter. In January 1999, his father was sentenced to five years in a federal prison. In addition to his basketball and academic commitments, Oliver was now left to watch over his two younger brothers.

As his senior year approached, it appeared his father may not have to serve his whole prison sentence. Dean desperately wanted his father to be able to attend his games, but it was unclear whether that would be possible. Oliver even considered redshirting. Finally, in November 2000, his father was released from the federal prison in Pekin, Illinois. Accompanied by some of his Iowa teammates, Dean picked him up and promptly went to Carver-Hawkeye Arena to play a game of pick-up basketball.

Dean spoke to Andrew Bagnato of the *Chicago Tribune* about what it meant for his father to be able to watch him play in person again. "The things you take for granted, I don't take for granted anymore," Oliver said. "Like hearing his voice in the crowd at games. Usually, it's like, 'Awww, Dad, shut up. I know what I'm doing.' Now, I'm just glad when I hear him."

His father, Dean, Sr., shared similar sentiments with Bagnato. "Watching him practice, I guess I am kind of living through his eyes. I guess I just kind of revel in it. Now that I'm out again, I treasure every minute that I'm here."

With his father out of prison, Dean was set to begin his senior season. Many new faces played key roles in the 2000-01 team. Coach Alford's first full recruiting class was one of the top-ranked classes in the nation. Oliver now shared the backcourt with former Indiana star Luke

Recker. Junior college transfer Reggie Evans started at power forward. Freshmen Glen Worley and Jared Reiner played substantial minutes, as did Kentucky transfer Ryan Hogan.

The 2000-01 season started off as one of Iowa's best in years. Oliver provided senior leadership, Recker was a needed boost to the offense, and Evans was a rebounding beast. The team started off 17-4 and 6-2 in the Big Ten.

Then Luke Recker was lost to injury, and the team spiraled, ending the season tied for sixth in the Big Ten. Their first-round game in the Big Ten Tournament was against Northwestern. Oliver played 39 minutes in a win over the Wildcats and then played all 40 minutes the following day, as Iowa upset Ohio State in the quarterfinals. He added 15 points and eight assists in a decisive victory over Penn State to earn Iowa a trip to the championship game against Indiana. Oliver played 39 minutes as Iowa upset the Hoosiers for their fourth win in as many days. The Hawkeyes won their first Big Ten Tournament title and earned an automatic trip to the NCAA Tournament.

Oliver proudly hoisted the Big Ten championship trophy into Carver-Hawkeye Arena for a reception afterward. That same day, they learned their first NCAA Tournament opponent would be Creighton. Iowa defeated Creighton in New York to earn a match-up with No. 2-seeded Kentucky. Though Oliver tied a school record for an NCAA game with six three-pointers, the Wildcats prevailed despite Oliver's 26 points in the final game of his Hawkeye career.

> **Dean Oliver was only the third player in Big Ten history to record 1,500 points, 500 assists, and 200 steals.**

Oliver had an outstanding career. He is one of only nine Hawkeyes to be named team MVP in three seasons, and he is also one of nine Hawkeyes to earn three All-Big Ten selections. He still ranks in the top ten in school history in career points, assists, steals, and games played.

After a brief NBA career with the Golden State Warriors, Oliver enjoyed a long career playing basketball in Europe. Dean Oliver now has a young son, Isaiah. Surrounded by the two most important things in his life, family and basketball, Dean Oliver is moving forward with the next phase of his life. "I think my life has changed the same way most fathers' lives change once they have a child. I don't get as much sleep as I used to. I listen to Choo Choo Soul more than Kanye West now," Oliver said.

It's been a remarkable journey for the terrific point guard from Mason City.

Accolades
• Third Team All-Big Ten (1999, 00, 01)
• Team MVP (1999, 00, 01)
• Ranks in the top ten in school history in career scoring, steals, and assists
• Led team in scoring (1999, 00)
• Led team in assists (1998, 99, 00, 01)

No. 20 DEAN OLIVER									
Year	GP	FG-FGA	FG%	FT-FTA	FT%	Reb	Avg	Pts	Avg
1998	31	79-211	37	96-126	76	78	2.5	274	8.8
1999	30	105-262	40	111-155	72	106	3.5	357	11.9
2000	30	125-339	37	118-154	77	87	2.9	408	13.6
2001	35	157-401	39	143-186	77	98	2.8	522	14.9
Totals	126	466-1,213	38	468-621	75	369	2.9	1,561	12.4

How He's Remembered

"To me, Dean Oliver kind of epitomizes what it means to be a Hawkeye."

Pat Harty

"He had some big shoes to fill because Andre [Woolridge] had just left. He came in and did a great job. I remember him playing in a state tournament game his senior year in high school. Just watching him play that game, I was excited he was going to be a Hawkeye. He came in and did a great job of running the team. He ended up having a great career. One thing about Dean, he came real close to breaking my steal record; I think he was two or three short, so I still give him a hard time about that. He just couldn't quite get there. But even just playing one year, I had a lot of fun getting to know him and then got to play against him a couple years in the NBA when he was with Golden State. It was fun to see him in the NBA. I think barring a couple of injuries and a bit of bad luck, he'd still be playing in the NBA."

Ryan Bowen

"Dean came in with probably as much hype as any athlete in a long time at Iowa, but I actually saw him as an eighth grader and saw terrific passing skills. But for his size, he was maybe as good of a point guard as Iowa's ever had."

Mac McCausland

Jersey #20 Honorable Mention

Dick Crayne – Football (1933-35)

Perhaps no other fullback in Iowa history can match the accomplishments of Dick Crayne. He was a First Team All-State fullback for Fairfield High School, and he played both football and track for the Hawkeyes. His Hawkeye career began and ended with 139- and 140-yard rushing performances against Northwestern. As a sophomore, he gained 655 yards, which was the most by a Hawkeye in 12 years. His career highlights include an 85-yard kick return and what is believed to be the longest punt in Iowa history. Standing in Iowa's end zone, he punted a ball against Indiana that rolled out of bounds at the Hoosier five-yard line. Crayne was All-Big Ten as a junior and Third Team All-American as a senior. He was highly regarded by his teammates. Despite playing in the same backfield as the great Ozzie Simmons, Crayne was twice named team MVP. Upon graduation, Crayne became Iowa's first first-round draft choice in the NFL.

Wilburn Hollis – Football (1959-61)

Wilburn Hollis came to Iowa from Boystown, Nebraska. After sitting behind Olen Treadway as a sophomore in 1959, Hollis ascended to the starting quarterback position as a junior and helped lead Iowa to one of its most successful seasons. He rushed for two touchdowns against Wisconsin in 1960 and threw the game-winning touchdown with 52 seconds remaining in a 28-21 victory. That performance earned Hollis National Back of the Week honors from the *Associated Press*, and Iowa was elevated to No. 1 in the nation after the win. Iowa spent three weeks at No. 1 and won the Big Ten title with an 8-1 record. The 6'2", 200-pound Hollis earned All-Big Ten and Third Team All-American honors. Unfortunately, injuries would derail his senior season. Hollis, a team captain in 1961, fractured his right wrist in the second game of the season, and his very successful Iowa career came to a premature end.

Andre Jackson – Football (1972-75)

Despite winning only nine games over his four years, linebacker Andre Jackson left an indelible mark on the Iowa defensive record book. As a freshman in 1972, he recorded 22 tackles in a 6-6 tie with heavily-favored Michigan State. This was the first of six times in his career where he tallied 20 or more tackles in a single game. Jackson holds the record for most tackles in a season (171 in 1972) and currently stands behind only Larry Station in career tackles (465). His senior year, Jackson was named team captain and team MVP.

#21: PRAISING CAIN

"Obviously, we had an outstanding basketball team. People will tell you that I might have gotten more press than everybody else because of the Olympics and all of that, but I evaluate us as a team. Some of us were All-Big Ten or All-American, but we didn't have any really big names on our basketball team. We were a unique group of five guys who came to the same location and played basketball at the same time. As a team, we were extraordinary."

- Carl Cain

Iowa's basketball fortunes in the mid-1950s may have hinged upon a high and tight fastball.

"I dabbled a little bit in other sports in high school," explained Carl Cain. "I did a little high jumping in track. Baseball was really my preferred sport, but I had an incident where I was playing and got beaned and couldn't keep my foot in the 'bucket' anymore. Throw me a little curve and I start bailing out.

"After that, all the people who knew anything about baseball said, 'If you can't, with whatever help is available, get over this fear of being hit again, then you can throw that notion of playing baseball out of your mind.' I really had the greatest love for baseball, but that incident put me on the track of devoting all my energy to playing basketball. So basketball was basically the sport that I played."

Carl Cain grew up in Freeport, Illinois, in the late 1940s and early '50s down the street from another future Hawkeye, McKinley (Deacon) Davis. Davis was a year older than Carl, and together they led Freeport to the 1951 Illinois High School basketball championship. The next fall, Deacon enrolled at the University of Iowa on a basketball scholarship offered by Iowa head coach Bucky O'Connor. This heavily influenced Carl's choice of colleges.

"Deacon went to Iowa City to have a recruiting visit," recalled Cain. "We lived next door, and we were best buds, so he said, 'Hey, do you want to ride up there with me?' I said, 'Sure, I do.'"

"I didn't do a whole lot of traveling, so I figured I'd go," Cain continued. "After Bucky O'Connor finished his work with Deacon on the recruiting end of it, we were about ready to leave Iowa City and go home. Bucky turned to me and said, 'Carl, I'd like to think that when you finish down there at high school in Freeport next year, you'll think about coming up here to the University of Iowa.'"

"I was kind of impressed with that," Cain explained. "You know, this guy was offering me a chance to consider coming to school up here, and he didn't know much about me. But I was impressed, and it stuck in my mind. And so it was very easy for me to make that decision."

"Cool Carl," as he was called by some, had to sit out his freshman year according to NCAA rules at the time. Four other freshmen – Sharm Scheuerman, Bill Seaberg, Bill Logan, and Bill Schoof – did the same. The talented quintet waited until the 1953-54 season to make their debut. What a debut it was!

Three of them were regular starters through the year; Cain at forward, Seaberg at guard, and Logan at center. Scheuerman and Schoof played in a reserve role for most of the year, but after two consecutive February losses, Coach O'Connor decided to start the entire sophomore group. The "Fabulous Five" were officially assembled.

> **Four of the "Fabulous Five" were from the state of Illinois.**
> **Only Bill Logan was from the state of Iowa.**

"As sophomores," Cain recalled, "we went to Bloomington, Indiana, to play Indiana University. That was the game that our coach started us five sophomores. They were defending national champions who had most of their people back, and we weren't even supposed to be in the same gym. But we beat them by about 15 points. And people said, 'Whoa, this is an extraordinary group here.' That's the game that I remember."

Though Indiana went on to win the conference, a statement had been made by the second-place Hawkeyes. The two leading scorers, Logan (14.3 points per game) and Cain (12.9), were only sophomores. Scheuerman was quietly developing into the cerebral point guard with pinpoint passing. Bill Seaberg was the marksman of the group, setting a school record for shooting percentage. Unlike today's game, only the conference champion advanced to the sixteen-team NCAA Tournament. That would be the last time the five saw their season end without post-season play.

By their junior year, all but Schoof were regular starters. For the first time since the days of Dick Ives and Murray Wier, the Hawks became conference champs. Bolstered by eight consecutive wins throughout February, Iowa finished with a second consecutive 11-3 record. Logan again led the team in scoring, with Cain behind him at 13.4 points per game.

Their first game in the NCAA Tournament was a 29-point blowout win over Penn State, with Cain scoring 21 points to lead the team. The following day, Iowa defeated Marquette to earn their first Final Four trip in school history. Colorado matched up against San Francisco, while Iowa went against the LaSalle Explorers in the other bracket. Iowa's run ended against defending national champion LaSalle in a hard-fought, three-point loss. They would falter again in the consolation bracket at the hands of Colorado.

Heading into their senior year, Cain and the Hawkeyes had naturally garnered their share of national attention and respect. This resulted in a No. 2 national ranking to begin the season. They would eventually realize their expectations, but the season was not without its challenges.

Eight games into the 1955-56 season, the "Fabulous Five" had five losses against only three wins. After some soul-searching and a special team meeting, the team refocused on the season. It worked; they didn't lose again for 76 days.

Beginning with a January 9 win over Ohio State, the team reeled off fourteen straight wins before the tournament. The season culminated with a March matchup with Illinois. Both teams stood at 11-1, and the outright Big Ten lead was on the line. The Illini had taken Iowa's place in the national rankings at No. 2, while Iowa stood at No. 10. The game was nationally televised, and a trip to the NCAA Tournament was on the line.

All morning, Iowa fans stormed the Field House in anticipation of the 1:30 p.m. tip-off. The game was close that afternoon until Iowa broke it open with a 59-point second half. It was sweet justice for the nine Illinois natives on Iowa's roster, many of whom had been overlooked by the Illinois coaching staff as high school seniors.

"We were big rivals of Illinois," Cain recalled, "because four of us five starters were from Illinois. I remember one year we were playing Illinois for the Big Ten championship, a Saturday afternoon game on television. You know, our team was one of the early groups to play on television. But we were playing in Iowa City for the Big Ten championship, and we just really clicked again and kind of blew Illinois away."

Cain attributes the team's ability to bounce back from its early-season woes directly to the camaraderie the team had built over four years.

"We liked each other," he explained. "We hung out together. That freshman year when one of us, for example, would decide to sell programs at the football games, all of us sold programs. I mean, we were very clannish. We stayed in the same dormitory. That's another part of what made our team so good. One guy wasn't doing this while another guy was doing that. If you'd find one of us doing something, you'd find the other four doing the same thing."

Iowa's first opponent in the 1956 NCAA Tournament was Morehead State, that year's highest-scoring team in the nation. Cain was the high scorer on that particular day, with 28 points to lead Iowa in the first-round victory. The Kentucky Wildcats came to Iowa City for a second-round game. Again, Cain set the stage for an Iowa win with a career-high 34 points. The Hawkeyes were headed to Kansas City for their second consecutive Final Four.

Iowa handed Temple an 83-75 defeat to place themselves on the biggest stage of all, the national championship game against Bill Russell and San Francisco. Ultimately, Russell and company proved to be more than Iowa could handle on that given day. Cain and Seaberg led Iowa with 17 points, but San Francisco pulled out an 83-71 win. Both Cain and Bill Logan earned All-American honors for their senior year, and, for the second time, Cain was named the team's most valuable player.

Though the "Five" ended their fabulous Iowa careers that March, Cain remained on the national stage by representing the USA on the 1956 Olympic Team. "I'd just graduated from the University," said Cain. "There was no such thing as going to the Olympics as a freshman or a sophomore like Larry Bird or Michael."

USA Basketball won the gold medal in Melbourne, Australia. The 1956 Olympic team won eight games by an average of 53.5 points per game. Despite the team's success, however, Cain paid a heavy price for his trip.

"I hurt my back during the Olympics," noted Cain. "I had planned to go to the NBA. In fact, I had been drafted by the Rochester Royals. I subsequently found out that I had ruptured a disk, and that far back medical science had not evolved to the place of successful back surgery as it has today. My plan was to come back from the Olympics and go to Rochester to play basketball in the NBA. But when I got back, I'm damaged goods."

"We couldn't sign contracts because the draft had occurred before we went to the Olympics," Cain said. "The Olympics were very, very strict about professionalism. You had to be a pure amateur. So Bill Russell, K.C. Jones, and I were the three collegiate athletes on the '56 Olympic team. We had to sign affidavits before we went to the Olympics that we had never been paid to play basketball before and had no intentions in the future of being paid to play basketball. I'm sure you know how ridiculous that was. Everybody in America knew the Celtics couldn't wait for Russell to get back."

> **Carl Cain and Chuck Darling are the only two Hawkeyes to represent the USA basketball team in the Olympics.**

Cain continued, "I returned home [from Melbourne], got married, and then moved myself to California. Very shortly after arriving in the Los Angeles area, I got a job as a probation officer for the County of Los Angeles. I did that for about ten years. Then I moved back to Chicago and got in the insurance business, and that resulted in my being transferred as a District Manager to Des Moines. I remained in Des Moines and did various kinds of work for the next almost 30 years. I retired in September of 1995 after about 23 years as the Manager of Consumer Affairs for MidAmerican Energy."

"I'm out here living in Pickerington, Ohio, which is a suburb of Columbus," Cain explained. "My wife and I, after being retired for a few years, decided we'd sell this nice ranch house we'd lived in for all these years and move out to Ohio where our kids are. We did that about seven years ago."

Cain summarizes his Iowa career very simply. "I've been away from that environment and those experiences for well over 50 years," he said, "and I have never been one to do a lot of living in the past, but I certainly remember we had a great experience and a great career at Iowa."

Bill Logan, Carl Cain, and Bill Seaberg in 2002

Carl Cain is not one to seek praise. He was never in it for the glory; he was in it for the team and the player camaraderie. His humble nature tends not to dwell on his many athletic accomplishments. That's okay. Generations of Iowa fans will do it for him.

Accolades
• First Team All-American (1956)
• First Team All-Big Ten (1956); Second Team All-Big Ten (1954, 55)
• Won gold medal with USA Olympic Team (1956)
• Selected to Iowa's All-Century basketball team (2002)
• No. 21 retired by Iowa basketball in his honor

No. 21 CARL CAIN

Year	GP	FG-FGA	FG%	FT-FTA	FT%	Reb	Avg	Pts	Avg
1954	22	106-248	43	71-119	60	-	-	283	12.9
1955	26	133-333	40	94-140	67	244	9.4	360	13.8
1956	26	165-403	41	81-112	72	257	9.9	411	15.8
Totals	74	404-984	41	246-371	66	501	9.6	1054	14.2

How He's Remembered

"I can remember Carl maybe my first game ever watching TV, and he just amazed me with his sleekness and athleticism on that 'Fab Five' team. He was definitely the leader, but a very quiet, confident person as I got to know him later on in life. He just enjoyed his time at Iowa."

Mac McCausland

"Carl was one of the first great leapers. People who watched Carl play would say he'd go up in the air, and he seemed to stay in the air longer than anybody else. And that was exactly right; he was a very smooth ball player. 'Cool Carl Cain' was kind of his nickname. One of the trademarks of our team was that we were a good fast-breaking team, and Carl would fill that third lane just like nobody. He got down the court, and we could either give it to him for the layup or we'd lob it to him. Carl was extremely quick. He was fast and quick."

Sharm Scheuerman

"Carl Cain was extremely fast, very athletic. Carl was just so quick, so graceful. He's still a very good friend, and it's just wonderful talking to those guys whenever I get a chance."

Bill Seaberg

"Carl was a great leaper, a great rebounder. In the clutch, you knew Carl was going to be there. He was super on the fast break and extremely quick. He was at full motion in two strides."

Bill Schoof

Jersey #21 Honorable Mention

Devon Mitchell – Football (1982-85)

Devon Mitchell walked on to Iowa's football program in 1981. After redshirting, he started nine games his freshman year. A game-saving tackle against Indiana that year earned him *The Sporting News* defensive play of the week. As a junior, he missed the Freedom Bowl with an injury but came back as a senior to help lead Iowa to the Rose Bowl. He was named Second Team All-Big Ten, Honorable Mention All-American, and team MVP in 1985. Mitchell and Nile Kinnick share the school record with 18 career interceptions. Mitchell was drafted in the fourth round by the Detroit Lions. He was born in Kingston, Jamaica.

"Nate Creer, Devon Mitchell, and Owen Gill were all teammates at Brooklyn Tilden High School [in New York]. I remember going with Bernie Wyatt as a graduate assistant, a part-time coach, as a full-time coach to recruit and learn the ropes. I remember going to practice and watching those three guys practicing on a thing; it was on a field that was called a football field. There was dirt; there were rocks; there was broken glass. Literally, this is how bad it was. But we were watching those three players going, 'Wouldn't it be something if we'd get all three of these guys to come to Iowa?' And all three of them ended up coming."

Dan McCarney

Tony Stewart – Football (1987-90)

New Jersey native Tony Stewart ran for 326 yards as a freshman, including 102 yards against Wisconsin in his first start. He became the first Iowa sophomore to rush for over 1,000 yards in a season, despite missing two games with a knee injury. His junior and senior years were spent sharing time with Big Ten MVP Nick Bell. Even though he led Iowa in yardage only one year, he became Iowa's all-time leading rusher – twice. In the 1991 Rose Bowl, he broke Owen Gill's record of 2,556 yards. He lost yardage his next carry and then regained the top spot to end with 2,562 total yards.

#22: A FABULOUS SHOOTER

"Bill Seaberg was one of the finest guards that I could have played with – an extraordinary shooter. He had good range. We didn't have the three-point stuff back then of course, but he was a fantastic shooter. Great, great guy, great athlete, great basketball player."

- Carl Cain

For a basketball team to live up to the moniker "fabulous", it needs all the right ingredients. To begin, you need a presence in the middle. From 1954 to 1956, that was Bill Logan. You need a high-flying slasher who can create his own shots – that was Carl Cain. You need unselfish role players such as Bill Schoof. You need a heady floor general to distribute the ball – that was Sharm Scheuerman. Finally, you need someone who could extend the defense with his shooting. That was Bill Seaberg. That, Iowa fans, was the original "Fabulous Five."

For Bill Seaberg, it all started in Moline, Illinois. "I was like most guys," Seaberg said. "I played baseball, football, basketball, and track in high school. I even ran cross-country to get in shape for basketball. Basketball was my priority."

> **When he was young, Bill Seaberg chipped ice off the alley so he could shoot baskets during the winter months.**

Seaberg played high school ball in Moline's Wharton Field House. With a seating capacity of up to 6,000 people, Seaberg later considered it an advantage to have played in such an environment prior to the raucous crowds of the Big Ten. "When you play in that large of a group, you get accustomed to the crowds and noise. It was really quite a basketball facility for a high school," Seaberg stated.

All-Century Team Induction

"My junior year, we played the Illinois state championship game against Freeport," recalled Seaberg. "Freeport had Deacon Davis and Carl Cain, who both went to Iowa. They beat us quite badly because we had an overtime game against Quincy on that afternoon and we were just beat. But that was a highlight of my high school career, getting second in the state my junior year. My senior year, we lost in the semifinals to Rock Island. They had Sharm Scheuerman, and he and I went on to be teammates at Iowa. So it's a small world after all."

At 6'0" and 170 pounds, Seaberg came to Iowa after showing interest in Kentucky and Minnesota. Seaberg recalled, "Bucky O'Connor came to visit me a couple times. Then on the third time, I committed to play at Iowa with him. He told me that Sharm was going, Carl Cain was going. He thought he was having a good recruiting class. And I said, 'Well, I'll join them.'"

At the time, freshmen were ineligible to play college basketball. Seaberg and the rest of the freshman class had to settle for a year on the practice court before taking the Field House court for the first time.

Their opportunity finally arrived in late 1953. Seaberg, Carl Cain, and Bill Logan all made the starting lineup early in their sophomore year, with Scheuerman and Schoof coming in off the bench. That changed one memorable evening in Bloomington, Indiana. After losing to Ohio State and having been beaten badly by Illinois at home, Coach O'Connor decided to make a change. He chose to go with an all-sophomore lineup of Cain, Seaberg, Logan, Scheuerman, and Schoof. With defending national champion Indiana at ten wins against one loss on the season, O'Connor probably felt that he had little to lose.

It was a brilliant move. Iowa stunned the conference-leading Hoosiers on their home court, 82-64. Seaberg led all scorers with 21 points. The promising sophomores were more than just good on the practice court. They led Iowa to a 17-5 season and a runner-up showing in the Big Ten. Cain was named team MVP, Logan averaged over 14 points per game, and Seaberg set a school record for shooting percentage. A good team was developing into something fabulous under their young head coach, Bucky O'Connor.

> **As a sophomore, Bill Seaberg set a new school record for field goal percentage at 47%. It broke Chuck Darling's previous record of 42%.**

"The main asset Bucky had," said Seaberg, "is he was a good psychologist. He knew when to crack down on us and when to ease up. He knew by the time we were juniors, and especially our senior year, we knew what we were doing out there. And he just let us play the game. He knew what our talents were. He knew we were close knit; we still are. And we knew what our roles were on that floor. We knew who was going to lead the fast break, who was going to shoot from outside, when to get the ball inside. We just all had a good feel for the game, and Bucky knew this. Once in a while when we'd get lazy or something, then he'd crack into us, but he just knew when to let us play and when to get tough with us."

The following two years were perhaps the most decorated in all of Iowa basketball history with two Big Ten championships and two consecutive Final Four trips. From an individual perspective, Seaberg's junior year was his most accomplished. He was named team MVP and also Third Team All-American. Despite the honors and accolades, it was always about the team with this group of Hawkeyes.

"We always encouraged each other if someone had a bad game," Seaberg recalled. "Once in a while Carl would score 20 or 25, then I'd score 20 or 25 the next game, then Logan would score. We just kind of moved it around. If they gang up on me then, boom, you'd go over to Sharm. He'd get it in to Logan. The opponent could not focus on any one or two guys on our team and stop our offense. We all knew the importance of defense, and we helped each other out. I'd press out front, and if someone would get around me, I knew there would be someone behind me that would pick them up. So we could press and push them out towards that half-court line so they couldn't get comfortable shooting. We had good balanced scoring."

"I think my senior year, I was around 17 points per game in the Big Ten, and we just dominated. Carl was up there; Logan always led us in scoring," Seaberg continued. "Schoof and Sharm contributed; they could score and also knew when to pass. They were excellent passers. We just knew how to get open and somehow that ball was going to get to us, plus we never stopped fast-breaking. We would run anybody off the court."

After going to the Final Four in 1955, the "Fab Five" came into their final season a bit too relaxed. "I think we were a little complacent our senior year," Seaberg noted. "We were ranked No. 2 to begin the season when we went on that road trip and lost three on the West Coast. We came back and decided we better play ball. We should've won that Michigan State game but lost by one point at home. We got very serious and had a team meeting after that and just really buckled down. I said, 'Okay, everybody take advantage of their talents and use them, coordinate with one another and get serious about this, and no let-ups from here on out.'"

They didn't let up, winning the Big Ten for the second straight time and returning to the Final Four. Seaberg's career culminated in the 1956 national championship game against San Francisco and the famous Bill Russell. Iowa led by 11 points in the first quarter, but then Russell took over. San Francisco grabbed the lead and never relinquished it. Iowa trailed by seven late in the game and could never pull any closer to the back-to-back NCAA champs. Seaberg and Cain led Iowa in scoring with 17 points each. "We were close," Seaberg simply stated about the 1956 NCAA championship game.

In the 83-71 San Francisco win, Russell recorded 26 points and an incredible 27 rebounds, which is still a Final Four record for a single game. "Playing against Bill Russell meant a lot at the time," said Iowa teammate Bill Schoof, "and of course now it has meant so much more because of what he has accomplished. I guess I've always had tremendous respect for people who changed the way things are done…and Bill Russell actually changed the way teams play basketball. When we played, we were taught to never leave your feet on defense except to get a rebound. There was no such thing as the blocked shot. It didn't happen. If you were doing that, you were leaving your feet and doing something wrong. The way Russell played defense was something new."

In addition to the Indiana game as sophomores, two other Big Ten games stand out as being particularly memorable to Seaberg. "I loved playing against Illinois," he said. "They had all Illinois kids and none of us [Illinois natives] were recruited by the coach at Illinois. I remember our senior year for the Big Ten championship at Iowa, the crowd started pouring in there about nine o'clock in the morning. The game wasn't until about one or two o'clock. It was just jam packed, and we beat 'em. We were close to them at halftime, and then we poured it on in the second half and beat them by about 25 points. I also recall Minnesota our junior year up there for the Big Ten championship. They had capacity crowds of around twenty to twenty-one thousand. A great team, but we were able to beat them."

Upon graduation, Seaberg set his sights away from the basketball court. He declined an $18,000 offer to play for a professional team in Ohio and instead decided to transition to the business world. He moved to Colorado to pursue a position in the real estate business where he has worked for nearly 40 years.

Today, Bill and his wife, Ida, have five children and 13 grandchildren. They own a home in Evergreen and a ranch in Telluride where they spend time during the summer, hunting season, or any other time to enjoy a great view of the San Juan Mountains.

"I talk to Carl a couple times every year," said Seaberg. "I see Sharm once in a while; he's in Denver. Schoof's coming to visit me in September. I played golf with him down there recently, and we're still close. I don't see Logan that much. He's down in Florida. It's wonderful. You call up and say hi, and there are no strangers among us."

This class of players from the mid-1950s set the gold standard for Iowa Hawkeye basketball. With back-to-back Big Ten championships and Final Four appearances to their credit, this special group of student athletes left an indelible mark in Hawkeye basketball lore.

Accolades
- Third Team All-American (1956)
- Second Team All-Big Ten (1955, 56)
- Team MVP (1955)
- Selected to Iowa's All-Century basketball team (2002)
- No. 22 retired by Iowa basketball in his honor

No. 22: BILL SEABERG							
Year	GP	FG-FGA	FG%	FT-FTA	FT%	Pts	Avg
1954	Statistics not available						
1955	22	107-258	41%	82-104	79%	296	13.4
1956	26	126-331	38%	110-141	78%	362	13.9

How He's Remembered

"The 'Fabulous Five' was a great team. They played as a team. I don't think Seaberg averaged many points, but he and Sharm Scheuerman were a great set of guards. I don't remember Seaberg being a great scorer, but he was certainly a great playmaker. Team was the name of the game with those guys. Nobody cared what they scored, as long as they won the game."

Buck Turnbull

"Bill might have been the best pure shooter that I saw play basketball at that time. Had the three-point shot been in effect during our careers, Bill may have averaged 25 points a game. He was a pure shooter, but was a tough, tough competitor. Not many people realize how good a defensive basketball team we had at Iowa when we played there. Sharm and Seab were shutdown guards. I mean, they were really tenacious on defense."

Bill Schoof

"Well, I'm still a Hawkeye, and I was so very much honored when they put me on that All-Century Team with Carl Cain and Bill Logan as my teammates. It was always a thrill playing at Iowa, and I enjoyed the people there."

Bill Seaberg

Jersey #22 Honorable Mention

Eddie Phillips – Football (1980-83)

Eddie Phillips, a 6'1", 210-pound running back, came to Iowa right as Hayden Fry's program took flight. Despite leading the team in rushing for only one season (1982), Phillips left four years later as Iowa's all-time leading rusher. His career highlights include appearances in the Rose, Peach, and Gator Bowls. In 1982, he rushed for 198 and 158 yards on consecutive weekends against Minnesota and Illinois. He tore knee ligaments in a loss the next week at Purdue but played again in the season finale against Tennessee. In 1983, he ran for 172 yards (including 80 yards on the game's opening play) versus Minnesota to become Iowa's all-time leading rusher. He ended his career with 2,177 yards and 18 touchdowns.

Tavian Banks – Football (1994-97)

Despite playing in a reserve capacity for three years, Tavian Banks played a large role in the Iowa football program's success in the 1990s. He returned 28 kicks as a freshman to go along with five rushing touchdowns. In 1995, while starter Sedrick Shaw set an Iowa season rushing record, Banks added 400 more yards. As a junior, Banks led the team in scoring and rushed for 182 yards against Iowa State. In 1997, with Shaw having graduated, Tavian Banks made short order of Iowa's season rushing record. That year, Banks reached 1,000 yards quicker than any other back in NCAA history. This included an Iowa-record 314 yards on 29 carries against Tulsa. Banks' rushing total of 1,691 yards in 1997 ranks second on Iowa's single-season rushing list. He finished in the top ten nationally in rushing, scoring, and all-purpose yards that season. He also holds Iowa's career touchdown record with 36.

"Watching him hit the corner was something of beauty. When he turned the corner, it was over and he was gone. Tavian was just a special, special athlete...Banks could just fly. He had the natural gift of making people miss and accelerating. The thing some people don't remember about Tavian is that he was a really, really good soccer player. His soccer coach used to tell me that he could have played college or national-level soccer because he was so talented. And he really enjoyed playing soccer."

Tom Kakert

#23: IOWA'S OWN "FLINTSTONE"

"When he came in, I likened him to kind of a small Michael Jordan. I don't want to compare him to Michael Jordan, but he played like that. Great athlete, could shoot, run the court, everything."

- Sharm Scheuerman

Throughout its history, Iowa basketball has had its share of "blue-collar" athletes. Players such as Bill Logan, Kevin Kunnert, Ed Horton, and Jess Settles all knew how to crash the boards and play solid defense. They weren't flashy but were extremely productive. They were the timecard-punching, lunchbox-carrying types, so to speak.

Then there are the "high-flyer" Hawkeyes. They come through the program less often, but when they do, they wow fans with their athleticism, creativity, and scoring ability. Players such as Carl Cain and Ronnie Lester set the standard. Then Roy Marble came along and raised the bar.

Roy was part of Coach George Raveling's highly-coveted 1985 freshman class, which also included B.J. Armstrong, Ed Horton, Kevin Gamble, and Les Jepsen. Because of Marble's frame, his athleticism, his scoring abilities, and his jersey number, talent scouts saddled him with the "next Jordan" label while he was still in high school. It was a comparison that would follow him throughout his career at Iowa.

Roy Marble was runner-up for Michigan's Mr. Basketball in 1985; future teammate B.J. Armstrong finished fifth in the balloting. Roy was another product of the basketball factory which is Flint, Michigan, joining a long line of major college stars to come out of that city. Flint is also the hometown of Barry Stevens and Jeff Grayer from Iowa State and Michigan's Glen Rice. Four Flint natives, collectively known as "The Flintstones", were the bedrock of Michigan State's rise to prominence in the late 1990s. Whether it's great coaching or something in the water, Flint routinely produces great basketball players, and Marble was no exception.

Roy led his Beecher High School team to an undefeated 27-0 record as a senior, averaging 26.5 points and 13 rebounds per game. He was a three-time All-State selection and earned both Parade and McDonald's All-American honors.

> **Roy Marble once shot 18 of 19 from the field in a high school game.**

He made an immediate impact on Raveling's 1985-86 team by leading Iowa in scoring at 12.5 points per game. Today, that stands as the sixth-best freshman scoring average in Iowa history. While Armstrong and Horton were adjusting to the college game, Marble hit the ground running. After playing only six minutes the first two games, he responded with games of 29 and 28 points his third and fourth games. He broke Ronnie Lester's record for points by an

Iowa freshman and was named a First Team Freshman All-American by NBC. By every measure, it was an impressive freshman year.

Prior to the 1986-87 season, Raveling left Iowa and headed west to coach USC. Iowa athletic director Bump Elliott brought new head coach Tom Davis to Iowa City. Davis was known for an up-tempo, pressing basketball style which seemed to be a very good fit for the young and athletic Hawkeyes.

"The acrobatic Marble returns for a second season after leading the Hawkeyes in a number of categories as a rookie while becoming Iowa's all-time top scoring freshman with 399 points," wrote *Iowa City Press-Citizen* columnist Al Grady in the 1986-87 Iowa Basketball Preview. "Like [Gerry] Wright, Marble likes to play up around the rim, but he is an accomplished outside shooter. What he needs, like most youngsters, is more consistency."

Davis was just the coach to develop Marble's fundamentals and athleticism in his trademark pressing style. Davis and the Hawkeyes went 18 games into the 1987 season before their first loss. Meanwhile, Marble was Carver-Hawkeye Arena's version of Chicago's No. 23 with his high-flying plays and high-scoring games. The Hawkeyes finished second in the conference to Indiana and earned a No. 2 seed in the NCAA Tournament.

After defeating Santa Clara in the opening round, the Hawkeyes earned a hard-fought win over Texas El-Paso to advance to the Sweet Sixteen. Marble scored a team-high 28 points against the Miners to advance to the West Region semifinals in Seattle. Oklahoma was Iowa's next victim in a thrilling 93-91 overtime win. Only UNLV stood in the way of Iowa's fourth Final Four appearance. Despite leading by 19 points in the first half, however, Iowa suffered a bitter defeat at the hands of the Runnin' Rebels.

For the second year in a row, Marble led Iowa with 14.9 points per game. Despite the loss to UNLV, Iowa's basketball future looked promising with Marble, Armstrong, and Horton yet to play their junior seasons.

As a junior, Marble raised his scoring average to 15.4 points per game and was a Second Team All-Big Ten selection for the second straight year, but some fans still expected more. "People have been constantly saying, 'What's the matter with Roy Marble?' I've found that question continually puzzling because, in my mind, he's been playing well," Coach Tom Davis said. "It points out one of the negatives of a lot of publicity early in your career. When you get built up so much so early, it becomes almost impossible to live up to."

The Hawkeyes redeemed themselves against UNLV in the 1988 NCAA Tournament. After a first-round, 102-98 defeat of Florida State, Iowa thumped the Runnin' Rebels, 104-86, in Los Angeles to make it back to the Sweet Sixteen. Iowa's run in the NCAA Tournament ended in Seattle at the hands of Lute Olson and Arizona, however; it was their second loss of the season to the Wildcats.

Horton, Armstrong, and Marble began their senior seasons in 1988. Similar to two years prior, they strung together a long winning streak to start the season at 13-1. This included wins over Iowa State, Michigan State, and North Carolina.

The dramatic win over 12-1 North Carolina was especially memorable since it came in Chapel Hill. Tied at 97 with 22 seconds remaining, North Carolina's Jeff Lebo missed a jump shot. After a short scramble under the basket, a foul was called on the Tar Heels. Horton appeared to be the Iowa player fouled, but after indicating to the referee that he was the player that was fouled, Marble was awarded the free throws. Marble scored his 23rd point of the game, and Iowa won, 98-97.

Marble became Iowa's all-time leading scorer later that month in a home win against Wisconsin. He also became the first Hawkeye to score over 2,000 career points in a loss to Michigan. More importantly, Marble seemed to finally be at peace with the labels that had been placed upon him. "I'm not another Michael Jordan, or a little Dominique [Wilkins]. I'm just Roy now. Roy Marble," he announced.

1989 was a particularly strong year for Big Ten basketball. Indiana won the conference. Two of the eventual Final Four participants (Illinois and eventual national champion Michigan) were from the Big Ten. Despite finishing fourth in the Big Ten with a 10-8 conference record, the Hawkeyes still earned a No. 4 seed in the NCAA Tournament.

The 1989 NCAA Tournament would bring the senior class full circle. Horton, Armstrong, and Marble began their NCAA Tournament history in 1986 with a 66-64 loss to N.C. State. It also ended that way. After a 14-point win over Rutgers, Iowa bowed out with a double-overtime loss to N.C. State. The senior trio made their presence known, scoring 76 of the team's 96 points.

> **Roy Marble scored 37 points in a game against Illinois in 1989.**
> **He also had six steals versus Northwestern in 1988.**

Roy Marble continues to support the Hawkeye basketball program. His son, Roy Marble Jr., recently accepted a scholarship offer to play basketball at Iowa, despite the inevitable comparisons that attending his father's alma mater will create. However, if there was one thing that Roy Marble Sr.'s Hawkeye career proved, it was that a player can craft his own legacy, even in the face of lofty comparisons.

Was Roy Marble the best scorer in Iowa basketball history? Not necessarily. Over a dozen Hawkeyes have a higher career scoring average than he does. Was he the most creative with the ball? Perhaps not – many Iowa basketball history buffs would think of Murray Wier for that distinction.

However, Roy Marble had a special blend of abilities that rarely come together in a single individual. He could play inside and outside with equal ease, and his high-flying style lit up the Iowa scoreboard. It can be argued he had as much versatility as any Hawkeye before or after him. He helped lead his team to great success and was named team MVP three times.

"Any kid in our era loved Roy Marble and thought he was the best thing ever," said Jess Settles. "Roy Marble was Iowa's Michael Jordan in the eyes of all of us kids growing up."

How appropriate it is, then, for Roy Marble to be named the greatest Hawkeye at No. 23.

Accolades
- Holds school record for career scoring
- Second Team All-Big Ten (1987, 88); Third Team All-Big Ten (1989)
- Team MVP (1987, 88, 89)
- Led team in scoring (1986, 87, 89)
- Selected to Iowa's All-Century basketball team (2002)

No. 23 ROY MARBLE									
Year	GP	FG-FGA	FG%	FT-FTA	FT%	Reb	Avg	Pts	Avg
1986	32	157-300	52%	85-118	73%	157	4.9	399	11.5
1987	35	199-357	56%	118-173	68%	178	5.1	520	14.9
1988	34	190-343	54%	141-190	74%	147	4.3	522	15.4
1989	33	241-459	53%	172-226	76%	186	5.6	675	20.5
Totals	134	787-1459	54%	516-707	73%	668	4.9	2,116	15.8

How He's Remembered

"Roy really came into Iowa at a time when the game was turning from a fundamentals game to an athletic game in the mid '80s. He was Iowa's first what I call 'non-traditional' basketball player. Not a great shooter, not a great ball handler, but a terrific scorer as proven by the fact that when he left, he was Iowa's leading scorer. Individually, if you break down his game, you just didn't see a lot of things that make him great. But when you add it all together, he was pretty unstoppable."

Mac McCausland

"Roy Marble did a basketball clinic over at Louisa-Muscatine High School when I was in about seventh grade. I remember he taught me how to place my hand on the basketball to shoot free throws. He said that you have to put your two fingers where the air bubble is so you can look down and know your hand is square on the ball. From that day on, that's what I did. I remember being in Iowa games, looking down, and thinking about Roy Marble when I was shooting free throws. I also remember the beginning of my sophomore year we were playing an exhibition game in Des Moines. He came in the locker room, put his hand on my shoulder, and said, 'Hey, this is Jess.' He said this to John Streif, our trainer. 'This is the guy who's going to break all of my records.' I had had a good freshman year, put up some decent numbers, and I just very humbly smiled at him and thought, 'I hope that happens.' He was very encouraging and really wanted us to have a phenomenal year."

Jess Settles

"Roy was a tremendous athlete. I kid with him nowadays, because I said, 'Well, Roy, you know, you had a major accomplishment [in breaking my career scoring record] of course, and I'm not trying to take anything away from you, but you did have the three-point shot to help you out. I had to get it the hard way. If they had the three-pointer when I was playing, who knows where I'd be.' So I tease him about that."

Greg Stokes

"Roy was so athletic – that's the thing I always come back to. He went from an athlete who happened to play basketball to a good basketball player by the time he left Iowa and ended up being a first-round pick because he developed his jump shot. He was really a key force on those Tom Davis teams. He got things done on the glass, he was a pretty good defender, and he really worked hard at his game to get his jump shot down, because he was a very inconsistent shooter when he came in. He led Iowa in scoring his freshman year as a true freshman, which doesn't happen too often. He really kind of gave them a scoring punch as the rest of those guys developed around him. He was someone opponents always had to game plan for on the court. He could just do so many things; he was able to step out to the arc and shoot the ball, and he could take people off the dribble and dunk on you. He was a good player, a really good player."

Tom Kakert

"I just relished watching Roy play, because he came in the kind of player we hadn't seen at Iowa in a long time, if ever. I was trying to think, who brought the whole package like Roy Marble did – a guy who's big enough to play inside at 6'6" but also a guy who's quick enough and had deep enough range to where he could play guard? He really did bring the whole package from Flint, and there have been many great players who've come out of the state of Michigan. Iowa was very fortunate to land Roy Marble."

Gary Dolphin

Jersey #23 Honorable Mention

Bob Clifton – Basketball (1950-52)

Bob Clifton earned All-State honors in basketball and averaged 20.8 points per game as a senior at Boone High School. He led Boone to the state tournament for the first time in 16 years. His high school coach, Bucky O'Connor, left for the University of Iowa in 1948, and Clifton soon followed him to Iowa City. He played under O'Connor on Iowa's freshman team before starting for three years on the varsity squad. Clifton scored 25 points against Michigan in his first Big Ten game. He improved his point-per-game average from 8.5 to 9.0 to 11.8 in his three varsity seasons respectively, and Iowa's standing in the Big Ten improved each year as well. Clifton's game blossomed in his senior season under O'Connor, who was in his first year as Iowa's varsity coach. As a senior in 1952, Clifton helped the Hawkeyes to a second-place finish in the Big Ten standings, and he was recognized as a Third Team All-American. He was drafted by the Fort Wayne (now Detroit) Pistons in 1952.

Gerry Jones – Basketball (1965-67)

Standing 6'4" and weighing 180 pounds, Gerry Jones came to Iowa from Carver High School in Chicago, Illinois. He began playing in 1964, the same year Ralph Miller became Iowa's new head coach. His sophomore year, Jones averaged 14 points per game while playing alongside Iowa teammates George Peeples, Chris Pervall, and Jimmy Rodgers. His junior year, however, Jones was ruled academically ineligible for much of the Big Ten schedule. Iowa still went 17-7 under Miller that year and finished third in the Big Ten. To his credit, Jones regained eligibility for his final year and averaged 18.6 points per game. With newcomer Sam Williams also in the lineup, Iowa again finished third in the Big Ten despite graduating four starters the previous year. Jones was named team MVP in 1967 and still holds the tenth-highest career scoring average at Iowa (16.2 points per game.)

Shonn Greene – Football (2005-06, 2008)

Shonn Greene played sparingly his first two years before sitting out the 2007 season for academic reasons. While getting his grades in order and working in a furniture store that year, Greene remained committed to the Hawkeye program. He returned for a stellar 2008 season – a season in which he set Iowa's season rushing record with 1,850 yards, earned unanimous First Team All-American honors, was named the Big Ten MVP, and won the Doak Walker Award as the nation's best running back. He was the first Hawkeye to win this prestigious award, and he finished sixth in the Heisman Trophy balloting. Greene was a punishing runner for the Hawkeyes, yet he displayed great balance and elusiveness for a 235-pound back.

"Don't try to tackle Shonn Greene with one arm because you will lose it."

Paul McGuire, ABC Sports

#24: ALL-AMERICAN BY ALL MEASURES

"Nile Kinnick was the personification of what they now refer to as a student-athlete."
- Bob Brooks

Nile Kinnick was voted as the greatest player in the first 100 years of Hawkeye football in 1989. But his legacy extends well beyond that. He was a scholar, a patriot, and an inspiration to Iowans everywhere. He was spiritual, intelligent, talented, and humble. He was everything we want our sports heroes to be and more. He remains, in many ways, the patron saint of Hawkeye football, and there is no man ever associated with the program more suited for that distinction than Nile Clarke Kinnick, Jr.

Kinnick's grandfather, George Clarke, was an Iowa graduate and the 21st Governor of Iowa, while Kinnick's father, Nile Kinnick, Sr., lettered in football for Iowa State in 1913 and 1914. With such strong bloodlines, it is not surprising that Kinnick was an exceptional student-athlete. Nile was a typical Iowa boy. He was born and raised in Adel, Iowa, and his first job at the age of nine was as a paperboy for *The Des Moines Register*.

As a follower of Christian Science, however, Nile was almost fanatical about self-improvement, athletically and academically. Despite a small 5'8", 170-pound frame and below-average speed, Kinnick developed an incredible skill set. He could pass a football and shoot a basketball with either hand. He excelled at three sports; he was a teammate of Hall of Fame pitcher Bob Feller on his Junior Legion baseball team. Nile scored 485 points for the Adel basketball squad as a sophomore, and he led the football team to an undefeated season.

Kinnick spent his senior year at Benson High School in Omaha, where he was First Team All-State in both football and basketball. Teammate Bob Hobbs recalled, "At Benson, Nile was a coach on the field. He directed the team, analyzed the opposition, advised the coach, instilled confidence in everyone…In basketball, he carried the team to the state tournament."

The University of Iowa's sports department was severely struggling during this time. The University built a brand new football stadium in 1929, only to have financing the project become difficult in the 1930s. In fact, the first game in the new stadium was played just a couple weeks prior to the October 1929 stock market crash. Iowa was even temporarily suspended from the Big Ten to begin 1930. Ironically, the school's struggles were something that attracted Kinnick, who sought the difficult challenge of lifting a school that was down.

Kinnick was recruited to Iowa City by Coach Ossie Solem. He played freshman football, basketball, and baseball, but before Nile's first varsity football season as a sophomore, Coach Solem left for Syracuse. In 1937, Solem wrote, "I was sure that Kinnick was destined to be the greatest back in all Iowa history, and I am more convinced than ever that he will be." Solem was replaced at Iowa by Coach Irl Tubbs.

As a sophomore, Kinnick played nearly every minute of the Big Ten season. He scored Iowa's only touchdown in the conference opener, a 13-6 loss to Wisconsin. Sportswriter Roundy Coughlin wrote, "This Nile Kinnick of the Iowa team stands out today as the best all-around sophomore football player in America. Kinnick is a punting fool, folks – in fact, the best punter to come into the Big Ten in years and years, and he is a rugged type of youth that can tackle and block and do everything. He looks like the coming football star of the college world. Wisconsin would of knocked the pants off Iowa if they didn't have this boy Kinnick in that lineup."

> **Nile Kinnick averaged 6.1 points per game in Iowa's 1937-38 basketball season, which ranked second at Iowa and 15th in the Big Ten.**

The following week, Iowa lost to Michigan, 7-6, despite a 74-yard punt return for a touchdown by Kinnick. "Kinnick is only 19, but he directs the weak Iowa team with the skill of a veteran. He passes accurately and returns punts almost as well as his brown-skinned predecessor, Oze Simmons," *United Press* reported. "Kinnick weighs 167, runs with rhythmical stride, and has a neat change of pace. His passing is good enough to make him a dangerous triple-threat. For quarterbacking, he has an agile mind that placed him in the upper one percent of his class in the commerce college."

Despite going winless in the Big Ten in 1937, Iowa's Nile Kinnick was an All-Big Ten selection. He was the only sophomore voted onto the team. He was also a Third Team All-American. Iowa assistant coach Ernie Nevers, a football legend himself, said, "Kinnick is the greatest first-year man I ever coached. He's a natural player and does things right instinctively."

The following season was disappointing for Kinnick. He suffered an ankle injury in the opening game against UCLA and never recaptured the form of his sophomore season. Still, he played every game and ranked third nationally in interceptions with six. Kinnick also finished fourth nationally in punting average with 41.1 yards per punt in 1938. None of this was enough to save Coach Irl Tubbs' job, as he was let go after the season.

In an attempt to reverse fortunes for the 1939 Iowa squad, the University lured Dr. Eddie Anderson from his head coaching position at Holy Cross. He was an Iowa native who had played for Coach Knute Rockne and Notre Dame. Anderson was the Irish team captain in 1921, the last time Notre Dame came to Iowa City. As a medical doctor, Anderson would spend some days at the hospital seeing patients and then switch gears to head the Iowa football coaching staff in the afternoons.

Although around 85 men turned out for spring practice in 1939, Anderson's brutal workouts ran over half of them off. He believed in toughness, and for good reason. Hank Vollenweider, Kinnick's teammate on the 1939 Hawkeyes, noted that Iowa's uniforms in that era had very little in the way of padding. The helmets worn were simply leather headgear without facemasks, so broken noses and poked eyes were commonplace. The players would put cotton behind the elastic on the top part of the helmet, so that when they got bloody noses, they could use the cotton to stop the bleeding and therefore not be taken out of the game. Longtime Iowa announcer Bob Brooks recalled, "With these guys, there was no facemask or anything. Shoulder pads were about the size of cotton swabs, and helmets were leather."

Anderson immediately identified Kinnick as his team's leader. "Slap him in the stomach and you'll break your wrist. He's just that tough," Anderson said of Kinnick. Kinnick declared, "For three years, nay for fifteen years, I have been preparing for this last year of football…I anticipate becoming the roughest, toughest all-around back yet to hit this conference."

Little was expected of the 1939 Iowa team; most pundits understandably picked the Hawkeyes to finish near the conference cellar. Coach Anderson, however, was quietly confident. "We are going to win the conference championship. Don't laugh, I mean it," Anderson told an Iowa City sportswriter. "We've got some fine men on this squad, and I've got the best quarterback in the country in Nile Kinnick. He isn't as fast as most of the others, but he can throw a football and he can think."

The Hawkeyes opened their schedule with an easy win over South Dakota, but the season really heated up the following week, both literally and figuratively. Iowa's first Big Ten opponent, Indiana, came to town to take on the Hawkeyes in 94-degree heat. Iowa had not beaten the Hoosiers since the days of Aubrey Devine and Duke Slater in 1921. The lead went back and forth between the two teams until the very end. Down three points with little time remaining, Iowa faced a fourth down deep in Indiana territory. On fourth and goal from the 15-yard line, Kinnick connected with Erwin Prasse in the end zone for a three point win. The third touchdown pass from Kinnick to Prasse that day produced Iowa's first Big Ten win at home in six years.

After a road loss to Michigan, Iowa stayed on the road to face Wisconsin. Kinnick threw three touchdowns to lead the Hawkeyes to their first win in Madison in ten years. Badger coach Harry Stuhldreher declared, "Kinnick is one of the finest all-around backs I've seen in a long time. You find a player like him once in a generation. Usually when you find a great football player, he is great because he has one exceptional talent. Kinnick is exceptional at everything. In addition, he is a great morale man. He is another coach on the field. Kinnick could play on any team. He beat us, and that's where the credit should go. I think he is a great player."

A notable trend was developing. As injuries were mounting, a number of Hawkeyes had begun playing the entire 60 minutes of each game. Against Wisconsin, Kinnick and four other players went the distance, and Coach Anderson began referring to them as the "Ironmen." The moniker stuck. Kinnick and seven other Hawkeyes played the entire 60 minutes the following week, as Iowa ground out a 4-0 victory over Purdue.

Nearly every Heisman winner has his signature moment or game. Doug Flutie had the Miami Hurricanes, Desmond Howard struck a pose in the end zone, and Ron Dayne took over the all-time rushing record (against Iowa no less). In Nile Kinnick's case, it happened when third-ranked Notre Dame came to town.

"With a few breaks, we may give Notre Dame a fit," Kinnick predicted. His forecast came true after the Hawkeyes knocked off the heavily-favored Irish in a tight, hard-fought game.

Kinnick's four-yard touchdown run and extra point provided all the scoring Iowa needed in the 7-6 win. As usual, Kinnick played a large role on special teams. He punted a school-record sixteen times for an average of nearly 46 yards per punt. His last punt of the day covered 63 yards and boxed the Irish deep in their own territory as time ran out.

The final home game of the season brought Minnesota to Iowa City. These weren't the Gophers of present day; the Gophers of that era were a bona fide dynasty. They won mythical national titles in 1934, '35, and '36. In 1939, they led the Hawkeyes, 9-0, after three quarters.

From there, Kinnick took over with passes and a run to lead Iowa 80 yards to the end zone. The scoring play was a 48-yard bomb to Erwin Prasse. Later in the quarter, Kinnick again connected on a 28-yard scoring pass; this time it was to Bill Green, and it gave Iowa the winning margin. The Hawkeyes beat Minnesota for the first time in ten years, 13-9, and for the first time ever, Floyd of Rosedale became a resident of Iowa City. Fans stormed the field and carried Kinnick to the locker room.

"There's a golden helmet riding on a human sea across Iowa's football field in the twilight here. Now the helmet rises as wave upon wave of humanity pours onto the field. There's a boy under the helmet, which is shining like a crown on his head. A golden No. 24 gleams on his slumping, tired shoulders. The boy is Nile Clarke Kinnick, Jr., who has, just now, risen above all the defenses that could be raised against him," wrote James Kearns of *The Chicago Daily News*. "Here is Kinnick at the peak of his great career, leading a frenzied little band of Iowa football players to a victory which was impossible. They couldn't win, but they did."

Nile Kinnick called the victory over Minnesota the sweetest win of the year.

Kinnick succumbed to a separated shoulder in the season finale against Northwestern, which ended an incredible streak of 402 consecutive minutes played. The Hawkeyes finished with a 6-1-1 record and a No. 9 national ranking. "We cared not who did it or how, just so it was done," Kinnick said of the Ironmen. "We had a fierce desire to win."

Nile Kinnick rushed for five touchdowns, threw for 11 more, and drop-kicked 11 extra points in 1939. He was involved in all but 23 of Iowa's points by passing or rushing. In other words, 82 percent of Iowa points scored came from the hand or foot of Nile Kinnick. For comparison's sake, as great as Brad Banks and Nate Kaeding were in 2002, they only produced 63 percent of Iowa's points combined that season. On defense, Kinnick was just as effective; he led the nation in interceptions. On special teams, he led the nation in kickoff return yardage.

All in all, it's easy to see why he nearly ran the table on all the major college football awards that year. He was a consensus First Team All-American and won the Walter Camp and Maxwell awards. *Associated Press* even named Kinnick the top male athlete for 1939. His competition for that award included Yankee great Joe DiMaggio (who hit .381 that summer), heavyweight boxing champ Joe Louis, and golfing legend Byron Nelson.

Foremost among these awards was the 1939 Heisman Trophy, which was given to the most outstanding all-around college football player. Many people say Kinnick's Heisman Trophy acceptance speech was the most eloquent ever uttered. The University of Iowa plays audio clips from this speech at the beginning of every home game. The perspective Kinnick maintained and the sentiments expressed when he was picking up his numerous trophies illustrate that he truly was wise beyond his years. "Young men would rather fight and bleed for a trophy of this kind than for all the war medals in the world," Kinnick said in accepting the Walter Camp Trophy. "I thank God that this past year I have been dodging tacklers and not bullets, throwing passes and not hand grenades." It becomes apparent why people who knew him swore that Kinnick was headed for greatness far beyond the football field.

Kinnick's last football game was the College All-Star Game in an exhibition against the 1939 NFL champion Green Bay Packers. He took the train back to Iowa City with his teammate Erwin Prasse. "He said, 'Erwin, my football career is over,'" Prasse recalled. "Later, I looked up and he wasn't in our train car. I went looking for him. There was a car full of deaf students, and Nile was back there talking with them in sign language. I said, 'Nile, when did you learn sign language?' And he said, 'I memorized the finger movements in a book I read last year.' I tell you, the guy was unbelievable."

> **In 1972, when the University was about to rename Iowa Stadium after Kinnick, legendary Penn State coach Joe Paterno wrote, "I know as a young boy growing up, Nile Kinnick was a hero to me…the possibility of naming your stadium in honor of Nile would be a wonderful idea, especially in these days when our young people have a tendency to play down the great qualities men like Nile stood for."**

Kinnick declined professional football offers to instead enter law school with a keen interest in politics. He spent one year as a law student and two years as an assistant football coach at Iowa before enlisting in the Naval Air Corps Reserve. World War II was now underway, and unfortunately, this would be the last chapter in Kinnick's short life.

On June 2, 1943, Kinnick was conducting a training mission in the Gulf of Paria off the coast of Venezuela. He had been flying for over an hour when his Grumman F-4 Wildcat airplane developed a serious oil leak. Without lubrication, his engine failed, leaving Kinnick no choice but to attempt a wheels-up landing in the water about four miles from the *USS Lexington*. It is suspected that Kinnick was knocked unconscious and drowned. His body and his plane were never recovered. Nile Kinnick was only 24 years old.

Kinnick is someone you're glad to claim as a native Iowan. He was a true representation of all that is good about student-athletes and humanity in general. Parents are well-advised to tell the story of Nile Kinnick to their children. His life is not just a sports story, and it transcends the Iowa fan base. Kinnick's is a story about humanity. It's a story about perseverance and hardship. It's a story about triumph and tribute. It's a story about faith and philosophy. Most of all, it's a story about a man who made the state of Iowa proud at a time when they needed it most.

Accolades

- Won Heisman Trophy as the nation's most outstanding football player (1939)
- Consensus First Team All-American (1939); Third Team All-American (1937)
- Inducted into the College Football Hall of Fame (1951)
- No. 24 retired by Iowa football in his honor
- Iowa Stadium renamed Kinnick Stadium in his honor
- Selected as the Most Outstanding Player of the first century of Hawkeye football (1989)

No. 24: NILE KINNICK

Year	Rush Att	Rush Yds	Rush Avg	Pass Compl	Pass Pct	Pass Yds	Pass TDs	Rush TDs
1937	95	214	2.3	36-87	.414	566	1	2
1938	53	136	2.6	21-49	.429	241	1	0
1939	106	374	3.5	31-93	.333	638	11	5
Totals	254	724	2.9	88-229	.384	1,445	13	7

Year	Int	Punts	Avg	Punt Ret	Avg	KO Ret	Avg	XPts
1937	3	55	42.7	36	8.9	4	28.5	0
1938	7	41	41.1	11	6.5	3	24.0	0
1939	8	71	39.9	19	12.0	15	25.1	11
Totals	18	167	41.1	66	9.4	22	25.6	11

How He's Remembered

"The country is okay as long as it produces Nile Kinnicks. The football part is incidental."

Bill Cunningham, *Boston Globe*

"Talk about a gracious, poignant Heisman acceptance speech. But then at the very end he gets a little political, and he does it in a very respectful manner. I know that time is lost and this country may never see those times again, but you begin to realize that he thought and acted far ahead of his time. It truly just laid out for everyone who Nile Kinnick is. Great football player? Heck yeah. Fantastic son? Yes. Spiritual man? You bet. I read a book called, 'A Hero Perished: The Diary and Selected Letters of Nile Kinnick,' and it just gave me a better respect for the man whose name hangs on that stadium."

Mark Allen

"He was such a smart player. Nile Kinnick might have been the greatest athlete ever to play at Iowa. Dan Gable has been called the greatest athlete ever [in Iowa]. Nile Kinnick probably would have been right there with him, in that Nile could play multiple sports and he also got it done in the classroom. With the 3.4 GPA and the Phi Beta Kappa scholar status, many of the old-timers that I've talked to felt that Nile Kinnick was destined for greatness in politics. He could've been Governor, he could've been a U.S. Senator, even could have been President of the United States. Who knows how that would have changed history?"

Gary Dolphin

"Nile was an excellent athlete, really. He didn't have the natural gifts of some scatterbrains, who can do many things by virtue of their physical gifts, but he coupled keen ability and intelligence with what he had. He was an excellent field general – the people on the field would 'buy' his analysis, his instant analysis. There was no question or argument, because over and over he had demonstrated that he did know what was going on...He did it all in such a nice way. Nothing he achieved ever rang any bells with him personally. He did it because he was able to do it – it needed to be done and he did it. He proved one thing, that college athletics could be beautiful. Everything that can be said that is good about college athletics he was. He didn't represent it – he was it."

Tait Cummins

"From the accomplishments of a single season, Nile Kinnick became the most famous player in Iowa history, and he is still one of the best-remembered college athletes in the United States... His death was a sad and ridiculous accident, one that left him unfinished and so beyond our full grasp. But better that than at 24 to have died completed, with nothing more to become."

Paul Baender

Jersey #24 Honorable Mention

Bobby Hansen – Basketball (1980-83)

Bobby Hansen led West Des Moines Dowling to the 1979 Iowa state championship. Twelve months later, he was a key freshman reserve for Lute Olson's Final Four squad. Hansen was named team MVP and was a Third Team All-Big Ten selection in 1983, when he helped guide the Hawkeyes to the Sweet Sixteen. He graduated from Iowa ranked in the top ten in career scoring with 1,145 points. Bobby Hansen played nine seasons in the NBA, including seven playoff seasons with the Utah Jazz. He finished his professional career with the Chicago Bulls, where he teamed with B.J. Armstrong on the 1992 NBA championship team. Hansen is currently the radio analyst for Hawkeye basketball games.

"You just don't step on the floor as a freshman on a Final Four team and play unless the coach thinks you're up to the task of melding in with veteran leaders. Bobby always played beyond his years, just like Nile Kinnick. He's a guy who wasn't in awe of upperclassmen. He felt that it was his time whether he was a freshman, sophomore, or junior, he could play at that level. To me, that's a great attitude, that's a guy who plays with extreme confidence, and that's a guy who's a winner. There's a reason Jerry Sloan drafted Bobby Hansen. Sloan saw that toughness in Bobby."

Gary Dolphin

James Moses – Basketball (1989-92)

Originally from California, James Moses scored 1,343 points as a guard for the Hawkeye basketball team, which places him 14th all-time. He twice led Iowa in steals in 1990 and 1992. James Moses was the 1991 team MVP. The biggest basket of Moses' career came on the road against No. 4 Indiana in 1991. With one second remaining in overtime, Moses tipped in a missed shot by Chris Street to give Iowa an 80-79 win and sew up a trip to the NCAA tournament.

Luke Recker – Basketball (2001-02)

Luke Recker was Indiana's Mr. Basketball in 1997, and he played his first two seasons with the Hoosiers. He was a Third Team All-Big Ten selection in 1999 with Indiana before transferring to Iowa. Recker averaged 18.1 points per game the first 20 games of his junior season, leading Iowa to a 16-4 record, before missing the rest of the season with a fractured kneecap. He was a Third Team All-Big Ten selection as a senior, making consecutive buzzer-beating shots in the 2002 Big Ten Tournament. Recker hit game-winning shots against Wisconsin in the quarterfinals and Indiana in the semifinals. He was Iowa's team MVP in 2002. Recker still holds the Iowa school record for free throw percentage in a career.

#25: BLACK 'N' GOLD BOMBER

"My introduction to Iowa football was Kenny Ploen and Randy Duncan. I can vividly remember watching my first Rose Bowl in 1959 and seeing this guy just wing the ball down the field and watching Bobby Jeter take handoffs from this wonderful No. 25. I didn't know a whole lot about him at the time, but I knew one thing, he looked awfully good in that gold helmet and leading the Hawks to a pounding of their Pac-10 opponent. I can remember being so proud because I'm all about the state of Iowa and Randy of course is from Des Moines. He's gone on to prominence after his football career as an outstanding attorney in the capital city, so Randy Duncan got it done on both sides of the line of scrimmage in life and athletics."

- Gary Dolphin

He led his team to three straight top five finishes in the nation and was then named the No. 1 overall pick in the NFL Draft. How many quarterbacks in college football history can claim that? Only one – Iowa's Randy Duncan. Duncan had a career of unparalleled success, and he was an integral part of three of the greatest teams in school history.

Despite his current status as a Hawkeye legend, Iowa nearly lost Duncan – twice. He was a multi-sport star at Roosevelt High School in Des Moines. He played a key role in his team's state basketball championship as a junior, and he followed this up by leading his football team to a state runner-up finish in 1954. He was a First Team All-State player in both sports and was recruited collegiately in both.

Duncan almost committed to the University of Colorado before choosing the Hawkeyes. Bump Elliott, then an assistant coach for Forest Evashevski, sealed Duncan's commitment. "I changed in favor of Iowa because of Bump Elliott. I thought he was the greatest human ever to walk the face of this earth," Duncan said.

> **Randy Duncan played high school basketball against Ken Ploen.**

Randy Duncan graduated high school at mid-year and enrolled at Iowa in the spring of 1954. Because freshmen were ineligible for varsity competition, this meant that he had to wait 18 months before playing varsity football. It was during this frustrating time that Iowa nearly lost Duncan again. "I was going to quit so many times. I didn't think I'd ever learn to play defense well enough to see any action. Time after time, I was going to quit and transfer to Iowa State," he said. "It sure as hell doesn't help your confidence having Calvin Jones knock you into the stands and not be able to play games for two springs and a fall."

Duncan also began at Iowa with the intention of playing two sports. For at least one year, that's what he did. "I played basketball at Iowa for one year," Duncan said. "My sophomore year I was going to play again, but we went to the Rose Bowl. By the time we got home from that, it was January and I just couldn't get back into basketball shape, so I quit after my freshman year."

The 1956 season began with Duncan fighting to be the back-up quarterback to senior Ken Ploen. Duncan eventually won the job and early on showed Iowans flashes of greatness. His very first college game against the Hoosiers, however, wasn't one of them. "The first game I don't even remember. I got hit in the head and don't recall anything about the game at Indiana," stated Duncan.

The injured Duncan fell to third-string for Iowa's next game against Oregon State. "I sprained my ankle pretty badly and had my ankle shot up for that game," he recalled. "Bump saw me working out and said, 'You're not going to play today.' Then Kenny got hurt and they carried him off. Mike McFarland, another quarterback, was in there for a while." In the fourth quarter, Iowa trailed 13-0 when Coach Forest Evashevski turned to Duncan. "Finally, they put me in and we scored two touchdowns," Duncan said, and Iowa salvaged a 14-13 win.

Duncan stated that he did play in parts of every Iowa game as a sophomore. The culmination of that season came in Iowa's first trip to the Rose Bowl. On January 1, 1957, Iowa played Oregon State for the second time that season. The Hawkeyes led, 14-7, when Ploen hyperextended his knee in the second quarter and had to be carried off the field. Duncan entered the game and played the rest of the half, leading Iowa to a touchdown and a 21-7 halftime lead. Ploen recovered for the second half, and Iowa marched to its first Rose Bowl victory.

Randy Duncan had established himself as the heir apparent to Ploen, though there was no mistaking the two of them. They were two distinctly different players. Ploen was as good on defense as he was offense. Duncan also played safety, but he was more oriented to offense. Ploen was a better runner than Duncan, but Duncan was a much stronger and more accurate passer. With tailbacks like Willie Fleming and Bob Jeter, Duncan could afford to focus on being a passing threat first and foremost. That's what he did.

In 1957, Iowa was 4-0 when they played a controversial game in Ann Arbor. The Hawkeyes trailed Michigan, 21-7, in the third quarter before rallying with a late pair of touchdowns. Duncan tied the game at 21 on a quarterback keeper with 9:12 left in the game. Iowa regained possession with about three minutes left, but Duncan had to leave the game with leg cramps. Evy controversially decided to run out the clock and accept the tie, arguing that a tie severely damaged Michigan's shot at a Big Ten title while leaving Iowa in contention for the conference crown.

Evy's plan worked, and two weeks later, the Hawkeyes met Ohio State in Columbus for the Big Ten title. Iowa led 13-10 late, but the Buckeyes scored the winning touchdown with 3:53 left to claim a 17-13 victory. After the Hawkeyes ended the season with a win over Notre Dame, Irish coach Terry Brennan said, "This Iowa team was good as any we've met this year. I'm not taking anything away from Ohio State, but Iowa marched all over the field against them last week, and there is no doubt in my mind that Iowa would have been rated the No. 1 team in the nation if it had won that game."

With a 7-1-1 record, Iowa's 1957 season had proved the previous Rose Bowl team was no fluke. The Hawkeyes finished the season ranked fifth in the Coaches' Poll. Duncan set Iowa season records in total offense, passing yards, completions, and completion percentage. He was also named All-Big Ten. Even with Outland Trophy winner Alex Karras leaving school, the prospects for 1958 were as high as ever.

The week before the 1958 season opener, Evashevski issued a stern warning to the team about complacency and overconfidence. While Iowa had a nice shutout win over nationally-ranked Texas Christian University, the Hawkeyes were then played to a draw by the lightly-regarded Air Force Academy. Evy's warnings suddenly resonated, and the Hawkeyes refocused and set their sights on the Big Ten schedule.

After a win over Indiana, Duncan ran for a touchdown and threw a 68-yard touchdown pass in an upset at Wisconsin. The following week, Duncan completed 14 of 18 passes for 174 yards and two touchdowns, as Iowa held off No. 8 Northwestern, 26-20. His 14 completions were an Iowa single-game record. After the game, Iowa ascended to the No. 1 ranking in the Coaches' Poll; it was the first time that the Hawkeyes had secured a No. 1 ranking in a national poll.

Iowa defended their No. 1 ranking by ripping Michigan, 37-14, to give Evy his first win over his alma mater. Duncan threw two touchdown passes the following week to help Iowa topple Minnesota, 28-6. The victory over the Gophers clinched Iowa's second Big Ten title under Evashevski.

Duncan's best game probably came in the following week's loss to Ohio State. Although the Hawkeyes suffered a 38-28 defeat, Duncan completed 23 of 33 passes for 249 yards and one touchdown. The 23 completions set a Big Ten record for Duncan, who also ran for a touchdown in the loss. After the game, Ohio State fullback Bob White, who had torched the Hawkeyes two straight seasons, told Duncan, "You fellows are still champs. We sure will be for you in the Rose Bowl."

> **During Randy Duncan's three seasons at Iowa, the Hawkeyes compiled a 24-3-2 record.**

The 1959 Rose Bowl was perhaps the pinnacle of Evashevski's success at Iowa. For the second time in three seasons, the Hawkeyes left Pasadena with a dominant Rose Bowl victory when they demolished California, 38-12.

It was a rewarding end to Randy Duncan's career at Iowa. The Hawks finished 1958 as the top offensive team in the nation, outgaining the next team by over 25 yards per game. Duncan led the nation in passing yardage. He finished second in the Heisman Trophy balloting and helped put Iowa on the college football landscape for the foreseeable future.

"They had a very strong two-pronged attack: a passing attack and a running attack," recalled teammate Wilburn Hollis. "Duncan was really an offensive weapon as a passer. If he wanted to mix 'em up, he'd hand the ball off to Jeter or Fleming. Then they'd run the defense crazy."

Duncan credits Coach Evashevski with playing a major role in his development. "Because he was on my back so much, I wanted to prove to him I could be a player," said Duncan. "That was his style. If you ran 70 yards for a touchdown, he would chew you out for not making it 80 yards. His philosophy was 'keep driving, keep driving.' Don't praise anybody. Get [the players] pumped up, and always have somebody that's waiting to take your job. He always wanted competition at every position."

Evashevski may have been harsh in his tactics, but in this case, he followed it up with lavish praise. "For throwing ability, Randy Duncan has got to have a place in Iowa football history, because I think he holds most of the records," Evy said after the 1960 season. "Randy had the ability to throw the long soft ball, or drill the hard, fast one. He had enough strength in his arm to split an end eight or ten yards out, drive him into the sideline and hit the receiver without the high trajectory that would mean the danger of an interception."

Randy Duncan was a unanimous First Team All-American in 1958. He was the first player in school history to earn that honor.

The following spring, Green Bay made Duncan the NFL's No. 1 draft choice. But Duncan chose the same path as Ken Ploen two years earlier and went into the Canadian Football League. He played two years for Vancouver and then played for the Dallas Texans of the NFL. While in Dallas, he began taking law classes at Southern Methodist University. After Duncan retired from football, he came back to Des Moines, finished law school at Drake University, and then entered private law practice.

Randy and his wife Paula have three grown children. Duncan was inducted into the College Football Hall of Fame in 1997. He fondly recalls his whole family cheering him from the balcony at the Waldorf Hotel in New York City.

Randy Duncan still resides in Des Moines and attends a number of Iowa football games. After all these years, he's glad he stuck with the Hawkeyes. "I'm proud that I'm from the state of Iowa and got to play for my own home state," said Duncan. "I'm proud that I still live in Iowa. I'll always be an Iowan and a Hawkeye, and I can't feel anything except great pride in being an Iowan and being able to represent the University of Iowa on a national level. It was a great time in my life."

Accolades
• Unanimous First Team All-American (1958)
• Finished second in the Heisman Trophy balloting (1958)
• Big Ten MVP (1958)
• Broke school records for career passing yards and passing touchdowns
• Inducted into the College Football Hall of Fame (1997)

No. 25 RANDY DUNCAN								
Year	Pass Att	Complet	Pct	Yds	Pass TD	Int	Rush	Yds
1956	41	17	.414	168	2	4	10	-14
1957	119	70	.588	1,124	10	12	35	59
1958	179	106	.597	1,397	12	9	39	65
Totals	339	193	.569	2,689	24	25	84	110

How He's Remembered

"It took Randy a long time to realize he was as great as he was."

Forest Evashevski (2006)

"Randy was a sophomore when I was a senior. Naturally, he showed great potential right off the bat. Not a great running quarterback but a good thrower. He had some games like Oregon State [in 1956] where he came in and actually won the game for us. He participated in the 1957 Rose Bowl. He had been in a number of different games. He was an intelligent guy, a good ball handler, and a great passer. And he could run; that just wasn't his strong point. I was a better runner than I was a passer, and he was a better passer than he was a runner. But it worked successfully for both of us."

Ken Ploen

"He was a good quarterback. He was one of the best."

Alex Karras

"With Jeter, Fleming, and Duncan, you had a pretty fearsome threesome."

Bob Brooks

"Evashevski constructed a wing-T offensive machine in 1958. Randy Duncan, All-America quarterback and Big Ten MVP, teamed with a strong line, a deep stable of backs and a group of ends known as the Gluefingers Gang to lead the conference in scoring, total yards, first downs, rushing, passing, and pass-completion percentage. Iowa went 8-1-1...and finished No. 2 to LSU for the school's highest-ever season-ending ranking."

Todd Jones, *Columbus Post-Dispatch*

Jersey #25 Honorable Mention

Dave Gunther – Basketball (1957-59)

Upon the departure of the "Fabulous Five" of the 1950s, Dave Gunther soon became the next great Hawkeye basketball player. Despite never matching the team success of previous years, this three-time team MVP became the face of the program by leading the team in scoring each of his three years and in rebounding twice. His career highlights include a 37-point performance versus Ohio State, which ranked second in school history at the time, and a 22-point outing in an upset win over Big Ten champion Indiana. He won First Team All-Big Ten honors as a senior, scoring 22 points per game. Gunther still ranks fifth in Iowa basketball history with an 18.0 point career scoring average. He also ranks highly in career rebounds with 690. A native of Le Mars, Iowa, Gunther was named to Iowa's All-Century Team in 2002.

Ed Horton – Basketball (1986-89)

Along with Roy Marble, B.J. Armstrong, Les Jepsen, and Kevin Gamble, Ed Horton was part of Coach George Raveling's most prized recruiting class at Iowa. Horton arrived on campus as the reigning Mr. Basketball from the state of Illinois. At 6'8" and 230 pounds, he was an imposing force around the basket for the Hawkeyes and a perfect complement to Armstrong's shooting and Marble's athleticism. Horton increased his scoring average to 11.3 points as a junior and 18.3 points as a senior. He was most effective on the boards and ranks third on Iowa's career rebounding list. His 350 rebounds in 1989 remains the fifth-best season total in Iowa history. Horton was named Iowa's MVP in 1989 and earned First Team All-Big Ten honors the same year. Horton was drafted in the NBA's second round by the Washington Bullets.

#26: A SIGNATURE CAREER

"Hancock starred alike at end and tackle. During his final year, he received nationwide acclaim as a great tackle."

- The Cedar Rapids Republican, **April 3, 1925**

The name John Hancock evokes images of the most famous signature on the Declaration of Independence or perhaps that of an insurance company. You might be surprised to learn that a former Iowa football star shares the name as well.

Iowa's John Hancock was born on April 13, 1901, in Marshfield, Wisconsin. He was a versatile player who could play both offensive end and tackle with equal skill. As a sophomore in 1922, Hancock was the starting right end when the Hawkeyes upset Yale in New Haven, 6-0. He would play a significant role as the 1922 Hawkeyes claimed the Big Ten championship. In 1923, Hancock's fourth-quarter 40-yard fumble return for a touchdown clinched a 20-0 victory over Ohio State in Columbus. That same year, his interception at the Iowa 22-yard line in the final minute helped seal a 17-14 victory over Northwestern in Coach Howard Jones' final game as Hawkeye head coach.

> **After John Hancock's junior season, Iowa nearly lured Knute Rockne away from Notre Dame to coach the Hawkeye football team. The news of Rockne's hiring got out prematurely, and on March 25, 1924, Rockne sent University of Iowa President Walter Jessup a telegram, officially declining the position. Coach Burt Ingwersen was hired the following month.**

In his senior season, John Hancock played at both the tackle and end positions and even managed to kick five field goals. One of those scores came in Hancock's last college game, as Iowa defeated Michigan, 9-2. For his efforts, he was named All-Big Ten and a Second Team All-American after the 1924 season. Hancock later played in the 1924 East-West All-Star game with Lester Belding and Aubrey Devine. He also threw the discus for the Hawkeye track team, winning three letters and capturing a title in the discus event at the 1925 Big Ten championships.

After graduation, Hancock became an accomplished coach. He was the head football coach at Mississippi State for three seasons from 1927 to 1929. In 1932, Hancock returned to the University of Northern Colorado, where he had earned a master's degree. Hancock served as the Bears' athletic director for 34 years, coached football for 21 years, and coached track and field for 30 years. But his greatest successes were as a wrestling coach, a sport in which he never competed at Iowa. Hancock led Northern Colorado to 29 straight conference championships and coached 12 All-Americans and two national champions.

John Hancock started the Colorado State High School Wrestling Tournament in 1936. As a result, Hancock has been nicknamed "the father of Colorado high school wrestling." The University of Northern Colorado's basketball and wrestling arena, the Butler-Hancock Sports Pavilion, is named in his honor. It's an impressive legacy for one of the founding fathers of Hawkeye football.

Accolades
• Second Team All-American (1924)
• All-Big Ten (1924)
• Started for Iowa's 1922 Big Ten championship team
• Inducted into the National Wrestling Hall of Fame (1998)

How He's Remembered

"Hancock finished his football career this fall with the reputation as one of the outstanding tackles of the west."

Waterloo Evening Courier (Dec 5, 1924)

"Hancock [is an] all-around star. Hancock scales close to 200 [pounds] and seemingly knows what to do with his huge strength. He handles himself well on the receiving end of forward passes, is strong on defense, and is, in addition, one of the best punters on the squad."

The Cedar Rapids Gazette (Sept 25, 1922)

"In the passing of...Hancock, Iowa will lose one of the greatest ends in the conference and a versatile tackle, who has also done work in the kicking department."

Davenport Democrat and Leader (Nov 9, 1924)

"Hancock is considered one of the greatest ends ever turned out at Iowa."

Waterloo Evening Courier (Nov 30, 1925)

Jersey #26 Honorable Mention

Norm Granger – Football (1980-83)
Norman Lance Granger was born in Newark, New Jersey, and chose Iowa over offers from Syracuse and Pittsburgh. He attended the same high school as Hawkeye great Andre Tippett. Granger became a four-year letterman and three-year starter at fullback for the Hawkeyes and a key component of Iowa's rise to prominence under Coach Hayden Fry. Granger was voted team captain both his junior and senior seasons and was named team MVP after the 1983 season. A member of three bowl teams, he played during Iowa's stunning 1981 defeat of Nebraska and returned a kickoff 99 yards for an Iowa touchdown against Indiana that same year. He was Iowa's leading rusher in the 1982 Rose Bowl.

Norm Granger lost his 1982 Rose Bowl ring soon after he was presented it. Twenty-four years later, a Hawkeye fan and collector from Cedar Rapids helped Granger get the ring back.

Jovon Johnson – Football (2002-05)

Jovon Johnson was a cornerback from Erie, Pennsylvania. He played all 13 games as a freshman for Iowa's 2002 Big Ten championship team. In addition, Johnson started every game for Iowa's Big Ten championship team in 2004. He intercepted passes in consecutive bowl games, the 2004 Outback Bowl and the 2005 Capital One Bowl. Johnson played cornerback and returned punts as a senior in 2005. He started 38 career games for the Hawkeyes, including 33 consecutive starts. Jovon intercepted 17 career passes from 2002-2005, falling just one short of the school record set by Nile Kinnick from 1937-1939.

™

#27: BIG MAN FROM BIG SKY COUNTRY

"I remember when I would come [to Iowa City] and watch Murray Wier and Chuck Darling…Chuck was a really great scorer – great hook shot, great scorer, great guy."
- Sharm Scheuerman

While Iowans are the backbone of the University of Iowa's sports programs, talented athletes from across the country have made large contributions to the success of Hawkeye sports. It is befitting that one of the biggest contributors to Hawkeye basketball came from Big Sky country. Chuck Darling dominated Big Ten play in his time from 1950-1952, and many years later, he was named to Iowa's All-Century Team.

While his family moved from place to place, Chuck Darling first made a name for himself as a high school basketball player in Montana. Playing for Rock Mountain High School in Helena, Montana, Chuck earned All-State honors as only a sophomore. He was developing the skills of a big-time player and a body to match. Darling grew an amazing six inches in a six-month period as a sophomore. Unfortunately for Rock Mountain High School, the Darling family moved to Colorado the following year. There, he won a state championship as a junior and only lost two games his last two years in high school.

Fortunately for Hawkeye fans, Darling settled on the University of Iowa for college. A number of circumstances led him to Iowa. His father had earned a graduate degree from Iowa, and Chuck had spent a brief time living in Iowa. Chuck also had an interest in geology. "I knew I wanted to get into that kind of work, and Iowa had a good geology program," Darling recalled. "Actually, it came down to either Iowa or Yale. I never regretted my decision, because I felt Iowa would be better for me. My mother never forgave me for not going to Yale."

Oddly, Chuck would play for three different Hawkeye coaches. This carousel of coaches began with Bucky O'Connor as his freshman coach. Freshmen weren't allowed to play at the time, so 1948-49 was essentially a year for the 6'8", 225-pound center to adjust to the rigors of college basketball. The following year, head coach Pops Harrison had a surgical procedure just before the season. A month into the season, complications from the surgery sidelined Harrison, so O'Connor moved from freshman coach to interim head coach. Darling was the starting center and averaged 9.2 points per game as a sophomore.

Athletic Director Paul Brechler surprisingly relieved Harrison of his coaching duties for Darling's junior year, and Rollie Williams took over. Chuck became a force during the 1950-51 season, leading Iowa with over 16 points per game and an Iowa-record 17.6 rebounds per game. His 25 rebounds against Purdue set an Iowa single-game record, and Iowa finished third in the Big Ten.

With four returning starters, Iowa entered Darling's senior season as a Big Ten favorite. Again, Bucky O'Connor assumed the head coaching position. One might think all the coaching changes would affect a team's chemistry and continuity, but that was hardly the case. The Hawkeyes began the season 12-0 and earned a No. 4 national ranking. Indiana handed Iowa its first loss of the season, but that was followed by five more wins. Iowa then lost to Illinois, which placed the Hawkeyes just behind the Illini in the league standings.

Since very few teams played in the post-season, Iowa needed to defeat Wisconsin in their final game of the season to keep their dreams of a Big Ten title and the school's first NCAA Tournament appearance alive. Unfortunately for the Hawkeyes, Wisconsin pulled a 78-75 upset, but Darling did everything he could have done. Darling scored 34 points and snared an amazing 30 rebounds against the Badgers in the final game of his college career. To this day, it's the one and only time an Iowa player has captured as many as 30 rebounds. In fact, only one person in Big Ten history has ever recorded more rebounds in a single game.

> **Chuck Darling likely topped his junior rebounding record as a senior, but the university does not have official rebounding stats from Darling's sophomore and senior years.**

Despite the late-season disappointment, Darling hauled in a basket full of accolades to end his Iowa career. He was named team MVP, Big Ten MVP, and consensus First Team All-American in 1952. He is still one of only three Big Ten MVPs from the University of Iowa.

Darling set or tied five Big Ten records in his career, including most points in a season and most free throws in a season. His 716 conference points in three seasons were also a Big Ten record. Darling topped Murray Wier's career scoring total at Iowa, despite only playing three years compared to Wier's four. While Wier led the nation in scoring, Darling came in third his senior year.

Though he had the opportunity, Darling never attempted to play in the NBA. Rather, he played in the National Industrial Basketball League (NIBL) for the Phillips Oilers. Here, he made the All-Star team all five years he played and was twice named league MVP.

Toward the end of his NIBL career, Darling had the opportunity to compete on the 1956 Olympic Team. He was joined by fellow Hawkeye Carl Cain on the squad. Though both men were hampered by injuries on the trip – Cain with a back injury and Darling with a sprained ankle – their team easily won the gold medal with victories in all eight contests.

After the Olympics, Darling played one final year for the Phillips Oilers and led them to their ninth straight league championship. When his playing days were over, Darling enjoyed a very successful business career working as an executive for Phillips Petroleum.

When Iowa basketball fans reminisce about the 1950s, Chuck Darling may not be the first name that comes to mind. The "Fabulous Five" established themselves as the team of the decade. As evidence, the jerseys of all five starters are retired. However, no one player's number shone brighter than that of No. 27 Chuck Darling. While his teams didn't rise to the heights of the subsequent Final Four teams, he was as good individually as anyone.

The Treasure State gave Iowa basketball quite a prize in Chuck Darling.

Accolades
- Consensus First Team All-American (1952)
- Big Ten MVP (1952)
- Ranks seventh in school history in career scoring average
- Won gold medal with USA Olympic Team (1956)
- Selected to Iowa's All-Century basketball team (2002)

No. 27 CHUCK DARLING

Year	GP	FG-FGA	FG%	FT-FTA	FT%	Reb	Avg	Pts	Avg
1950	19	67-212	32	41-65	62	-	-	175	9.2
1951	22	139-376	37	80-120	67	387	17.6	358	16.3
1952	22	204-489	42	153-218	70	-	-	561	25.5
Totals	63	410-1,077	38	274-403	68	-	-	1094	17.4

How He's Remembered

"He's just a class guy – very classy, unassuming, and lacking an ego. He has a quiet confidence, but it isn't an ego. And there's a difference."

Sharm Scheuerman

"Constant hard work and coaching have developed Darling's grace and poise on the floor as well as an almost unstoppable hook shot. His point-making ability is Darling's greatest asset, but he also adds strength with his rebounding and ball-handling."

Jack Palmer, *United Press*

"Chuck wears horn-rimmed glasses except when on the basketball court, and to see him studying on the train you wouldn't realize it was the same individual who was ramming home those powerful hook shots the night before…[Darling] pursues his studies as relentlessly as he does improvement in basketball."

Gus Schrader

"He's one of the finest centers in the country, if not the best. I think a lot of people have overlooked his fine defensive and team play because he's such a terrific scorer. He's one of the finest team players we've ever had. He's smart and he works hard. You only have to tell him something once."

Bucky O'Connor

#28: OF FAITH, FAMILY, AND FIELD HOUSE WINS

"Herb was just a very solid, outstanding player – a very, very good player. He could do the whole thing. He didn't have a big scoring average, but he could play the whole game as it should be played."
- Murray Wier

Every young basketball player dreams of hitting a game-winning shot to win an NCAA championship. In the long history of Hawkeye basketball, only one man truly knows what that sensation feels like. For his part, Herb Wilkinson always kept basketball in its proper perspective, and that allowed the Hawkeyes to snag one of the brightest stars in the history of the basketball program.

Herb Wilkinson was born into a Mormon family from Salt Lake City, Utah. He remained in Utah through childhood and into his freshman year in college when he attended the University of Utah. The Utes compiled an 18-4 record and thought their season was over after a first-round loss in the NIT Tournament. However, Arkansas was forced to withdraw from the NCAA Tournament after two of their starters were severely injured in an automobile accident, and Utah filled in as a last-minute replacement.

In the 1944 NCAA Tournament, Utah defeated Missouri to advance to the Final Four. The Utes then defeated Iowa State to advance to the NCAA title game in New York City. Utah squared off with Dartmouth for the NCAA championship, and the game was tied at 36 at the end of regulation. In the first overtime in NCAA title game history, Utah and Dartmouth were tied with three seconds remaining. Herb Wilkinson fired a jumper from the top of the key that bounced off the rim, hit the backboard, and rattled home, giving the Utes a 42-40 victory. But at the height of his basketball success, Wilkinson's career aspirations beyond basketball were charting a new path for him.

> **Herb Wilkinson grew up with a high jump pit in his backyard and placed fourth in the event at the 1945 NCAA track and field championships.**

Herb's brother, Clayton, was in Cedar Rapids, Iowa, completing a Mormon mission. Both Herb and Clay wanted to follow in their father's footsteps and become dentists, and Utah did not have a dental school. Iowa head coach Pops Harrison had seen Clay play basketball in an industrial league and sold him on a chance to play basketball and attend dental school at Iowa. Clay knew that his brother would like the same opportunity and told Harrison, "If I come, I'd like to bring my little brother with me." Harrison said that he'd see what he could do.

The same day that Harrison met with Clay, Utah won the NCAA championship. Herb Wilkinson stated, "The next day, my picture was in the papers with my teammates raising me on their shoulders and carrying me off the floor. Pops right away called Clay and said, 'Is that your little brother?' Clay said yes, and Pops said, 'Hell, bring him along.'" Harrison recruited Clayton, and Clayton in turn recruited his brother to come to Iowa with him.

"The way it seemed was Herb simply decided to go straight from Utah to Iowa, but that's only part of the story," Hawkeye teammate Murray Wier recently recalled. "By God, we got both of them. What an addition! At that time, players didn't have to sit out a year, so Herb was eligible right away."

That marked the beginning of the Wilkinsons' basketball careers in Iowa City. Both Herb and Clayton found themselves in a young starting lineup that fall of 1944. Herb was a tall guard at 6'4", whereas Clayton played center. Sophomore Jack Spencer joined Herb in the backcourt, while sophomore Dick Ives and junior Ned Postels played the forward positions.

Herb Wilkinson's success at Utah followed him to Iowa City, as the Hawkeyes won their first ten games. Dick Ives led the team with 12 points per game, but the Wilkinson brothers' contributions were significant. Clayton added 11.5 points per game and earned Second Team All-Big Ten. It was Herb Wilkinson, however, that gained the most individual accolades. As a sophomore and in only his first year at Iowa, Herb was named First Team All-American. His 10 points per game weren't even a team high, but he was recognized for his leadership and overall floor play. Especially on defense, where a player's value doesn't always show in the box score, Wilkinson played with rugged determination. Together, the Wilkinsons helped lead Iowa to its first outright Big Ten title, which also earned them a spot in the NCAA Eastern playoffs.

It was soon discovered that Ned Postels and Herb Wilkinson had scholastic commitments that would conflict with the team's trip to New York City. The players voted on whether to participate in the tournament, and the Hawks eventually declined the invitation. Later, the team issued a statement that said, "If the whole team couldn't make the trip, there was no use making it." It was actually the second straight year Iowa declined to participate in the NCAA Tournament for that very reason.

Four starters of that young Iowa team returned the next season. With the addition of outstanding sophomore Murray Wier, the team raced to a 14-1 record. Yet they couldn't recapture the Big Ten crown as they had the year before. Upon losing their last three games, the team dropped from first to third place in the Big Ten. Herb Wilkinson was again recognized after the season by earning First Team All-Big Ten and Second Team All-American honors.

> **Herb Wilkinson is the only Hawkeye to earn All-American honors in three seasons. He is also the only Hawkeye to be named First Team All-Big Ten three times.**

From a team perspective, Herb's third and final season at Iowa was not as successful as the first two. The team finished sixth place in the Big Ten with a 12-7 overall record. However, during his time at Iowa, the Hawkeyes posted an outstanding 53-12 record.

"We were good enough to win the Big Ten title all three years," Herb recalled. "It's kind of sickening that we didn't. But Clay had to have an operation – he'd fallen on his tailbone one year – and Danner had some back problems. Still, we were good enough to win the championship more than just that first year."

After leaving the Big Ten ranks, Herb Wilkinson was offered a contract with the Minneapolis Lakers. As a devout Mormon, however, he did not agree to play games on Sundays. "One Sunday game I wasn't there and the owner asked where I was," Herb recalled. "The coach said he doesn't play on Sundays, and the owner sent me a note saying I had to play on Sundays or he would release me. I'm not sure he was serious, but I quit basketball and went off on a mission for two years."

Murray Wier recalls Herb's commitment to his Mormon faith. "The Mormons were very much involved with their church," he said. "I remember at a timeout some of us were ticked off about something and used some foul language. Herb and Clayt never did. I never heard either one of them say a swear word – never. Meanwhile, the rest of us may have been cussing up a storm. I guess we took their part of it, too. I remember Herb would say, 'Cheese and crackers!' We were like, 'What in the hell are you talking about?'"

Herb Wilkinson fulfilled his lifelong dream of becoming a dentist and oral surgeon. He also became an ordained minister. He credited winning the NCAA championship with inspiring him to achieve his career goals. "Anything like that gives you more confidence to do other things in life," Wilkinson said. "You think, 'Gee, if we won the NCAAs and weren't expected to, we could probably do a lot of other things we didn't think we could do.'"

Herb Wilkinson's basketball career had come to a close. He was truly a Hawkeye great who won over 80 percent of his games at Iowa. As a tribute to his career at Iowa, the University honored him with one of 20 spots on Iowa's All-Century Team.

Herb Wilkinson was a man of strong faith, he was close to his family, and he achieved great success in basketball. And he always ranked them in that order.

Accolades
• First Team All-American (1945); Second Team All-American (1946, 47)
• First Team All-Big Ten (1945, 46, 47)
• Team MVP (1946)
• Selected to Iowa's All-Century basketball team (2002)

No. 28 HERB WILKINSON			
Year	GP	Pts	Avg
1945	18	173	9.6
1946	18	151	8.3
1947	Statistics not available		

<u>How He's Remembered</u>

"His work at guard has been the rock upon which many of the Midwest's best scorers have foundered. Iowa's opponents have averaged only 36.1 points and the rock-ribbed Hawkeye defense is built around Herb Wilkinson."

Walter Byers, *Mason City Globe*

"Wilkinson was Iowa's mainstay. The 23-year-old dental student…was a constant scoring threat for the Hawkeyes and specialized in holding down the score of the opponent's stars."

Ed Sainsbury, *Mason City Globe-Gazette*

"Herb was an exceptional player and a great guy to have around."

Murray Wier

"Herb…was a terrific ball-handler and floor leader. He also earned a reputation of being able to make long shots that would deflate opposing defenses, in addition to his ability to score inside because of his size."

Mike Finn and Chad Leistikow, *Hawkeye Legends, Lists & Lore*

#29: THE REAL DIEHL

"Bill Diehl was a good athlete, a good leader, and a good student, and he came along at the right time for Iowa football."

- Al Couppee

Great skill players are often dependent upon their linemen to give them an opportunity for success. It should come as no surprise that Nile Kinnick was the beneficiary of some fine blocking by several outstanding linemen. One of the linemen that paved the way for Iowa's only Heisman Trophy winner was Bill Diehl, who anchored the center and linebacker positions for the Hawkeyes from 1939-1941.

William Diehl was a Third Team All-State center as a high school senior for Cedar Rapids Roosevelt in 1937. Diehl initially left the state to play for the legendary Pop Warner at Temple University. However, after Diehl's freshman season at Temple, Warner retired from coaching. Diehl promptly transferred back to his home state to play for the University of Iowa and their new head coach, Dr. Eddie Anderson.

Diehl immediately became a starter as a sophomore for the 1939 Ironmen. He started at center on offense and turned into a middle linebacker on defense. Diehl first made his presence felt in an oppressively hot game against Indiana. The Hawkeyes had not won a home conference game in six years and had not beaten the Hoosiers in three times that long. The game was a wild, back-and-forth affair. Indiana raced out to a 10-0 lead, Iowa responded to grab a 20-10 advantage, and then the Hoosiers battled back to take a 29-20 lead. At the end of the third quarter, Indiana held a nine point lead and possessed the ball at the Iowa 32-yard line.

The Hawkeye team was hot, weary, and battling injuries. A Hoosier score would almost certainly create too large a deficit for Iowa to overcome. It was at this moment that Bill Diehl made one of the most important plays of his career, picking off the Indiana quarterback and giving the ball back to the Hawkeyes. Iowa responded with a 12-play drive for a touchdown, which cut Indiana's lead to 29-26. That set the stage for Kinnick's game-winning touchdown pass a few minutes later and a thrilling 32-29 Hawkeye win.

> **After the high scoring victory over Indiana, Bill Diehl showed up with his face full of bruises. Nile Kinnick saw him and joked, "Diehl, did they keep score on your face today?"**

Diehl started the first four games of the 1939 season. His fourth start was against the Wisconsin Badgers in Madison, and Diehl was dominating, especially on defense. Wisconsin sportswriter Roundy Coughlin wrote, "Diehl at center for Iowa played a wonderful game. I don't know how many tackles that guy made, and when I say 'tackles', I mean tackles. And his [snapping] was perfect." Unfortunately, with only a few minutes left in Iowa's victory over the Badgers, Diehl suffered a sprained shoulder and a season-ending knee injury, which required off-season surgery.

As a junior, Bill Diehl continued to anchor the Hawkeye defense. In Iowa's first conference game in 1940, the Hawkeyes again squared off against Wisconsin. Diehl played with a vengeance against the team to which he had suffered his knee injury the previous year. He recovered a fumble at the Wisconsin 20-yard line that led to Iowa's first touchdown, and the Hawks rolled to a 30-12 win.

> **Bill Diehl played all sixty minutes against the Badgers in 1940. Since he did not perform the feat for the Ironmen, it was the first sixty minute game of his career. He also played the full sixty minutes two weeks later against Minnesota.**

Diehl suffered the second season-ending knee injury of his career in Iowa's great 7-0 upset of Notre Dame in 1940. Again, he needed extensive off-season knee surgery to correct the problem. Diehl garnered such respect from his Hawkeye teammates that they elected him captain of the 1941 squad. Iowa struggled to a 3-5 record that season, as the Hawkeyes played four of their six Big Ten games on the road.

Bill Diehl was talented in basketball and baseball in addition to football. He initially came to Iowa on a basketball scholarship, but knee surgeries prevented him from ever suiting up in basketball for the Hawks. Diehl was a reserve outfielder for the Hawkeye baseball team in 1940 and 1941.

Pearl Harbor was attacked on December 7, 1941. Immediately after the 1941 football season, Diehl left the University of Iowa, just one semester shy of graduation, to enlist in the military. However, he was still able to participate in the 1942 College All-Star Game. After that, he played for the Eastern Army All-Star team, a team of college all-stars that played three games against NFL teams. The Eastern Army All-Stars went 2-1 against the NFL, defeating the Brooklyn Dodgers and the New York Giants and losing to the NFL champion Chicago Bears, 14-7.

Diehl spent the war with a tank destroyer unit in Europe and was discharged as a captain in 1946. He returned to the University of Iowa for his final semester of school and served as the first baseman on the baseball team, earning his only varsity baseball letter. After graduation, he worked as a salesman for MacAllister Machinery and eventually was promoted to vice president of the company. He raised three children with his wife, Mary, whom he married at the Little Brown Church in Nashua back in 1941 when Diehl was team captain.

Bill Diehl was a huge asset to Iowa football. As a linebacker, he was one of Iowa's best defensive players from 1939-1941. As a lineman, his blocking helped make Nile Kinnick a national sensation. And as an Ironman and team captain, Diehl established himself as an outstanding Hawkeye in one of the most unforgettable eras in Hawkeye history.

Accolades
• Played for two Hall of Fame coaches – Pop Warner and Eddie Anderson
• Started for Iowa's 1939 Ironmen team
• Team captain and MVP (1941)
• Selected for the College All-Star Game (1942)

How He's Remembered

"Diehl is not a flashy player. He is, however, a coach's player. Thus far he has done everything one could ask of a sophomore center. His [snaps] have been accurate, his downfield blocking good, and his defensive play as a linebacker has been outstanding."

Mason City Globe-Gazette (Oct 20, 1939)

"A wise-cracker on the practice field to keep the squad in good spirits, Bill is nevertheless a conscientious player and perhaps the most alert defensive player on the team."

Iowa City Press-Citizen (Oct 16, 1941)

"I think the squad made a wise selection [for 1941 team MVP]. Diehl played great football for three years and is certainly deserving of the honor. We're sorry to lose him."

Eddie Anderson

"In my mind's eye, I could once again see Diehl, the linebacker, slicing across the line of scrimmage and cutting a ballcarrier down like an axe to a tree."

Al Couppee

#30: DRESSED FOR SUCCESS

"I maybe should be in the Guinness Book of World Records. I may be the only athlete in intercollegiate sports, male or female, who was named the most valuable player on a team that didn't win a conference game."

- Bill Reichardt

"I'm Bill Reichardt, and I own the store."

Some athletes are so successful at their second career that you almost forget they had a first one. Many Iowans might remember Bill Reichardt primarily as the professionally dressed pitchman, advertising his clothing store as the ideal place to buy a fine suit. But decades earlier, Reichardt was a shifty runner that lifted the Hawkeye football team from 1949-1951 and received the Big Ten's highest honor.

William John Reichardt had an early association with Hawkeye football. He grew up in Iowa City, just two blocks from the home of Iowa's head coach, Dr. Eddie Anderson. As a nine-year-old friend of Anderson's son, Reichardt had a close association with the 1939 Ironmen. He was occasionally referred to as the team's "curly-haired mascot."

In high school, Reichardt was a First Team All-State player at Iowa City High. He was inducted into the Iowa High School Football Hall of Fame in 2009. After Reichardt's senior season in 1948, his mother wanted to get him out of Iowa City, so he actually accepted a scholarship offer at the University of Southern California. But when Coach Anderson heard that his former mascot was leaving, Anderson and others met him at the train station and persuaded him to stick with the Hawkeyes.

Bill Reichardt first saw game action as a sophomore in 1949. The Hawkeyes got off to a 4-2 start that season, including a 35-9 win over Indiana for Iowa's largest margin of victory in 26 years. But the key game in 1949 was the Hawkeyes' incredible shootout with the Oregon Ducks. Iowa had never defeated a Pacific Coast team, and the Ducks were the defending Pacific Coast Conference champions.

Oregon jumped out to a 24-6 lead, but the Hawkeyes scored two touchdowns to cut the deficit to 24-20 early in the fourth quarter. The Ducks quickly responded, however, with a touchdown drive to extend their lead to 31-20 with just over nine minutes left in the game. For the moment, it appeared that the Iowa rally had been too little, too late.

Reichardt fielded the ensuing kickoff at the one-yard line, started up the sideline, cut to the middle of the field, and broke away from the pursuing defenders. Ninety-nine yards later, Reichardt had the stadium record for longest kickoff return and cut Iowa's deficit right back to four points. Four plays after that, Iowa recovered a fumble at the Oregon 19-yard line. Three straight Reichardt runs gave Iowa the 19 yards they needed and a 34-31 lead. That score held up, and Iowa had secured the largest comeback victory in school history.

Reichardt never lacked confidence. After the game, a reporter asked him, "Did you think you were going all the way with that kickoff?" "You're [expletive] right I did," Reichardt snapped. "But don't forget to mention the blockers who paved the way."

> **Iowa started the 1950 season with a bang, upsetting Bill Reichardt's former suitor Southern California in Los Angeles, 20-14. As a result, the Hawks, who had been three touchdown underdogs to USC, were ranked 15th in the first ever Coaches' Poll.**

The low point of Reichardt's career came halfway through his junior season when Ohio State and Heisman Trophy winner Vic Janowicz destroyed the Hawks, 83-21. It was understandable that Iowa was a large underdog the following week in Minneapolis against the Gophers. But Reichardt's strong play keyed a Hawkeye upset of Minnesota to give Iowa its first road victory over their rivals since 1921. Reichardt's great running earned him an All-Big Ten nod at the end of his junior year.

Bill Reichardt's crowning athletic achievement was winning the Big Ten's Most Valuable Player award in 1951. This accomplishment is seldom mentioned without also noting that, in an unusual quirk, Iowa did not win a conference game that season. The Hawkeyes' conference record in 1951 was 0-5-1. It should be noted, however, that Reichardt displayed remarkable toughness and versatility on his way to earning that award. As a senior, he rushed for 737 yards, had 115 yards receiving, kicked a 35-yard field goal, and converted 18 of 22 extra points.

On a cold, windy day, Reichardt played his final home game against arch-rival Minnesota. For three quarters, Minnesota dominated play, taking a 20-0 lead into the final period. But the relentless Reichardt had one more comeback in him. The Hawkeye defense got the rally started by blocking a Gopher punt at the Minnesota 24-yard line. It took just three Reichardt carries to break into the end zone for the first Hawkeye score. Gus Schrader of *The Cedar Rapids Gazette* wrote, "Reichardt had been a demon all afternoon, but now he virtually went crazy." On Iowa's next possession, he carried the ball five more times to set up a ten-yard touchdown pass with 4:26 to play. Reichardt missed the extra point under a heavy rush, though many Hawkeye backers thought the Gophers were offside on the play.

Nevertheless, the Hawks had momentum. Reichardt kicked off for a touchback, and the Hawkeyes again held Minnesota without a first down. Iowa marched to the Minnesota 36-yard line with under two minutes remaining in the game. "Reichardt smacked through a gaping hole at center and crunched through the Gopher secondary like a 47-ton tank," Schrader described Reichardt as he galloped for the tying score. Minnesota had seen enough and deliberately ran out the rest of the clock. The Hawkeyes settled for a draw, though the electrifying comeback allowed Iowa to maintain possession of Floyd of Rosedale. Performances like that one helped Reichardt to be named a Second Team All-American in 1951 and to narrowly defeat Illinois linebacker Chuck Boerio for the Silver Football.

After his Hawkeye career, Reichardt played just one season for the Green Bay Packers before leaving football and serving three years in the Army. He opened Reichardts, Inc. in 1953, a men's clothing store in Des Moines where "no sale is ever final." Reichardt owned the store for 44 years and quickly became a pillar of the Des Moines small business community. He also dabbled in politics, serving six years in the Iowa state legislature from 1964 to 1970 and running for governor of Iowa in 1994.

In addition, Reichardt was very involved in issues affecting young people. He published many articles pertaining to competitive athletics and juvenile crime. Reichardt founded the Little All-American Football League and the Des Moines Youth Soccer League and coached in the football league for 29 years. He also participated in many other youth organizations and was a guest speaker at numerous events to benefit young people.

> **Bill Reichardt rushed for 1,665 yards in his career. That career total was a modern-era record and the third-highest total at Iowa all-time, behind only Aubrey Devine and Gordon Locke.**

Reichardt warned of the dangers of playing football, particularly for young people. "Football is a violent game. And it's not a matter of if you get hurt; it's when you get hurt. One of the purposes of the game is to hurt you, ring your bell," Reichardt said. "If you want to be a football player, you have to develop physically. It's not a game for the timid; it's a game for the tough."

Despite all of his accomplishments as a football player, businessman, and youth advocate, Reichardt was probably best known publicly as a commercial spokesman for his clothing store. But privately, Bill Reichardt was just a man that genuinely wanted the best for young people. "He would rather give you advice than sell you a suit," friend William C. Knapp admitted.

That's a reputation that will never go out of style.

Accolades
• Big Ten MVP (1951)
• Second Team All-American (1951)
• All-Big Ten (1950, 51)
• Selected for the College All-Star Game (1952)
• Inducted into the University of Iowa Hall of Fame (2001)

No. 30 BILL REICHARDT

Year	Att	Yards	Avg	Recept	Yards	Avg	TDs
1949	68	343	5.0	3	24	8.0	4
1950	138	585	4.2	11	95	8.6	0
1951	178	737	4.2	11	115	10.5	2
Totals	384	1,665	4.3	25	234	9.4	6

How He's Remembered

"One of the best players to wear an Iowa uniform."

Ron Maly

"He really could hit. He was tough to get off his feet. He's a real good one."

Stan Wallace, Illinois halfback

"He's the hardest driver I've ever seen. He just pounds and pounds away long after he's tackled."

Ed O'Shaughnessy, Michigan center

"Reichardt is a terrifically strong, hard running fellow. He's a swell blocker, too, and he's even good as a halfback on defense."

Dick Harlow, former Harvard coach

"I feel we haven't heard the last of Bill Reichardt. Certain people, when they die, start the clock over. I'm not the only one who knows a million stories about Bill, and as they become embellished, enlarged, and enhanced, no one is going to be around to challenge and deny them. They're just going to get better."

W.A. Krause

Jersey #30 Honorable Mention

Al Couppee – Football (1939-41)

Albert Wallace Couppee was born in Council Bluffs, Iowa, in 1920. He was a sophomore quarterback for Iowa's 1939 Ironmen team and was a lead blocker for Nile Kinnick during Kinnick's run for the Heisman Trophy. Couppee led the Hawkeye football team to two straight victories over highly-touted Notre Dame and provided a key fourth-quarter interception late in the 1940 game to pace the Hawks to a 7-0 victory. Couppee went on to star in the broadcasting booth after his pro football career with the Washington Redskins. He provided superb play-by-play of University of Iowa football and basketball for more than a decade prior to taking his talents to San Diego, where he was an announcer for both the Chargers and the Padres. Couppee was inducted into the University of Iowa Hall of Fame in 1996. He also authored a book titled "One Magic Year, 1939, An Ironman Remembers".

Kenny Arnold – Basketball (1979-82)

Kenny Arnold came to Iowa from Calumet High School of the Chicago Public League. He was a reserve as a freshman for Iowa's Big Ten championship team in 1979, and he claimed a starting spot in his final three years at Iowa. Arnold led Iowa's 1980 Final Four team in scoring, and he led the 1980 and 1981 Hawkeyes in assists. He scored 1,112 points in his career, which ranks 29th in school history. Arnold was a Third Team All-Big Ten selection as a senior in 1982. Years later, his courageous battle against brain cancer united and inspired his fans and former teammates.

#31: BY LAND OR BY AIR

"He was the best combination of runner and receiver of any back that I saw at the University of Iowa. There were others who were maybe better receivers. There certainly were those who were better runners; but as a combination runner and receiver, Ronnie Harmon was the best."

- Ron Gonder

Ronnie Harmon defined versatility on the football field. He remains in the top ten in both career rushing and receiving yards at Iowa, and he was perhaps the most talented offensive player of the Hayden Fry era. A native of Laurelton, New York, Harmon was an integral part of four bowl teams for Coach Fry from 1982-1985.

Although he originally came to Iowa to play running back, Harmon played receiver as a true freshman. The position move allowed him to see the field immediately, and he hauled in 19 receptions and three touchdowns as a freshman. Two of his touchdowns came in the 1982 Peach Bowl win over Tennessee. He extended his playing time as a sophomore with 35 receptions, over 200 yards rushing, and 12 kickoff returns, while Coach Hayden Fry gradually shifted Harmon back to running back. Harmon was making a name for himself as a "big play" specialist. As a sophomore, he ran or caught a pass for more than 20 yards seventeen times.

He started off his junior year in a big way also. Having moved to the starting tailback position, he scored on an 86-yard rushing touchdown and then a 68-yard pass in the opener against Iowa State. He had become Hayden's dual threat player on a high-powered offense. He would finish the year ranked second in the nation in all-purpose yards and tenth in kickoff return yardage.

Harmon played a key role on the 1984 team with both his presence and absence. Iowa sat at 5-1 in the conference with Wisconsin coming to Kinnick. On successive plays, Harmon and quarterback Chuck Long were injured. Harmon's injury, a broken leg, kept him out until the next year. Iowa tied Wisconsin and then lost their next two games. Once in the driver's seat for the Rose Bowl, Iowa settled for an invite to the inaugural Freedom Bowl.

> **Ronnie was one of five Harmon brothers. In addition to Kevin, who also played for Iowa, Greg played semi-pro for the Brooklyn Kings. Derrick was a standout running back at Cornell and earned a Super Bowl championship ring with San Francisco.**

As a running back, he was never one to try to run over defenders. He had a very distinctive look and style of running with the ball. With hip pads that always extended above his waistline, he didn't have blazing speed but ran with a very low center of gravity. This allowed him to turn on a dime.

"I never liked running into people," Harmon told Dave Dorr of the *St. Louis Post-Dispatch* in 1985. "If you can make two or three guys miss, it feels really good. I get a thrill out of that, and everybody else does too."

With Harmon healthy and Chuck Long returning for his final season, prospects for the 1985 team were high. Together, they pulled off one of the most memorable plays that year. Down with only seconds to go against Michigan State, Iowa was faced with a third and one at the Spartan two-yard line. Chuck Long faked a handoff to Harmon. Spartan defenders converged onto Harmon as he dived into the pile and sold the fake perfectly. Long rolled around to the right and pranced into the end zone untouched.

"Long faked a handoff to Ronnie Harmon, and almost everyone in Johnson County bought the fake as Harmon tried to leap through the line," wrote Mike Hlas of *The Cedar Rapids Gazette*. The play gave Iowa a 35-31 win and preserved the No. 1 national ranking they had earned the previous week.

The 1985 team was one of the best Iowa has ever produced. Iowa fans saw their team blow out Iowa State, 57-3, in Ames. Rob Houghtlin kicked Iowa to a 12-10 thriller over No. 2-ranked Michigan in a game for the ages. Iowa pounded Illinois, 59-0, and ended the regular season with a 31-9 win over Minnesota. The Hawkeyes won the Big Ten title outright for the fourth time in school history and earned a trip to Pasadena. Harmon ranked sixth in the nation in all-purpose yardage, and the Hawks had the second-highest scoring offense in the nation. Iowa took their No. 3 national ranking and their 10-1 record against UCLA in the Rose Bowl.

There's something to be said for saving your best game for last. Unfortunately, Harmon saved his worst for last. He had just earned All-American and All-Big Ten honors, but he fumbled four times in the first half against the Bruins. He had previously fumbled only once all season. Iowa lost the game, 45-28. Harmon's performance immediately generated questions about how he could have played so poorly. Some of those questions still linger today.

After a disastrous Rose Bowl performance, Ronnie Harmon went on to have a very successful NFL career. He was a first-round selection of the Buffalo Bills, and he played 12 seasons professionally, mostly with the Bills and the San Diego Chargers. His best seasons were with the Chargers. He was selected for the 1992 Pro Bowl after he finished the year ranked in the top ten in the NFL in receptions and receiving yards, and he played in Super Bowl XXIX against the San Francisco 49ers. Harmon led the Chargers in the Super Bowl with eight catches for 68 yards in a losing effort.

> **Ronnie Harmon is the only Hawkeye to surpass 10,000 all-purpose yards in the NFL.**
> **He gained 10,265 combined yards rushing, receiving, and returning.**

When you think of Ronnie Harmon, think not only of what could have been in the 1986 Rose Bowl. Consider that, despite missing a number of games his junior year due to injury, he still ranks in Iowa's top ten in both rushing and receiving. Consider that, despite four fumbles, he still caught a Rose Bowl-record 11 passes. Consider that Coach Kirk Ferentz invited him to be an honorary captain in 2006. Not only was No. 1-ranked Ohio State in Iowa City that evening, but ESPN College GameDay was also on hand. The whole nation was watching.

If Coach Ferentz can move beyond one bad game 25 years ago, so can Iowa fans.

Accolades
- First Team All-American (1985); Second Team All-American (1984)
- All-Big Ten (1984, 85)
- Ranks in the top ten in school history in career rushing yards and career receiving yards
- Played 12 seasons in the NFL; selected to the Pro Bowl (1992)
- Selected to the all-time University of Iowa football team (1989)

No. 31 RONNIE HARMON

Year	Att	Yards	Avg	Long	Recept	Yards	Avg	TDs
1982	8	13	1.6	26	19	299	15.7	3
1983	22	185	8.4	27	35	729	20.8	7
1984	190	907	4.8	86	32	318	9.9	12
1985	223	1,166	5.2	46	60	699	11.7	10
Totals	443	2,271	5.1	86	146	2,045	14.0	32

How He's Remembered

"Ronnie might be the most physically gifted player of the Hayden Fry era. He could really do it all as a back. In fact, he was so good that Harmon played receiver his first year on campus because they just had to get him on the field. It's really too bad that a lot of Iowa fans' memory about Ronnie are the fumbles in the Rose Bowl loss to UCLA, because he is one of the best backs to ever wear an Iowa uniform."

Tom Kakert

"The most exciting running back I've ever been associated with."

Hayden Fry (1985)

"He caught passes, and he was a superior running back. Harmon was also a great receiver. How he fumbled four times in the Rose Bowl, nobody could explain that, because he wasn't a fumbler, really. That's what he's remembered for, but he was a great all-around player. In fact, Coach Fry said he was one of the best players he ever coached."

Buck Turnbull

"Ronnie Harmon probably was the most exciting running back I remember at Iowa. He brought people to their feet. As I'd look out onto the stadium from the press box, Ronnie Harmon would get the ball, and you'd see more people jump to their feet to watch how the play was going to finish out than any back I can remember."

Frosty Mitchell

"Harmon is never content to catch a pass and be tackled…He seems to be convinced he could run around or through the whole Russian army!"

Gus Schrader

Jersey #31 Honorable Mention

Bill Logan – Basketball (1954-56)

Bill Logan, a 6'7" center, played on consecutive Final Four teams as part of the "Fabulous Five"; as is the case with the other four, Logan's number 31 is retired. The Keokuk native was the only Iowa native among the starters. He is one of only seven Hawkeyes to lead the team in scoring three different seasons. Logan was a First Team All-Big Ten selection as a junior and a senior, and he was a Second Team All-American as a senior. He still holds the 12th-highest career scoring average at Iowa. Logan is on Iowa's All-Century team.

"Bill Logan was outstanding. He was a good scorer inside, and it's amazing how much speed he had for a big guy. He wasn't one of those lumbering centers that just loafed down the court; he was very energetic and hard-working. He was just a very sound, intelligent player."

Bill Seaberg

Mel Cole – Football (1978-81)
John Derby – Football (1988-91)

Mel Cole and John Derby were Hawkeye linebackers that played a decade apart. Cole was team MVP in 1981; Derby was team captain in 1991. Cole was All-Big Ten in 1981; Derby was All-Big Ten in 1991. Cole led the Hawkeyes in tackles in 1981; Derby led the Hawkeyes in tackles in 1991. Cole won a Big Ten title in 1981; Derby won a Big Ten title in 1990. Cole started at linebacker in the 1982 Rose Bowl; Derby started at linebacker in the 1991 Rose Bowl. Cole made a game-changing interception in a 1981 road upset over Michigan, which propelled Iowa to the Rose Bowl; Derby made a game-clinching interception in a 1990 road upset over Michigan, which propelled Iowa to the Rose Bowl. Cole ended his career in 1981 as the 11th-leading tackler in school history with 244 career tackles; Derby ended his career in 1991 as the 12th-leading tackler in school history with 262 career tackles.

Matt Roth – Football (2001-04)

Matt Roth came to Iowa as a highly-regarded linebacker from Villa Park, Illinois. Roth played mostly on special teams as a true freshman before Coach Kirk Ferentz moved him to defensive end prior to his sophomore year. Roth finished his second year with a team-leading ten sacks in a reserve role, as Iowa won the Big Ten title in 2002. A feisty demeanor and an ability to get to the quarterback became Roth's trademark. He started every game in 2003 and earned All-Big Ten honors. He was a Second Team All-American as a senior in addition to being named All-Big Ten for the second time. Iowa finished with a combined 38-12 record during Roth's four years at Iowa.

#32: DOWNTOWN IOWA CITY

"We'd had a poor season the year before, and in looking back to our success in 1970, you'd have to say Fred Brown was the missing piece to our puzzle. He fit in perfectly."

- Chad Calabria

In football, it's sometimes difficult for one player to dramatically change a team's overall record. It's simply a matter of numbers – 22 players are on the field at once. In basketball, with only five starters, that is not as much the case. A single player can drastically influence a team's success. As a case in point, look no further than the 1970 Iowa basketball team.

Four starters returned in the fall of 1969 from an eighth-place Big Ten squad the year before. These four would start again as seniors with one new addition – a junior college transfer named Fred Brown. He was that one player who could help turn around the program.

Fred Brown attended high school in Milwaukee, Wisconsin, where he twice led his team to a state championship. Though Brown didn't attend the University of Iowa straight out of high school, Iowa's coach, Ralph Miller, stayed in contact with him. Fred was a 6'3" guard who could do it all at Southeastern Community College in Burlington, Iowa. He could handle and distribute the ball like a point guard, yet he was also their leading scorer. He averaged 21 points per game his freshman year and 27 points per game as a sophomore on his way to being named to the national junior college all-tournament team.

Enter Fred Brown to the Hawkeye program. Brown was the newcomer with four returning starters. John Johnson – the team's leading scorer – played one forward position with Glenn Vidnovic at the other. Dick Jensen played center, while the fourth senior, Chad Calabria, was Brown's backcourt partner. This group of five players, in addition to sixth man Ben McGilmer, would soon become Coach Miller's "Six Pack" team of 1970.

Brown's time at Iowa sputtered early; he was sick for his first two games as a Hawkeye. However, by the third game of the season against Duquesne, Iowa fans began to see first-hand the ability of Iowa's new point guard. Though Brown scored no points in the first half against the ranked Dukes, he scored 18 points in the second period to lead the Hawks to a win.

Like Brown, the Hawkeye team struggled early in the 1969-70 season. Iowa lost four of their first seven games, and a win against Hawaii drew their record even as the Hawkeyes entered Big Ten play. The 1970 conference slate began with a home game against league-favorite Purdue. Iowa weathered a 53-point onslaught by Purdue's Rick Mount to upend the Boilermakers, 94-88; Mount would score 61 points in a second loss to Iowa later that season.

The Hawkeyes began to pick off conference opponent after conference opponent, and Brown's quick transition to Big Ten play was a big factor. Coach Miller had successfully dipped into the junior college pool before by acquiring star players such as Sam Williams and John Johnson, but Brown fit in with the team immediately. "Fred has made one of the finest adjustments I have ever seen a junior college boy make," Coach Miller said. "Every game you see some improvement."

It was like a light came on and the Hawkeyes' offense began to master the finer points of the game. The team – especially Brown – passed the ball unselfishly to find the open shooter. Coach Miller later said they were the best passing team he ever coached. They also set school team records for field goal and free throw percentages.

The 1970 Hawkeyes had become a "pick your poison" opponent. Hold John Johnson under 20 points, and Fred Brown would make up the difference. Hold them both in check, and Calabria would come up big, and so on. Led by Johnson's 27.9 points per game, they simply outscored people. Iowa rolled to a perfect 14-0 conference record and their first outright Big Ten championship since the "Fabulous Five" in the mid-1950s.

Miller's "Six Pack" would go down as the highest-scoring team in Big Ten history. That's no small task for a team that had a 5-9 conference record the year before. Iowa's 1970 record of 102.9 points per game in Big Ten play still stands. It's a record that may never be broken. "We couldn't have done it without Fred Brown," Coach Miller said. "He was the glue that held the team together."

> **Iowa scored more than 100 points fourteen times during Fred Brown's junior season.**

Iowa's amazing run of 16 straight wins came to an end in the NCAA Tournament, when eventual NCAA runner-up Jacksonville edged the Hawkeyes, 104-103. Fred Brown's basket with 18 seconds remaining gave Iowa a lead until Jacksonville regained the lead with only two seconds remaining. It was a crushing defeat; both players and fans alike felt this Iowa team could have gone all the way in the tournament. Brown led the Hawkeyes with 27 points in the loss. Iowa thumped Notre Dame, 121-106, in a consolation game to ease the sting just a little, but the Hawkeyes' magical season was over.

Despite averaging over 17 points per game in 1970, Brown was only the third-leading scorer on his own team. That is how the season went for the high-scoring Hawkeyes of 1969-70. Brown was a Second Team All-Big Ten selection, and his contributions were undeniable. He knew his role and played it to perfection.

"I wasn't the type of player who wanted to score points," Brown said. "I just filled a need. Those other guys had all been there. I could pass well, and the other guys wanted to shoot. Because I was the point guard, I had the ball. So I got it to them."

Those are the words of a coach's dream. At the conclusion of the 1970 season, however, Ralph Miller announced he was leaving Iowa for Oregon State. He was replaced by Dick Schultz, but the loss of four senior starters and the top reserve hit the team hard. Those five seniors combined had averaged 77.7 points per game the previous year. In addition, Jim Speed, a junior college transfer who was expected to contribute at forward, contracted meningitis just before the season. The illness caused Speed to spend a month in intensive care and eventually rendered him blind, which shook the entire team emotionally.

With a short-handed squad, Coach Schultz knew the 1970-71 Hawkeyes would have to be built around Fred Brown. That fact was reflected in the team's nickname, "Fred Brown and the

Ugly Ducklings." Expecting the team to roll through the Big Ten was too much to ask, but the Hawkeyes had a few bright moments. Brown had a career-high 36 points in less than 31 minutes to help Iowa upset previously-unbeaten and No. 15-ranked Illinois. Illini coach Harv Schmidt said, "That Brown is something. They go to him for the big ones, and he comes through…I've said all along Brown is the best true guard in the country."

Brown poured in 35 points in his final home game, an 86-82 loss to Michigan. It was Iowa's eighth loss of the season by four points or less. "Predictably, Fred has been the target of enemy defenses the entire season, for Iowa has no other player who has maintained a scoring average in double figures," Al Grady of the *Iowa City Press-Citizen* wrote. "If you played Iowa, chances are your defensive strategy would be to let some of the other guys shoot as much as they wanted but try to keep Fred Brown from getting his hands on the ball, or play a zone so Brown can't go one-on-one. Despite these defenses, Fred may wind up averaging more points per game than any player in Hawkeye history."

In his final game against Purdue, Brown "only" needed 23 points to surpass John Johnson for the highest career scoring average in school history and 27 points to win the 1971 Big Ten scoring title. Sadly, he could only muster 13 points against the Boilermakers, his lowest point total since his second game with the Hawkeyes. He finished the year averaging 27.6 points per game. Though Iowa finished seventh in the Big Ten, Brown was named team MVP, First Team All-Big Ten, and First Team All-American in 1971.

As great as his collegiate career was, Fred Brown may be best remembered for his successful professional career with the Seattle Supersonics. He was drafted by the Supersonics as the sixth overall pick in the 1971 NBA Draft; it is the highest that any Hawkeye basketball player has ever been drafted. Brown played 13 seasons in Seattle and was captain of the Supersonics' 1978-79 NBA championship team. Brown retired as Seattle's leader in games played, points, field goals made and attempted, assists, and steals. He was even reunited with former Iowa teammate John Johnson for a time. Brown ended his professional career in 1984, and Seattle retired his No. 32 jersey two years later.

> **Seattle's "Downtown" Freddie Brown once scored 58 points in a game against Golden State.**

After his playing days were over, Brown entered the banking business for 15 years. He served as senior vice-president for a banking firm in Washington, Idaho, and Oregon. He never strayed far from the game he loved, however, and he coached three of his sons in basketball.

In 2002, the University again recognized his career by providing a spot in their All-Century team for Iowa's one and only "Downtown" Freddie Brown. "The people in Iowa were good family folks and had been great to me," Brown recalled. "I loved being down there in that atmosphere, and it was a wonderful experience. I made a lot of wonderful friends, who I still stay in contact with today. The people will always be my greatest memory and then the playing. Playing in the Big Ten was just a dream come true."

Accolades
• First Team All-American (1971)
• First Team All-Big Ten (1971); Second Team All-Big Ten (1970)
• Ranks third in school history in career scoring average
• Selected to Iowa's All-Century basketball team (2002)
• No. 32 retired by the Seattle Supersonics in his honor

No. 32 FRED BROWN

Year	GP	FG-FGA	FG%	FT-FTA	FT%	Reb	Avg	Pts	Avg
1970	24	180-360	50%	69-86	80%	91	3.8	429	17.9
1971	24	268-535	50%	126-152	83%	111	4.6	662	27.6
Totals	48	448-895	50%	195-238	82%	202	4.2	1,091	22.7

How He's Remembered

"Some called him 'Freaky Freddie' in his time at Iowa and with good reason. He was a flat-out scorer, who was part of the great team of 1969-70 that went undefeated in the Big Ten. Fred was the third-leading scorer that year, but after John Johnson, Chad Calabria, and 'Stick' Vidnovic graduated...he took over the bulk of the scoring load and averaged nearly 28 points a game his senior year."

Tom Kakert

"That 1970 team was probably the best team Iowa ever had. John Johnson and Fred Brown combined were a great twosome. If they had the three-point shot back then, there's no telling what Freddie would have averaged."

Buck Turnbull

"Freddie was as good of a shooter as I saw in the '70s, even when you consider Rick Mount and Pete Maravich played then. It is interesting when you look at the number 32; Fred Brown had 32, Vince Brookings had 32, and Kent McCausland had 32. All three understood what shooting was about, and they all wore number 32."

Mac McCausland

"Fred Brown might be the best basketball player Iowa ever had and, whether he is or isn't, he certainly is the most exciting player here since Murray Wier...Some of his moves and some of his shots have bordered on the impossible. He has given Hawkeye fans two memorable years of thrills, win or lose."

Al Grady

Jersey #32 Honorable Mention

Emlen Tunnell – Football (1946-47)

A native of Garrett Hill, Pennsylvania, Emlen Tunnell played one season of football and basketball at the University of Toledo, leading the Rockets to the 1943 NIT championship game. He enlisted in the Coast Guard during World War II before moving to Iowa City. Tunnell led Iowa in passing in 1946 and receiving in 1947. He set two school records in 1947 against Indiana with 155 yards receiving and three touchdown catches. He left before his senior season to become the first African-American to play for the New York Giants. Tunnell had a spectacular NFL career in which he was selected to nine Pro Bowls and intercepted 79 passes.   His 79 career interceptions rank second all-time in NFL history behind fellow Hawkeye Paul Krause's 81. Tunnell was a member of two NFL championship teams and was selected to the NFL's 1950s All-Decade team. He became both the first African-American and the first Hawkeye to be enshrined in the Pro Football Hall of Fame in 1967.

Mike Saunders – Football (1988-91)

Mike Saunders rushed for 123 yards and three touchdowns as a freshman against Minnesota. After being seated behind Tony Stewart and Nick Bell on the depth chart in his sophomore and junior seasons, he became Iowa's featured back as a senior in 1991. At 6'1" and 195 pounds, he was a very capable receiver out of the backfield; he caught a game-winning touchdown against his home-state Wisconsin Badgers in 1991. It was a fourth-down play with only 44 seconds remaining. Saunders had a career-high 167 yards and one touchdown against Northwestern that same year. In 1991, he became the sixth Iowa running back to top 1,000 yards in a single season. He was named All-Big Ten and team MVP his senior year after Iowa finished with a 10-1-1 record. He went on to have a successful career in the Canadian Football League.

Reggie Evans – Basketball (2001-02)

Reggie Evans, an All-American at Coffeyville Community College in Kansas, played two seasons for the Hawkeye basketball team. In 2001, he led the nation in rebounding average with 11.9 rebounds per game and in double doubles with 22. Evans also led the nation in free throws made and attempted. He set school season records in rebounds, free throws made, and free throws attempted. His 346 free throw attempts that season ranked second in Big Ten history. Evans led Iowa in points, rebounds, and blocks, and was the Most Outstanding Player of the 2001 Big Ten Tournament, when Iowa won four games in four days to earn an NCAA Tournament bid.

Reggie Evans was Iowa's team MVP, a Second Team All-Big Ten selection, and an Honorable Mention All-American in each of his two seasons with the Hawkeyes. He finished his Iowa career with 1,054 points, becoming just the fourth Hawkeye with a two-year career to top 1,000 career points. Evans won a gold medal with USA Basketball at the 2001 FIBA Under-21 World Championships. He has played eight seasons in the NBA.

#33: THE FACE OF A NEW PROGRAM

"When we first put Bob in the starting lineup as a freshman, it was like being in a street fight and having your big brother show up. He just lifted the play of everyone else on the field."

- Kirk Ferentz

The previous chapter stated that it can be difficult for a single football player to dramatically change a team's overall record.

There are exceptions.

Bob Sanders entered the Iowa program in 2000 with a bang – literally. At one moment, Michigan State kick returner Monquiz Wedlow was making his way through Hawkeye defenders. A split second later, he was sent sprawling backward by true-freshman Bob Sanders. Wedlow managed to get up, but he had provided thousands of Iowa fans with their first lasting memory of Bob Sanders. Appropriately, that game was Kirk Ferentz's first Big Ten win as head coach at Iowa. The face of his new program had emerged.

Despite all the breakdowns and analysis of high school prospects, recruiting is still an inexact science. By Division I college football standards, Demond "Bob" Sanders didn't have the "measurables," as they say, to be an impact player. He was a one-star recruiting prospect out of Erie, Pennsylvania, listed at 5'8" and 175 pounds. He played running back in high school, rushing for 15 touchdowns and 1,100 yards as a senior. Other than Iowa, Ohio University was the only other Division I college program that showed interest in him – the Bobcats, not the Buckeyes.

Kirk Ferentz's longtime friend and mentor, Joe Moore, coached Sanders in high school. Moore had experienced firsthand the effect Sanders' physical play could have on a team and convinced Ferentz that he could at least contribute to special teams. Despite the fact that Sanders was lightly recruited, Ferentz concluded that he was worthy of a scholarship offer. It paid off more than any of them had envisioned. In addition to being a defensive standout, Sanders did excel on nearly all special teams units. He was simply too valuable to be left on the sidelines.

"If [Ferentz] didn't offer a scholarship, I was going to walk on," Sanders told the *Iowa City Press-Citizen*. "[Coach Moore] was going to make me walk on. He said, 'You're not going anywhere but Iowa. You're not going to a Division II or Division III school. You're better than that, but no one knows it.'"

Sanders came to Iowa when it was at its lowest point in two decades. The Hawkeyes finished 3-8 in 1998 and 1-10 in 1999. The 2000 season didn't start much better, but by the middle of the season, fans sensed a change. Iowa was becoming much more competitive. Sanders played extensively on special teams and finally started the ninth game of the season against

Wisconsin. The following game, an upstart Hawkeye squad won at Penn State in overtime. Then they beat Northwestern (which knocked the Wildcats out of the Rose Bowl) before they lost a close game at Minnesota. Iowa went 1-7 without Sanders in the starting lineup before winning two of their last four games. Though Sanders started only four games at strong safety, he garnered Honorable Mention All-Big Ten honors.

Former Iowa State head coach Dan McCarney saw Sanders' exploits first hand. "I thought he was a sensational football player," McCarney said. "It was a great job of evaluation by Coach Ferentz and his staff. He was one of those guys who just inspired those around him. He was supposedly not tall enough, not big enough, all that stuff. All he did was go out there and excel and dominate on game day."

> **Bob Sanders recorded 25 tackles against Indiana in 2001 and was named National Defensive Player of the Week.**

The 2001 season was Sanders' first as a full-time starter, and he had an early impact. In the Big Ten opener against Penn State, he knocked running back Eric McCoo's helmet off during a tackle. "I never really thought I could do something like that," Sanders admitted. It was just the first of many vicious hits for Sanders in the 2001 season. He finished fifth in the Big Ten in interceptions and sixth in tackles, leading the Hawkeyes in both categories. The team finished with a 7-5 record and returned to a bowl game after a three-year hiatus. One of Sanders' interceptions came in the Alamo Bowl win over Texas Tech, when he sealed the victory by picking off Tech quarterback Kliff Kingsbury in the end zone as time expired. While winning the Alamo Bowl was a cause for celebration, Sanders was already focused on 2002. "Our next goal is to go undefeated," he said on the field after the game.

That was a highly ambitious goal, but Sanders and his Hawkeye teammates achieved what few thought possible in 2002. Iowa went undefeated in the Big Ten for the first time in 80 years and claimed their first conference title since 1990. While the Hawks boasted a potent offense with Brad Banks at quarterback and a juggernaut offensive line, the Sanders-led defense was equally impressive.

Although Sanders missed a game after suffering a painful ankle injury against Iowa State, he bounced back to guide the Hawkeyes through the Big Ten schedule. Against Purdue, the Hawkeyes trailed, 14-3, and Purdue was threatening to increase its lead until Sanders made a play late in the first half. He blocked a Boilermaker field goal attempt, and Antwan Allen returned it 85 yards for an Iowa touchdown. That play cut Iowa's deficit to 14-10 and allowed the Hawkeyes to stay in the game on their way to a dramatic 31-28 win.

The season's biggest showdown came when No. 13 Iowa traveled to Ann Arbor to face No. 8 Michigan. The Hawks were clinging to a 10-9 lead midway through the third quarter when they were forced to punt. Sanders sprinted down the field and drilled the Michigan return man as he caught the ball, forcing a fumble. Iowa recovered possession of the ball and used the short field to score a quick touchdown. That set the tone for the second half, and the Hawkeyes dominated the Wolverines from that point forward to win, 34-9. Michigan linebacker Carl Diggs summed up the Hawkeyes' hard-hitting attitude when he labeled them "the bullies of the Big Ten." If that was true, Sanders was the biggest bully on the playground.

Iowa clinched a share of the Big Ten championship in Minnesota. In the third quarter, the Hawkeyes were forced to punt to the Gophers. As usual, Sanders was the first Iowa player to reach the Minnesota return man. The ball carrier put a move on Sanders and made him miss. Sanders got back up off of the turf, ran down the ball carrier from behind, and forced a fumble that the Hawkeyes recovered. Sanders had a tenacious and aggressive style, and he was seemingly omnipresent. Most importantly, his style of play was infectious.

"Talking to his teammates, it was kind of fun to bring Bob up," Tom Kakert said, "because everybody else kind of wanted to be like Bob and get hits like Bob. It was almost like a competition. His value – I don't think you can calculate it."

> **In 2003, Bob Sanders led the NCAA in forced fumbles (six) and the Big Ten in recovered fumbles (three).**

Foot surgery kept Sanders out of most of the non-conference portion of Iowa's 2003 schedule, but he returned to lead Iowa to a winning Big Ten record in his senior season. He saved his best for last, powering the Hawkeyes to a win over Minnesota on Senior Day. Sanders had 16 tackles, two tackles for loss, three forced fumbles, a sack, and a fumble recovery against the Gophers. His most spectacular play of the day came when he forced a fumble by Minnesota running back Laurence Maroney inches short of the goal line in Iowa's 40-22 win.

Iowa finished with a 10-3 record in Sanders' senior season, and Sanders concluded his Hawkeye career with a win in the Outback Bowl. He was a Second Team All-American as a senior and was named All-Big Ten for the third straight season. "The man is – and this is meant in the best possible way – a freak," said Mike Hlas of *The Cedar Rapids Gazette*. "He is a 5'8", 194-pound explosive device."

Sanders was drafted by the Indianapolis Colts, where he has played for six seasons. In his second year with the Colts, he made 118 tackles and earned All-Pro honors. In 2006, he missed most of the season with a knee injury but came back to help the Colts make a run to the Super Bowl. Sanders had a forced fumble and an interception in Super Bowl XLI, leading the Colts to a victory over the Chicago Bears. The following season, he had 12 games with eight or more tackles, and he became the first Colts player to earn the NFL Defensive Player of the Year award.

Bob Sanders had a profound effect on Iowa's defense and special teams. Iowa's conference record improved from 0-8 the year before he came to 8-0 by his junior year. His fingerprints were all over the team's improved record and aggressive mentality. He was just what the Iowa coaching staff needed. Sanders was, indeed, the face of Kirk Ferentz's new program.

Just ask Monquiz Wedlow.

Accolades
- Second Team All-American (2003)
- All-Big Ten (2001, 02, 03)
- Ranks ninth in school history in career tackles
- Has played six seasons in the NFL; First Team All-Pro (2005, 07)
- Named NFL Defensive Player of the Year in 2007

No. 33 BOB SANDERS

Year	Solo Tack	Assisted	Total	TFL	Sacks	Int-Yds	Fum For	Blocks
2000	42	10	52	3/10	1/7	0-0	2	0
2001	78	44	122	6/14	1/7	4-24	1	1
2002	68	34	102	1/4	1/4	2-15	4	1
2003	48	24	72	6/18	1/3	1-0	6	0
Totals	236	112	348	16/46	4-21	7-39	13	2

How He's Remembered

"His impact on our team has probably been as significant as any one player we've had."

Kirk Ferentz

"If there's one guy that changed the attitude of Iowa football during the Kirk Ferentz era, it was Bob Sanders. The Iowa football program took off the minute Bob Sanders was put in the starting lineup. Early on, he probably made some mistakes, but you lived with them because of the tempo and passion that he played with. He was just a guy who went out there and just loved football, and he set the tempo in practice. I think that was one of the things that Kirk would always talk about. They'd have to dial him down in practice because he was just so intense and he practiced the way he played. He's one of those guys that will be a fan favorite forever."

Tom Kakert

"He reminded me a lot of the Stoops brothers, only with more athleticism. That's why he's starting, playing, and excelling in the NFL. He should give great inspiration that there's still room for those guys that supposedly aren't tall enough or aren't big enough to be outstanding college football players."

Dan McCarney

"My teeth rattle just thinking about Sanders. This guy hit harder than any football player I've ever seen. I remember a game at Kinnick where he had Penn State ready to get back on the bus before halftime. Sanders just flat out hammered people. He's such a soft-spoken guy when you talk to him, and he often answers questions with 'No, sir,' or 'Yes, sir,' something you don't hear anymore. If ever anybody caused receivers to grow alligator arms, it was Bob Sanders."

Keith Murphy

"You can teach people how to tackle, but you can't teach people to play with the fearless style that Sanders played with. I mean, the guy just laid it all out there. I also consider him an

overachiever at 5'8", to accomplish what he's accomplished. When he came to Iowa, he was fast, but he wasn't a burner. He worked so hard in the weight room, and by the time he was done at Iowa, he was one of the fastest defensive backs in the history of the program. To me, he epitomizes the football program under Kirk Ferentz. Iowa took a chance on him and look what happened."

Pat Harty

"Bob Sanders is a stud!"

Sign held by Iowa fan during game against Minnesota in 2003

Jersey #33 Honorable Mention

Michael Enich – Football (1938-40)

"Iron" Mike Enich was a First Team All-State fullback in 1936 from Boone, Iowa. He played his sophomore season for Coach Irl Tubbs, beginning his career as a reserve quarterback before moving to the guard position. In 1939, new Hawkeye coach Eddie Anderson placed Enich at tackle, where he proved to be one of the most durable Ironmen. He played six straight games without a substitution in 1939, joining Kinnick in that distinction. Enich was an All-Big Ten selection and a Third Team All-American in 1939. The following season, he was named team captain and MVP as a senior. Enich again earned All-Big Ten honors, and he was named a First Team All-American in 1940. "He was a tough tackle," said longtime Iowa broadcaster Bob Brooks.

William Kay – Football (1945-48)

Bill Kay, a 6'5", 220-pound tackle from Walnut, Iowa, initially came to Iowa to play basketball. He made his mark as a football player, however, earning Third Team All-American honors and being named team MVP as a sophomore. At the tackle position, Kay helped clear the way for Bob Smith in 1946, Iowa's first 500-yard rusher since Ozzie Simmons in 1936. As a senior in 1948, Kay was an All-Big Ten selection and a Second Team All-American. In his final game, he blocked a punt and recovered it in the end zone for an Iowa touchdown in a win over Boston University. He led the Big Ten in minutes played as a senior, averaging more than 55 minutes a game and twice playing all sixty minutes.

Bill Schoof – Basketball (1954-56)

Bill Schoof played on consecutive Final Four teams as part of the "Fabulous Five"; as is the case with the other four, Schoof's number 33 is retired. A forward from Chicago Heights, Illinois, Schoof could also play the center position. He averaged 6.7 points per game as a sophomore, 6.2 as a junior, and 10.8 as a senior. One of his best games came in the 1956 NCAA Tournament against Temple when he scored 18 points and grabbed 18 rebounds. His 18 rebounds remain a school record for rebounds in an NCAA Tournament game. Schoof also lettered in baseball for three seasons.

Owen Gill – Football (1981-84)

Owen Gill attended Tilden High School in Brooklyn, New York, with Hawkeye teammates Devon Mitchell and Nate Creer. Gill was named First Team All-State in football and track at Tilden, participating as a triple jumper on the track team. He played running back for Coach Hayden Fry and ran for 683 yards as a sophomore in 1982, which was the ninth-best total in modern school history. Despite being hampered by injuries in 1983, Gill led the team with 798 rushing yards, which was the fifth-best total in modern school history. He led Iowa in rushing as a senior as well, despite spending some of the season at fullback to accommodate Ronnie Harmon. Gill left Iowa as the school's all-time leading rusher with 2,556 yards, and he is the only Hawkeye in school history to lead Iowa in rushing in three bowl games. He was Iowa's team captain in 1984 and played in 41 of his final 42 games with the Hawkeyes. Gill also ran track in 1982 and 1983, placing fifth in the triple jump at the 1983 Big Ten meet.

#34: JACK OF ALL TRADES

"That doggone Dittmer. Every time I play against him, he does something sensational. In baseball he hits a home run, and in football he goes for the winning touchdown."
- Lawrence Day, Northwestern guard

Outstanding prep athletes often excel at multiple sports at the high school level. It is not uncommon to see a star high school athlete lettering in three or even four sports in a season. But participating in multiple sports at the Big Ten level is another story, and most athletes drop other ambitions to concentrate on just one collegiate sport. It can be argued that the pinnacle of overall athletic excellence at the University of Iowa was reached by the handful of men that have earned nine varsity athletic letters. No Hawkeye has been able to do that since Jack Dittmer dominated Iowa athletics from 1946-1950.

John Douglas Dittmer was accustomed to juggling multiple sports before he ever arrived in Iowa City. He earned 12 letters at Elkader High School in northeast Iowa during the years of World War II. When it was time to go to college, Dittmer had no doubts. "I didn't really go shopping around for any other schools, and there were some others that talked to me, but I told them that I'd already made up my mind that I was going to go to the University of Iowa," Dittmer said.

The Hawkeyes were a natural choice for Dittmer. "I used to watch Iowa all the time when I was growing up," he recalled, "and that was one reason why I decided that I was going there. Everybody seemed like they got treated very well." Proximity to home was also a big factor. Dittmer stated, "My folks and some of these other people around here could come and see me play if they wanted to." Then he added with a laugh, "After I made the team, of course!"

Making the team at Iowa was not a problem for an athlete as talented as Jack Dittmer. With freshmen temporarily made eligible due to the end of the war, he quickly established himself as a star second baseman for Otto Vogel's baseball squad. In football, success came more slowly. Dittmer, who had played halfback at Elkader, was an end in football at Iowa, and the Hawkeyes seldom passed under a run-first offense. Dittmer led the team in receiving yards as a freshman in 1946 with just 82 yards on five catches all season. Furthermore, his playing time was inconsistent behind players like Emlen Tunnell and a pair of twin ends, Harold and Herb Shoener.

Those three men moved on after the 1947 season, however, and by the following year, it was Dittmer's time to shine. He and fellow end Bob McKenzie formed a lethal combination, and an expanded offense helped the 1948 Hawkeyes set a school record for passing yardage. Though he fell eight yards behind McKenzie for the team lead in receiving, Dittmer did lead the team in scoring. His best game that season came at Fenway Park against Boston University, when he finished with 151 yards receiving. It was just the second time in modern school history that a Hawkeye receiver had topped 150 yards, and it is still the 22nd-best receiving game in school history.

Despite his slender build, Dittmer was a tough player. He never weighed more than about 160 pounds, yet he avoided major injuries over his collegiate career. "I always ran scared, so I never got hurt too much, 'cause they didn't catch me!" Dittmer laughed.

He was also a prankster with a great sense of humor. In a victory over Ohio State in Columbus, Dittmer was knocked unconscious by Buckeye fullback Joe Whisler. When Dittmer came out of his daze, his first remark was, "I wonder if they let Whisler out of the hospital yet."

> **Jack Dittmer was named a Second Team All-Big Ten end as a senior. He finished behind Gopher end Bud Grant, who would later coach the Minnesota Vikings to four Super Bowls.**

Dittmer lit up the school and conference record books as a senior. He graduated with five modern school receiving records: career receptions, yards receiving in a season and career, and touchdown receptions in a season and career. His 333 conference receiving yards as a senior in 1949 set a modern Big Ten record. In his final football season, Jack Dittmer was an Honorable Mention All-American.

As great as he was on the football field, Dittmer was even better on the baseball diamond. He was a Second Team All-American in the summer of 1949, as he led the Hawkeyes to the Big Ten title. Although Coach Anderson had previously discouraged athletes from playing multiple sports, Dittmer said that neither Vogel nor Anderson had a problem with sharing Dittmer's talents. "If they did, they never said anything to me about it," Dittmer said.

With four letters in both baseball and football in the bag, Dittmer had one more goal in mind. Shortly after the 1949 football season, it was announced that he was attempting to earn a spot on Pops Harrison's basketball squad. This was actually a second attempt at college basketball for Dittmer.

"Basketball was my favorite sport of all of them, to tell you the truth. I went out for basketball as a freshman, and I flunked a course that first year. I decided I wasn't going to do that anymore. I had to go to summer school to make that course up, and so I just stuck with football and baseball," Dittmer recalled.

But with his football career finished and his academics in order, Jack Dittmer again took up basketball, which put nine varsity athletic letters within reach. Only five men in Hawkeye history to that point had accomplished the feat, and the list included such legendary names as Clyde Williams, Aubrey Devine, and Erwin Prasse. Nine athletic letters remains a significant mark for obvious reasons. Since a player can earn up to four letters in a single sport, winning nine varsity letters requires an athlete to letter in three different sports over his Hawkeye career.

Dittmer's chase for his ninth athletic letter captivated the Iowa campus.

He played basketball like a football player, diving for loose balls and making hustle plays. Dittmer was a fan favorite, since Hawkeye fans knew the rarity of what he was trying to accomplish. Every time Dittmer entered a basketball game, the Hawkeye fans gave him a rousing ovation.

> **Jack Dittmer became the sixth and most recent Hawkeye to earn nine letters by lettering in football, basketball, and baseball during his senior year of 1949-1950.**

After graduation, Dittmer had a solid Major League Baseball career, playing six seasons in the major leagues. He played for five years with the Milwaukee Braves before finishing his big league career with the Detroit Tigers. Dittmer then moved back to his hometown of Elkader, where he worked for and later managed his father's auto business, Dittmer Motor Company.

Since no Hawkeye in the last sixty years has been able to earn nine letters, it is natural to wonder if anyone could duplicate Dittmer's achievement today. For anyone looking to follow in his considerable footsteps, Jack Dittmer recommends discipline on and off the field and a dash of good fortune, especially where injuries are concerned. "I'm sure it could be done, but this guy would have to be an awful good student and have to take good care of himself. There's a lot of luck involved in it," he noted. "I always took care of myself and tried to stay out of trouble and all, so that always helps and made everything that much better."

What he modestly neglected to mention, of course, is that anyone trying to duplicate what Dittmer did as a Hawkeye would also need the exceptional ability to excel at three different sports at the highest level. "I sure haven't seen many guys be a three-sport man down there at all for some time now," Dittmer observed. "But that's not saying there couldn't be a bunch of them coming up right now too."

"You never know."

Accolades
• One of six Hawkeyes to earn nine athletic letters
• Team MVP (1949)
• Played six seasons of major league baseball
• Inducted into the University of Iowa Hall of Fame (1993)
• Inducted into the State of Iowa Hall of Fame (1988)

How He's Remembered

"One of the great pass receiving ends to play for the Old Gold."

Bert McGrane

"Dittmer does not have to win his basketball letter to be remembered by Hawkeye followers. He has done enough in football and baseball to be talked about for years."

The Cedar Rapids Gazette (Nov 9, 1949)

"Such competitive spark is one of the reasons Dittmer has become one of the great receivers of college football and one of the great second basemen of amateur baseball. He's always trying."

Pat Harmon, *The Cedar Rapids Gazette*

"I think I handled myself all right…I used to get racked up pretty good sometimes, but I was very fortunate. I never had anything broken or anything. A few bruises, but that was about all. You could say I took good care of myself my whole life."

Jack Dittmer

Jersey #34 Honorable Mention

Scott Thompson – Basketball (1974-76)

Scott Thompson was a four-sport athlete from Moline, Illinois, prior to joining the Hawkeye basketball team. He played as a reserve guard his sophomore year before starting in his junior and senior seasons. In Lute Olson's second season at Iowa, Thompson led the Hawkeyes with 19.5 points per game. His play earned him team MVP and Second Team All-Big Ten honors. Thompson was drafted by the NBA's Detroit Pistons before beginning a successful career in coaching. He coached under both Digger Phelps and Lute Olson before becoming a head coach at Rice, Wichita State, and Cornell.

Jonathan Hayes – Football (1981-84)

Jonathan Hayes was an All-State football and basketball player from South Fayette, Pennsylvania. At 6'5" and 245 pounds, he played linebacker early in his career before moving to tight end; he once played both in the same game. The move to tight end paid off, and he was a key player in a high-powered Hawkeye offense. He caught 53 passes for 672 yards and seven touchdowns during his career and was a member of four consecutive bowl teams. He also collected 15 tackles on defense. Hayes ended his career with two touchdowns in a rain-soaked Freedom Bowl victory over Texas. He was named First Team All-American following the 1984 season. After college, Hayes went on to play 12 years in the National Football League and then began a career in coaching.

"From my point of view, he was second only to Marv Cook as a tight end during Hayden Fry's tenure at Iowa. Hayes was a highly skilled player who could do it all at tight end."

Tom Kakert

#35: COLFAX JOE

"Joe Laws played quarterback as every coach wants it played. He not only did his share of ball carrying, blocking, etc., but he played with every brain cell running at top speed, every minute of the game."
- **Francis Powers,** *Chicago Daily News*

The stock market collapse of 1929, coupled with Iowa's conference suspension for a month in 1930, led to a Hawkeye football depression throughout the 1930s. There were very few bright spots for the Hawkeye program during this decade prior to Iowa's magical season in 1939. But one of those bright spots was Joe Laws and his 1933 Hawkeye teammates, the first team since the depression began that Hawkeye fans could discuss with their heads held high.

Laws' football career paralleled Nile Kinnick's in several ways. Joe Laws was a native Iowan from Colfax High School. He signed on at Iowa when the program was at rock bottom. Not only did Iowa win just one game in 1931, but the Hawks would only tally one touchdown – all season. The Hawkeyes defeated George Washington University, 7-0, and were shut out in every other contest. In Laws' sophomore and junior seasons in 1931 and 1932, the Hawkeyes won just two games. But as with Kinnick, this only served to set up a dramatic senior season.

> **"Colfax Joe"** was a versatile football player, alternating between quarterback and halfback and playing wherever Coach Ossie Solem needed him. Laws also played two seasons for the Hawkeye baseball team, leading the team in hitting in 1932.

In Iowa's first football contest of 1933, the Hawkeyes met Northwestern at Soldier Field in Chicago. Iowa had lost to the Wildcats in the last game of the previous season, 44-6. But the Hawkeyes shocked Northwestern in 1933, as Laws' 31-yard touchdown run with nine minutes to play gave Iowa its only points in a 7-0 victory. It was Iowa's first conference win in four years!

The Hawkeyes' next conference game was Homecoming against Wisconsin. In front of the largest crowd to ever attend a football game in the state of Iowa, Laws led the Hawks to a decisive 26-7 triumph. Laws rushed for a touchdown in the first quarter, intercepted a pass and returned a punt for a touchdown in the third quarter, and added another interception in the final period. Wisconsin sportswriter Roundy Coughlin called Laws the best back he had seen in three years. Wisconsin's Hall of Fame coach, Clarence "Doc" Spears, called Laws one of the greatest backs he had ever seen.

After close road losses to Big Ten co-champions Minnesota and Michigan, the Hawkeyes hit the road again for their conference finale against Purdue. The Boilermakers were shooting for their third straight Big Ten title and sported a 20-game unbeaten streak.

Following a scoreless first half, Laws got Iowa on the board with a 27-yard touchdown run. Then in the fourth quarter, he sealed the game with a tremendous 60-yard punt return for a touchdown. Iowa captain Tom Moore said later, "It was so good that I just stood there open-mouthed and watched it." Iowa handed Purdue just its second home loss in eight years, as the Hawkeyes claimed a 14-6 win.

> After the game, Iowa City mayor Harry Breene told Joe Laws that he could have any city job but his own. Laws replied that he had always wanted to be a fireman, so he was named the town's honorary fire chief.

The victory over Purdue gave Iowa a winning record in the Big Ten; it was one of just two winning league records that Iowa would post in the 14 seasons between 1924 and 1939. Joe Laws led the Big Ten Conference in scoring in conference games, just two years after the Hawkeyes had scored one touchdown as a team for an entire season. Laws was named a Second Team All-American in 1933, capping the year by winning the Chicago Tribune Silver Football as the Big Ten's MVP.

Joe Laws had a distinguished career in professional football after graduating from Iowa. Laws put on an impressive performance in the 1934 College All-Star Game, helping the All-Stars fight the NFL champion Chicago Bears to a scoreless draw. He then signed a contract with Coach Curly Lambeau and played all of his 12 seasons in the NFL with the Green Bay Packers.

Laws participated in four NFL title games, winning three. He caught a 32-yard touchdown pass in the Packers' 1939 NFL championship game victory over the New York Giants. As a result, the NFL champion Packers played in the 1940 College All-Star Game, where Laws squared off against an All-Star team headed by Kinnick. The greatest game of Laws' pro career came in the 1944 NFL championship game. He led the Packers in rushing in Green Bay's victory over the Giants. Laws also intercepted three passes in the 1944 title game; his three interceptions are still a record in an NFL championship game.

By then, the Packer faithful had nicknamed him "Tiger Joe." Years earlier, "Colfax Joe" had displayed that same tenacity when he rose to prominence as the Big Ten's best player. For Hawkeye fans, Laws' lasting legacy was an assurance, even in the midst of a depression, that better days were on the horizon and that Hawkeye football would, one day, rise again.

Accolades
• Big Ten MVP (1933)
• Second Team All-American (1933)
• Played 12 seasons in the NFL; won three NFL championships with the Green Bay Packers
• Inducted into the State of Iowa Hall of Fame (1961)
• Inducted into the Green Bay Packers Hall of Fame (1972)

How He's Remembered

"[Few] men who wore the Gold and Black won more coveted recognition than Colfax Joe, and none went further, or higher, in professional football. In that field, no Iowan surpassed him."

Bert McGrane

"I still can see Joe Laws, that mighty atom of dynamite from Iowa, whip around and strike through a gap."

Noble Kizer, former Purdue coach

"Joe Laws [stood] in the safety position, yelling his lungs out and calling everybody on the Iowa team something. Joe was rough, tough, and cocky, but no man ever had a bigger heart. He played real football."

Dick Crayne

"We feel that in the superior attributes demonstrated by Mr. Laws both on and off the football field that he is eminently qualified through courage, prowess, integrity, and intellectual attainments to reflect the same high degree of excellence to any appointment within the gift of his state, his university, or this community, all of whom he has so signally honored, and by the same token delight to honor him."

Harry Breene, Iowa City mayor

Jersey #35 Honorable Mention

Kevin Gamble – Basketball (1986-87)

Kevin Gamble was an All-State basketball player for Lanphier High School in Springfield, Illinois, where he and future Hawkeye Ed Horton led their team to the state championship. Gamble was a First Team All-American at Lincoln Community College before transferring to Iowa for his final two seasons. He played very sparingly under Coach George Raveling as a junior in 1986, but he became a starter in his senior season under Dr. Tom Davis. Gamble scored in double figures 20 times in 1987 and was named team MVP. He hit a game-winning three-point basket with three seconds remaining in overtime to defeat Oklahoma in the Sweet Sixteen and secure a spot for Iowa in the Elite Eight. Gamble played ten seasons in the NBA, including six with the Boston Celtics.

Brad Quast – Football (1986-89)

Brad Quast, a football and scholastic high school All-American, was heavily recruited and chose the Hawkeyes over Michigan. After he committed to Iowa, Wolverine coach Bo Schembechler personally called him and stated, "Quast, you made a big mistake." Known as a great hitter, Quast was one of the few linebackers in Iowa history to start all four years. He was named the top freshman linebacker in the nation by *The Sporting News* in 1986, and he was an All-Big Ten selection in 1988 and 1989. His 435 career tackles ranks fourth in school history, and his 11 career interceptions ranks sixth. "The four years went too quick…it went too fast," Quast said. "I couldn't imagine going to another university and having the same amount of fun and experiences I did at Iowa. I got a top-notch education, played great football, and had a great time."

"Quast was very strong and quick at a young age. It's rare that someone can come in as a freshman and play at a high level in a physical position like linebacker. Brad could do that."

Mike Flagg, former Iowa teammate

#36: THE EYE OF THE SWARM

"Larry Station was one of the smartest football players and one of the most intense, with maturity way, way beyond his age."

- Dan McCarney

Middle linebackers often find themselves in the middle of the action. On 492 separate occasions from 1982-1985, Larry Station made the stop at the opposition's point of attack. He was a key member of Iowa's 1986 Rose Bowl team and one of the greatest defensive players in school history.

Station attended high school in Omaha, Nebraska, where he starred in football, track, and tennis. Many people, including Station himself, attribute his quick reaction time and footwork at linebacker to his training as a prep tennis player. "To me, they're very similar movements," Station told *The Des Moines Register.* "You have to keep your shoulders squared to the line of scrimmage or to the net. When you get to the point of attack, whether it's hitting the ball or making the tackle, you have to be under control."

Larry Station chose the Hawkeyes over Nebraska. "The number one reason for me going to Iowa was the fact that the fans were so loyal," Station said. "Iowa had not had a winning season in 20 years until the year before I came, but I heard at least that the fans would still come out and fill up the stadium and support the team. I was able to go to Iowa's last home game in 1981 when they played Michigan State, and the way it turned out, because Ohio State beat Michigan and Iowa won their game, they were going to the Rose Bowl for the first time in 20 years. And being in the crowd for that game and feeling the electricity in the stands – I was ready to sign up after that game."

Station played extensively as a freshman. His first start came against Northwestern in place of an injured linebacker. He made significant contributions in the Big Ten schedule with consecutive games of 15, 13, and ten tackles against Indiana, Michigan, and Minnesota respectively. Despite being injured much of the year himself, he earned Second Team All-Big Ten honors and led the team in tackles.

> **Larry Station had 23 games with ten or more tackles.**

Off-season surgery followed his freshman year, but he returned healthy for his sophomore season. Station recorded 138 tackles, the fourth-highest season total in school history. He had 19 tackles at Penn State and 20 against Purdue, as he led Iowa to a 9-3 record and their third consecutive bowl game. As a sophomore, Station earned All-Big Ten and Second Team All-American honors.

Iowa fans saw more of the same during Station's junior season. He set a career-high for tackles in a game with 21 at Minnesota. Station finished the 1984 season with 137 tackles, the sixth-highest season total in school history. He was named All-Big Ten for the second time and was a consensus First Team All-American. A holiday trouncing of Texas in the Freedom Bowl set up a potentially special senior season for Station and other classmates such as Chuck Long and Ronnie Harmon. The question was whether this talented class would all return to Iowa City for their senior year.

For Station, there wasn't much of a question. He was looking beyond his prospects in the NFL. "You never know what will happen in the way of an injury which could wipe out the future of a prospective pro player," Station said in 1984. "It's not a sound financial way to look into the future. You just can't rely on a pro team to draft you. I'm looking forward to a career in computer programming or a field of that nature."

In the end, the talented junior class of 1984 returned nearly intact for their senior season. The 1985 season was a memorable one. Iowa spent five consecutive weeks atop the national rankings for the first time ever. The season was headlined by No. 1 Iowa's showdown with No. 2 Michigan. Station made one of the most memorable plays in that game, and it came in the fourth quarter with Michigan leading, 10-9. Faced with a third and four, Michigan handed the ball to tailback Jamie Morris. Before he could get within two yards of the line of scrimmage, however, Station stopped him dead in his tracks. This returned the ball to Iowa for a game-winning drive that ended with Rob Houghtlin's memorable kick.

Former Iowa assistant Dan McCarney stated, "There was no blitz called. Everybody said it was a great call. It wasn't any blitz; it was just a base defense. He ran through and made the play, Larry Station being Larry Station, but it was one of the great plays in the history of Iowa football. It allowed the offense a chance to get the ball back and keep [Michigan] off the board late in the game."

"The thing I remember after that [third down] play is the noise," recalled Station. "It was just deafening. You could feel the electricity in the whole stadium. It was kind of scary, almost, to feel all that energy all around. It was definitely the highlight of my career."

> Larry Station is the only Hawkeye to lead Iowa in tackles four straight seasons.

The Hawkeyes went on to finish 7-1 in the Big Ten, defeating Minnesota for the outright Big Ten title. "After we defeated Minnesota at the end, we were champions, and just to be able to claim that title outright and get the championship ring – it was something I'd seen with the guys who'd won it the year before I got there, but I had yet to earn one," Station said. "Winning that championship was definitely my proudest moment."

Former Iowa broadcaster Ron Gonder fondly recalled Station's career as Iowa's 5'11", 225-pound defensive leader. "Larry was a guy who was rather short for a college linebacker, under six feet; but he was the quickest, most agile, most determined linebacker of perhaps any I saw of all my time in doing Iowa football play-by-play," Gonder said. "He was, of course, also a very, very intelligent player, which helped him to be a good linebacker. He was an all-academic player in addition to being an All-American player on the field…a brilliant mind and an outstanding athletic ability for someone who is a bit undersized."

Station was named a unanimous First Team All-American and was an All-Big Ten pick for the third straight time. He helped lead the Hawkeyes to the 1986 Rose Bowl, but what should have been the crowning moment of Station's football career turned out to be the worst. He suffered a serious back injury against UCLA in his final game as a Hawkeye, and the Bruins handed the

Hawkeyes an unexpected defeat. Station was only able to play one season in the NFL as a result of that injury.

"Probably of all of Hayden's players that you would have thought would have been a sure-fire, All-Pro NFL football player, you'd have guessed Larry Station," longtime Iowa announcer Frosty Mitchell stated. "But then came the injury, and that ended that."

Though a professional football career would have been rewarding to him, Station was prepared for exactly the scenario that unfolded. In addition to being an All-American athlete, he was also Academic All-American twice, so he had many options. Once his football career ended, he enrolled at Washington University in St. Louis and obtained a master's degree in business administration.

Larry Station was an important part of making the Hawkeye program what it is today. "I was part of building a good, solid football program," he said. "I think that was one of the best things about my experiences at Iowa because it's easy for someone to fit into something that is already successful, but to help create something to have a tradition of excellence is very gratifying."

Larry Station excelled in every aspect of being a student-athlete. He was Academic All-American not once but twice. On the field, he was a consensus First Team All-American not once but twice. He was Iowa's leading tackler all four years of his career. He received the defensive signals and was always in the middle of the action. Larry Station was almost an extension of the coaching staff on the field of play. He was truly Hayden Fry's "Eye of the Swarm."

Accolades
- Consensus First Team All-American (1984, 85)
- All-Big Ten (1983, 84, 85)
- Holds school record for career tackles
- Selected to the all-time University of Iowa football team (1989)
- Inducted into the College Football Hall of Fame (2009)

No. 36 LARRY STATION						
Year	Solo	Asst	Total	T/Loss	Int-Yds	Fum Rec
1982	51	37	88	4/-21	1/1	1
1983	81	57	138	8/-35	1/20	0
1984	85	52	137	8/-49	0	3
1985	91	38	129	15/-59	1/25	0
Totals	308	184	492	35/164	3/46	4

How He's Remembered

"Larry...would stand behind Barry Alvarez and me when we'd go inside drills, segment drills. He would step through every read. In other words, when he was in there, he was going. When the twos ran or threes ran and the ones were out, he'd stand behind us and instead of watching...he would step through every read. It was almost like there was never a play off in practice. He was that in tune to his reads. You talk about a marvelous young man and outstanding football player but even a better young man. Tenacity, toughness, smarts – [he was] amazing."

Dan McCarney

"Larry's a perfectionist. He's been able to do everything we ask of him on the football field. He's just a student of the game and has refined all his talents. He's a total player. He studies NFL films of other linebackers because he wants to learn more. Off the field, he is preparing himself for life past college. Larry Station is a success at everything he puts his mind to."

Barry Alvarez (1985)

"I heard Station talk when he was inducted into Iowa's Hall of Fame, and he talked about the fact that since others sort of downgraded him because of his size, it inspired him; and I think he played like that."

Ron Gonder

"Larry Station was just an absolutely vicious hitter. He was a fine person and absolutely Hayden Fry's best defensive recruit."

Frosty Mitchell

"I really try to lead by example. I try to work hard at practice in everything I do. When people see me giving that kind of effort and know that I've gained All-American honors, it makes them work all the harder. It becomes contagious."

Larry Station

Jersey #36 Honorable Mention

Peter Westra – Football (1927-29)

Peter Westra was a three-sport star at Sheldon High School in northwest Iowa before heading to Iowa City. He played two seasons at the guard position for the Hawkeye football squad, winning accolades for his play as a junior in 1928. Westra's All-Big Ten play propelled the Hawks to a 6-0 start, and he was named a First Team All-American after the season. As a senior, he shifted back to the tackle position, a position at which he was an Honorable Mention All-American. Westra was a cornerstone of the heaviest line in the Big Ten during his three seasons at Iowa, and the Hawkeyes had a 10-4-2 record in his final two seasons. After his Hawkeye career, Westra started in the Dixie Classic in Dallas, Texas, where the Midwest All-Stars defeated the Southwest Conference All-Stars, 25-12.

#37: CAPTAIN IRONMAN

"Prasse was primarily a finesse guy...he walked with the bounce in his stride that bespoke of speed and quickness, agility and endurance. He had basketball hands that made pass catching as natural as breathing."

- Al Couppee

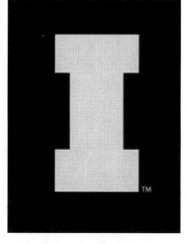

The captain of the 1939 Ironmen was more than just a great football player. He was a three-sport athlete at Iowa, excelling in baseball and basketball, and he was a natural leader who was admired by teammates for his toughness and modesty. While he was a great athlete, the selflessness and heroism he exhibited during World War II is as fondly remembered as anything he accomplished on the playing field.

Most of that description also fits Nile Kinnick, of course. But it more accurately describes Kinnick's teammate, Erwin Prasse. Prasse was one of the greatest athletes that ever graced the Iowa campus, and his leadership was instrumental in the success of the beloved Ironmen.

Erwin T. Prasse was the son of a German baker, which led to Prasse being nicknamed "Biscuits." He graduated from Schurz High School in Chicago and came to Iowa with a group of athletes recruited by Hawkeye coach Ossie Solem. When Prasse first arrived at football practice at Iowa, he saw the large farm boys and initially wondered aloud if he would last.

> Erwin Prasse's teammate, Hank Luebcke, pointed to a 5'8", 170-pound freshman and said, "If he can make it, you can." Prasse and that 170-pound freshman, Nile Kinnick, would lead the Hawkeye football team for the next three years.

The Hawkeyes struggled in 1937 and 1938, compiling a 2-13-1 record over two seasons. While Kinnick was hampered in 1938 with an ankle injury, Prasse earned All-Conference honors. When it came time to select the captain for the 1939 Hawkeye football team, the future Ironmen voted for Prasse, not Kinnick. But their teammate, George "Red" Frye, stated, "I don't think that [Kinnick's injury] had anything to do with the voting."

Instead, Frye recalled Prasse and Kinnick both as multi-sport athletes that were "well-liked and admired" by their teammates. But while Kinnick was somewhat reserved and introspective, "Prasse was a pool hall guy," Frye noted. Quarterback Al Couppee added, "Prasse was an outgoing, breezy guy with a great sense of humor."

"Kinnick had counted on being captain, and I thought he certainly would be. But he had a bad ankle in 1938, and I was named [captain]," Prasse noted. With typical modesty, he added, "Looking back now, what the hell difference did it make that I was the captain in 1939? The captain decides what you're going to do when the officials flip the coin, and that's it."

Prasse caught three touchdown passes from Kinnick in leading Iowa to a 32-29 victory over Indiana in 1939. Prasse's third and final scoring catch came on fourth down with only minutes remaining in the game. His three touchdown receptions would remain an Iowa (Kinnick)

Stadium record until 2005, when Ed Hinkel caught four touchdowns in a game against Minnesota.

In Prasse's final home game, Iowa trailed Minnesota after three quarters, 9-0. Kinnick hit "Biscuits" with a 48-yard touchdown pass to start the Hawkeye rally and cut the Gopher lead to 9-7. Another Kinnick touchdown would eventually hand Iowa a 13-9 victory, and the Hawks claimed the Floyd of Rosedale trophy for the first time in school history. Prasse played all sixty minutes in each of the last five games of the 1939 season. He was named a Second Team All-American in 1939 and was an All-Big Ten selection for the second straight year.

> **Erwin Prasse won nine athletic letters at Iowa, starring in football, basketball, and baseball. In 1938, he was named the MVP of Iowa's baseball and football teams, and he helped lead the Hawkeye baseball team to two Big Ten titles in 1938 and 1939.**

After graduation, Prasse played three seasons for the Oshkosh All-Stars of the National Basketball League, a forerunner to today's NBA. In 1940-41, Prasse played all 24 games for Oshkosh and started in all five playoff games, as the All-Stars swept to the NBL championship. His basketball career was cut short by St. Louis Cardinals manager Branch Rickey, who signed Prasse to an exclusive minor league baseball contract.

When World War II broke out, Prasse enlisted in the Army. "As soon as they saw his qualifications, they put him in officer training school...He was always willing to do what he had to do," his wife Norma remarked. In Europe, Prasse led a platoon to study the advisability of a major crossing of the Roer River in Germany. Norma Prasse said, "He took a boat over one night and heard German...He realized he couldn't speak it as well as he thought he could, but he understood, 'What was that?', so he got out of there." But after Prasse had crossed back over the river, the Germans spotted and fired at his platoon.

Prasse was hit by shrapnel in his right arm. His arm had been protecting his chest, which saved his life. The infantry was able to use the intelligence gathered by his platoon to make their crossing. Erwin Prasse was awarded the Purple Heart for his injuries and was later discharged with a rank (naturally) of Captain. His arm injury ended his professional athletic career, however, and he retired to family life with his wife and ten children in Naperville, Illinois.

Athletic ability, leadership, patriotism, courage...Nile Kinnick has been rightly admired for possessing these and many other fine qualities. But it should not be overlooked that Erwin Prasse and many of his Ironmen teammates possessed these qualities as well. As Kinnick stated in his Heisman Trophy speech, "A finer bunch of boys and a more courageous bunch of boys never graced the gridirons of the Midwest than that Iowa team of 1939."

It would be difficult to find a finer or more courageous Hawkeye than their captain, Erwin Prasse.

#37 – Erwin Prasse

Accolades
- Team captain (1939)
- Second Team All-American (1939)
- One of only six men to earn nine letters at the University of Iowa
- Played both basketball and baseball professionally
- Inducted into the University of Iowa Hall of Fame (1989)

How He's Remembered

"A sportswriter asked me if Prasse was overshadowed by Kinnick. 'Of course,' I answered, 'and so was everyone else on the team.' But none of them seemed to care...Prasse was an outstanding football player in his own right."

George Wine

"His friends would ask, 'How do you keep so thin?' He would say, 'I just keep moving.'"

Norma Prasse

"Being placed on honor teams is nothing new to big, blonde Prasse, the University of Iowa's three-sport man, who takes these honors in stride. Standing above the six foot mark and packing 185 pounds, Prasse has developed into an outstanding athlete the hard way, by digging ditches for a gas company and working at manual labor every summer...Here at Iowa, Erwin has set nine letters as his goal, and if nothing less than an earthquake hits him, he will reach that goal."

Loren Schultz, *Iowa City Press-Citizen*

"Prasse was a good guy, enjoyed life, good sense of humor, and as the elected captain of the 1939 Iowa football team, he carried this accolade and responsibility with easy humility and sincerity, but he was first of all tough. Like all athletes, Biscuits had the cocky belief in himself that enabled him to make difficult things look easy."

Al Couppee

Jersey #37 Honorable Mention

Matt Hughes – Football (1995-98)
Matt Hughes ran track and played defensive back and running back at Eastland High School in Texas. He came to Iowa in 1994 to play for a fellow Texan, Coach Hayden Fry. Hughes played sparingly on special teams as a college freshman, but he made an immediate impact as a sophomore. He had double digit tackles in each of his first nine games as a starter in 1996, and he had six more games of double digit tackles as a junior. Hughes led the Hawkeyes in tackles both seasons. He had eight tackles in the 1996 Alamo Bowl and twelve tackles in the Sun Bowl the following year; he led Iowa in tackles in both games. Hughes was Iowa's team captain in 1998, but he was slowed in the first half of the season by injury before coming on strong late in the year, recording 19 tackles in his final home game against Ohio State. Matt Hughes ranks eighth in school history with 354 career tackles.

#38: RUDY

"Stories like Bromert's are wonderful. They're a big reason I stayed in coaching all those years."
- Hayden Fry

A football player can go from hero to pariah in seconds. Kickers, in particular, are only as beloved as their last kick. Public sentiment for a team's placekicker swings from adulation to anger and back again more quickly than for almost any other player on the team. From 1995-1998, Zach Bromert experienced those pronounced highs and lows in his career as perhaps no other kicker in Iowa history had before.

Bromert's father was originally from Carroll, Iowa, but he was stationed in Florida in the Navy. Zach grew up in the Florida Panhandle and attended Pensacola Catholic High School. While he drew interest from major college programs, his high school team failed to make the playoffs and gave him few chances to kick and impress college coaches. Bromert did not draw a Division I scholarship offer, and he considered playing college soccer at Loras College instead. But his family, full of Hawkeye fans, encouraged him to walk on at Iowa.

Bromert did not suit up when Iowa opened the 1995 season against Northern Iowa. As a true freshman walk-on, he watched on television as the Hawkeyes took down Iowa State in Ames. But the stage was being set for Bromert's emergence. Brion Hurley missed the extra point following Iowa's last touchdown against UNI. In the Iowa State game, Hurley missed another extra point and a 29-yard field goal. Hurley was benched against the Cyclones in favor of backup kicker Todd Romano, who proceeded to miss two extra point tries himself. "The worst thing about the football game was the cotton-picking kicking game," Coach Hayden Fry said afterwards. "I guarantee that will be corrected, even if I have to kick it myself."

On Thursday night before Iowa's next game against New Mexico State, the coaches told the team that Bromert would start over Hurley and Romano on Saturday. "They told me, 'Hey, tell your aunt and uncle, but don't tell anybody else. We want to keep this on the down low and not try to cause any stir,'" Bromert recalled. "So I didn't really tell anybody except the guys on the team."

Zach Bromert, at 18 years old, had not yet dressed for a single game or even appeared on the roster. Three minutes into the game against NMSU, Sedrick Shaw ran for a touchdown, and Bromert, all of 5'7" and 150 pounds, trotted onto the field. "For that first kick, I was the most nervous I've ever been in my life," Bromert recalled. But his extra point was perfect, and his day had only begun.

> After his third extra point against New Mexico State, fans in the student section started bowing toward Bromert. He ended the game by converting all eight extra point tries and a 29-yard field goal.

In the fourth quarter, fans gave Bromert a standing ovation. While the coaches avoided causing a stir before the game by not telling the media about Bromert, Zach's performance against New Mexico State set off a media frenzy, as reporters scrambled to tell the story of the unknown kicker. Within hours, he had gone from complete anonymity to campus sensation. His small stature inspired fans. Comparisons of Bromert to Rudy Ruettiger, whose movie came out just two years earlier, were inevitable. "I got a lot of practice in front of a lot of people, so it was a great way to break in when there wasn't a ton of pressure," Bromert said. "It wasn't a Big Ten game yet, and I got a lot of reps in. It worked out great."

Fry announced that Bromert would take over the extra point and short field goal duties for the rest of the season, while Hurley would handle the longer kicks. Zach Bromert's role corrected a glaring weakness in the Hawkeye squad. He was extremely accurate, connecting on the first 22 extra points of his career before a high snap led to his only miss of the year. As a team, the Hawks accepted an invitation to the 1995 Sun Bowl, where Bromert and Hurley together set a modern school and Sun Bowl record by converting all five field goals in a 38-18 win.

Bromert was granted a scholarship for his sophomore season, and the Hawkeyes had an even better year in 1996. Bromert's three extra points were critical in Iowa's memorable victory at Penn State that season. "It was dumping rain," he recalled. "I remember Tim Dwight taking a punt back for a touchdown, and we kicked the extra point and won, 21-20. That was a major win. I think it gave us a lot of confidence that year."

Bromert was a key contributor to the 1996 Hawkeyes, who earned a trip to the Alamo Bowl. He kicked two field goals in Iowa's 27-0 victory over Texas Tech to end that season. Consecutive bowl victories would send expectations for the 1997 Hawkeye squad through the roof, as many fans expected a Rose Bowl contender in Bromert's junior year.

> **Zach Bromert set the school record with nine converted extra points in a 66-0 win over Northern Iowa in 1997, and he matched that feat two weeks later in a 63-20 victory against Iowa State.**

After a 4-0 start to the year, the Hawks lost consecutive games in Columbus and Ann Arbor to drop out of Big Ten title contention. Still, halfway through his junior season, Bromert had converted 20 out of 24 career field goals and 102 of 106 attempted extra points. He had been Mr. Automatic for the first two and a half years of his career. But then Zach Bromert lost his range and had the worst month of his kicking life.

Against Indiana, Bromert missed a 47-yard field goal attempt and slipped on a second field goal try, though it drew little attention as Iowa pounded the Hoosiers, 62-0. He had a field goal attempt blocked by Rosevelt Colvin and missed a second field goal in windy conditions the next week against Purdue, but the Hawkeyes easily upset the ranked Boilermakers.

Iowa's next game was in Madison, and Iowa had not lost to Wisconsin in twenty years. Yet for the second straight week and the third time in five weeks, Bromert's first field goal attempt was blocked. The Hawkeyes trailed the Badgers, 13-7, in the fourth quarter. Though Bromert hit a 41-yard field goal with eight minutes left to cut the deficit to three, he missed a field goal attempt from 43 yards away with less than four minutes to play, and Iowa lost, 13-10.

Snow and swirling winds confronted the Hawks the following week against Northwestern. Bromert missed two field goals in the near-blizzard conditions, and it only exacerbated the situation when backup kicker Chad Johnson also missed two field goals as Iowa fell, 15-14. Tavian Banks vented, "We've got about twenty kickers around here. You'd think they could find one who could make a field goal."

Bromert quickly got his kicking groove back, but the kicker took the brunt of the blame for the two losses and the overall disappointment of the season. For some fans, those four weeks, those eight misses, and those two losses are chiefly how they remember Bromert's career. Unfortunately, that's the fate of a kicker. You're only as beloved as your last kick.

"I've taken a lot of those lessons from those couple of weeks for the rest of my life," Bromert admitted. "You learn a lot about your teammates, you learn a lot about people around you, but most importantly, you learn a lot about yourself."

Zach Bromert led the Hawkeyes in scoring his senior season. He missed five extra point tries in 145 career attempts, which was only one more than the team had missed in the two games before he earned the starting job. He also converted 26 of 39 career field goals, a mark that looks much better outside of his one for nine spell in November 1997. "If you look at the two and half years going into those couple bad weeks and then the rest of my senior year, I didn't really miss that much at all," Bromert said. "So to go through those couple weeks, I think they were even that much harder to deal with, because I hadn't really had to deal with that much adversity. But when you go through it, you come out the other end a better person and a lot stronger."

Bromert graduated with a business degree and became a product line manager for Nike, working to develop better running shoes. He has no regrets about his time in Iowa City. "I'm extremely grateful to Coach Fry and his staff. They paid for my education. That's one thing that no matter what happens, I've always got my education. That's a big reason why I am where I'm at in my life today, so I'm extremely grateful," Bromert said.

In the roller coaster life of a kicker, Zach Bromert is back on top.

Accolades
• Ranks fifth in school history in career scoring
• Led team in scoring (1998)
• Started for three Iowa bowl teams
• Holds school record for extra points made in a game

How He's Remembered

"Bromert's emergence became a huge story. Add to it the fact that the guy is not on scholarship, is no taller than 5'8", and was not even listed in Saturday's game program. It all adds up to Bromert becoming an overnight success story."
Craig Sesker, *Burlington Hawk Eye*

"He wants to earn a scholarship. He wants to help the Hawkeyes win games. Bromert, plucked from obscurity Saturday...became an instant celebrity, saluted by fans and besieged by media hungry for information about the freshman walk-on from Pensacola."
Jim Ecker, *The Cedar Rapids Gazette*

"I think his last name begins with a 'B'. Now I just call him Automatic."

Tim Dwight

"I had a lot of good times at Iowa. Definitely had some rough patches, but, no doubt, I'm totally grateful for the program and the University and the fans for the opportunity they gave me. There are a lot of things I never would have experienced in my life if I wasn't given that chance. I look back on it as a major growing point in my life, and it made a big difference in who I am today."

Zach Bromert

#39: OVERLOOKED CONTRIBUTIONS

"Kenny looked less like an all-around athlete than most folks you'll ever meet...those appearances were extremely deceiving...the guy was stubborn as a bulldog and conscientious as a fox in a chicken coop."

- Al Couppee

A sculpture inside Kinnick Stadium depicts Iowa's 1939 score vs. Notre Dame.

Imagine making one of the biggest and most important plays in the history of Iowa football. Imagine recovering a critical fumble that led to one of the greatest, most memorable victories the University of Iowa has ever had. Now imagine that, several decades later, few fans even remember your name. In fact, imagine if the credit for your key fumble recovery is almost universally given to your teammates instead. Such is the story of Ken Pettit.

Ken Pettit was originally from Council Bluffs, Iowa. He played there one season before moving with his family to Logan, Iowa, where he would finish his high school career. Ken Pettit was an All-State player in football and basketball, and he played several positions for his high school football team.

Pettit was highly recruited by colleges across the Midwest. He hopped on a train for Chicago and planned to take a recruiting visit to Northwestern. But along the way, he stopped for a visit in Iowa City, and he never left. Pettit signed on with the Hawkeyes in 1937.

> **Ken Pettit's older brother, Roger, soon joined him on the Iowa football squad. Roger and Ken were teammates on the 1939 Ironmen.**

It's appropriate that the athlete featured at No. 39 made his mark as a member of the 1939 Ironmen. The previous season, Ken Pettit had lettered at the end position. But he played sparingly as a reserve end in 1939 behind Erwin Prasse and Dick Evans until injuries mounted on the line. Out of necessity, Coach Eddie Anderson shifted Pettit to the guard position. "I was happy to be switched to guard, because I thought I'd play more," Pettit confessed. His hunch was correct, and he was immediately called into action.

His first start in 1939 came against Purdue, and it resulted in an infamous mistake. The game with the Boilermakers was a defensive struggle, but Iowa had a rare scoring chance in the second half. Pettit committed a false start that wiped out a Kinnick touchdown. "Here's a guy who was playing his first football game at guard, played 60 minutes, played like a wounded grizzly, and about all he remembered was that goofy offside jump," quarterback Al Couppee remarked. Though Iowa defeated Purdue, 4-0, for the rest of his life, any time Pettit reunited with one of the Ironmen, he would apologize for his mistake.

Pettit would seemingly make up for his error the following week with one of the most overlooked plays in Hawkeye history. The Hawks were locked in a scoreless battle with Notre Dame late in the first half when a Kinnick pass was intercepted by Notre Dame's Steve Sitko near the Irish goal line. Bruno Andruska crashed into Sitko, popping the ball free. Dick Evans, Buzz Dean, and Ken Pettit chased the ball around, with Pettit falling on the ball inside the Notre Dame five-yard line. "Pettit is the guy who recovered the Notre Dame fumble on the Irish three-yard line from where we scored the only touchdown," Couppee noted.

Couppee then described Kinnick's legendary touchdown run. "Kinnick…cut back behind my block. Ken Pettit spotted a lineman slip through. Although Ken was supposed to pull from his left guard and lead Kinnick through the hole, blocking the linebacker, Pettit hit the Notre Dame guy who had slipped through and saved the play. Kinnick dropped his right shoulder, bounced off the linebacker and staggered into the end zone."

Afterwards, the *Associated Press* game recap would credit the fumble recovery to "Evans or Dean." That account would be duplicated a thousand times over as the story of the game spread. Just like that, Pettit's contribution to the stunning victory was glossed over and forgotten.

In Iowa's next game against Minnesota, Pettit played all sixty minutes for the third straight game, despite the fact that he badly injured his wrist. He did not allow the medical staff to x-ray his wrist after the game. Pettit feared that the wrist might be broken and that confirmation of a broken wrist would force him out of the season finale against Northwestern. Pettit somehow managed to play through the pain, and he put on a gutsy, 60-minute performance against the Wildcats to end the season.

As a senior in 1940, Pettit moved back to his natural end position. He once again established himself as Notre Dame's primary foil. The Hawkeyes traveled to South Bend, and the Irish were set on revenge for the previous season's upset loss. The Irish were once again undefeated, and with Kinnick gone, Notre Dame was prepared for vindication.

However, late in the fourth quarter, Iowa and Notre Dame were again stuck in a scoreless draw. And again, it was Pettit who was in the right place at the right time. He recovered a Notre Dame fumble at the Irish 24-yard line, and his recovery set up the one-yard touchdown by Bill Green that gave Iowa a 7-0 victory.

Iowa's 1940 win was dubbed "the Miracle Game at Notre Dame." For the second straight year, a Ken Pettit fumble recovery led to a touchdown that toppled the undefeated Irish.

After graduation, Pettit joined Nile Kinnick in the Naval Air Corps and traveled with Kinnick throughout most of Nile's flight training. Kinnick and Pettit became close friends; they attended social functions together, caught movies together, and even double-dated. Pettit was the only Ironman to meet Nile Kinnick's father; they met during Nile and Pettit's naval service.

Both Nile and Ken petitioned to join the Marines' air unit. The Navy released Pettit but held on to the former Heisman winner. "The Navy wouldn't release Nile, as they knew he was a definite asset," Pettit recalled. "This disappointed him. I have often wondered what his future would have been." As for Pettit, he flew several missions for the Marines during World War II, piloting top military officers around the South Pacific.

Pettit became a military flight instructor near the end of the war, and he nearly died when one of his students crashed his instructional plane. "The plane crashed and one of the propellers chewed into the fuselage and caught my right shoulder," Pettit said. "I was in the hospital for a full year." Pettit was eventually discharged from the service with the rank of Marine Captain.

Ken Pettit has never received the credit he deserves for his role in Hawkeye football history. Pettit was always quicker to remind teammates of his shortcomings than his successes, such as his fumble recoveries and 60-minute games played out of position. Still, overlooked contributions from men like Ken Pettit are what make teams like the 1939 Ironmen and the U.S. Marine Corps the legends that they are. And that's not hard to imagine at all.

Accolades
• Started for Iowa's 1939 Ironmen team
• Played 240 consecutive minutes
• Recovered key fumbles in upset victories over Notre Dame (1939, 40)
• Selected to the College All-Star Game (1941)

How He's Remembered

"Ken Pettit, doing a guard job that was tops, didn't get enough credit by far. It was Pettit who snared the ball on the four-yard line, rather than Evans or Buzz Dean, when Iowa grabbed its winning chance [against Notre Dame in 1939]. It was also Pettit who cleared the way with a riding block as Kinnick swung through for the touchdown."

Al Mitchell, *Mason City Globe-Gazette*

"It was fun to watch Pettit play poker; Ken concentrated, was intense, typical Pettit, angry with himself when he guessed wrong. He was just like that on the football field."

Al Couppee

"Guards can play hard and well and not have a monumental moment outsiders will recall. Pettit did have a moment. He recovered the fumble in the shadow of the Notre Dame goal [in 1939] and got a key block on Iowa's subsequent score."

Maury White

"Ken Pettit's spirit will give you an insight into why the University of Iowa football team is the surprise of the 1939 season...Ken came through with a perfect 60-minute performance against Purdue. Sportswriters lauded his play. But that wasn't particularly thrilling to Pettit. His biggest 'kick' came from 'the way Mike Enich played'...That is typical of the team spirit this fall."

Waterloo Daily Courier (Nov 13, 1939)

#39 – Ken Pettit

#40: FOREVER 40

"Chris exemplified the very best in competitiveness and team play...He's one of those kids that I think everyone would like to have on your team."

- Mike Krzyzewski

Some news can be so unexpected that a person remembers exactly where they were when they heard it. Hearing about the stunning and untimely death of Chris Street in 1993 is forever etched in the minds of many Hawkeye fans. Like Nile Kinnick before him, however, fond memories of Street remain long past his living years.

Christopher Michael Street grew up on a farm near Humeston, Iowa. Prior to Chris' sophomore year in high school, the Street family moved to Indianola. Chris excelled in athletics; he was an All-Conference baseball player as well as a First Team All-State quarterback. Basketball, however, was always Street's first love. He was named as a First Team All-State basketball player both his junior and senior seasons. His teams made it to the state tournament all three years at Indianola, finishing third both his sophomore and senior seasons.

> **Chris Street committed to Iowa after his sophomore season at Indianola. At the time, it was the earliest commitment ever to the Hawkeye basketball program. "I've been a Hawkeye fan ever since I was old enough to know what basketball was," Street explained.**

Street missed eleven games with a stress fracture in his foot his senior year. Two days after his cast was removed, Indianola had a road game at No. 1-ranked Ankeny. A win would give Indianola a share of the conference championship. "He was out there limping; he already had his scholarship to Iowa, and he had nothing to prove other than beating Ankeny and being the conference champion," his coach Bert Hanson said. "He was diving on the floor for loose balls. It was probably the most courageous, gutty performance out of an athlete, knowing the kind of shape the kid was in. That just showed the intensity, desire, and courage that kid had." Indianola won the game and a share of the conference title.

Street had the same influence on the Hawkeye basketball program. He started 15 games as a freshman and averaged five points and five rebounds per game. He started every game his sophomore season and averaged 10.6 points and 8.2 rebounds per game, which placed him third in Big Ten in rebounding. He was an Honorable Mention All-Big Ten selection his sophomore year and was developing into an impact player.

In Street's junior season, the Hawkeyes raced out to a 12-3 start and rose to No. 12 in the national rankings. Over his last six games, Street made 34 consecutive free throws which, as of 2010, still remains the school record. In his final game, a 65-56 road loss at Duke, he had 14 points and eight rebounds. His performance prompted CBS analyst Billy Packer to project a long professional career for Street. He was averaging 14.5 points and 9.5 rebounds per game, and nobody could have imagined he had just played his last game.

On January 19, 1993, Street and his girlfriend, Kim, had just finished a team dinner at the Highlander Inn. Chris had a night class on campus, so he and Kim hopped in the car for a short trip back. As they were turning left onto the four-lane highway, their car was struck by a northbound snow plow. Street was killed instantly.

James Winters, Street's roommate, later passed the scene. "I couldn't even recognize the car," Winters recalled. "We decided not to stop. We figured there was nothing we could do…I was getting worried, and I was telling the guys, 'I wonder if that was Chris' car.' They were saying, 'I don't even want to think about that.'" After Street failed to show up for his class, Winters and Kevin Skillett raced back to the scene. That was when they came to the horrible realization that their teammate and good friend had been involved in the accident.

Randy Larson, a Street family friend who co-owned The Airliner bar in Iowa City, received a call from the police notifying him of Chris' death. January 19 was the first Tuesday of the spring semester, so the bar was packed with around 600 students. Larson turned off the music, stood up on a chair, and choked out an announcement that Street had been killed across town.

"Five or six hundred people put down their glasses, picked up their coats and went home. Just like that. We closed. You would expect a bunch of the kids who had been drinking to kind of grumble about it or go off to other bars. But it was empty in a minute," Larson remembered. "They set their beers down and filed out in stone silence. I stood by the door, and half of them were crying. It struck me as they were leaving that no one was saying a word."

There was an outpouring of grief from across the nation. Iowa State coach Johnny Orr called Street "a great competitor who really made his team go. He was the kind of player you liked to have on your team but hated to play against, because he never quit." Former Iowa coach Sharm Scheuerman said, "His best years were in front of him. He was a hard-nosed Hawkeye." Hawkeye broadcaster Mac McCausland stated, "There was just no downside to ever seeing or meeting or being around Chris Street."

Chris Dufresne of *The Los Angeles Times* wrote, "What made Chris Street's death so difficult was that three million Iowans claimed him as either a son or a sibling. He grew up in their homes, around their kitchen tables. He was family, one of them, an Iowan. Most of them didn't know Street personally, but thought they did…He did what most Iowa boys dream of but few are talented enough to do. He grew up to play basketball at the University of Iowa."

The Hawkeye team postponed its next two games against Northwestern and Penn State to grieve and attend the funeral. Street wore his gold Iowa uniform with a black and gold warm-up jacket. He held a rose in one hand, and a Cabbage Patch doll dressed like an Iowa cheerleader was at his side. Two thousand, five hundred people attended Street's funeral, which included players and coaches from Iowa State and across the Big Ten. Chris' sister, Sarah, read a stirring eulogy during a highly emotional service.

Iowa's first game after Street's passing was a road trip to Michigan State. The Spartans built a 17-point lead, while the Hawkeyes struggled to focus on the task at hand. Michigan State still led, 70-55, with only 3:15 left in the game.

As if inspired by their fallen teammate, Iowa refused to fold. Three Hawkeye baskets and two Michigan State turnovers quickly cut the deficit to eight points. Iowa trailed by that amount with 1:07 left to play when a Val Barnes three-pointer forced a Spartan timeout. After one MSU free throw, Acie Earl made a traditional three-point play to bring Iowa within just three points with 48 seconds to play. The teams again traded scores before Val Barnes tied the game with a three-point shot with 22 seconds left. Acie Earl blocked Michigan State's game-winning attempt, and the Hawks had forced overtime.

> **Iowa scored nine of the first eleven points in overtime to finish a 30-8 run and secure a 96-90 overtime victory over Michigan State in the first game following Chris Street's death.**

"That was Chris Street's kind of game. He would have been proud of this," Coach Tom Davis said after the game. "He would have loved it. He was the toughest tiger in town."

The next game on the schedule was the first home game after Street's passing. It was against No. 5 Michigan, a team that had played in the national championship game the year before. Michigan's "Fab Five", as they were called, featured sophomores Chris Webber, Juwan Howard, and Jalen Rose. Reminders of Chris Street flooded Carver-Hawkeye Arena. The sold-out arena of 15,500 observed a moment of silence before the game, while Street's parents and two sisters had front-row seats.

The game was competitive and hard-fought. Iowa and Michigan were tied at halftime, and Michigan led, 75-73, with four minutes to play. Val Barnes and Acie Earl again made important baskets late in the game, while Kenyon Murray made key defensive plays. The Hawkeyes outscored the Wolverines 15-5 in the final four minutes to win, 88-80. Fans stormed the court, and the players weaved their way through the crowd to hand the game ball to the Street family. "To a person, they would not allow Michigan to win," Wolverine coach Steve Fisher remarked.

In Iowa's next home game against Indiana, the Hawkeyes officially retired Street's number 40. Iowa went on to the NCAA Tournament and lost in the second round to Rodney Rogers and Wake Forest. One wonders how Street would have fared against Rogers had he been around, but one wonders about a lot of things about Chris Street. "Who knows how good that kid was going to be? Guys with that kind of talent don't come along very often," Tom Davis said.

When Street was a sophomore, one of his teammates decided to transfer. Chris complimented him and wished him the best, but then he noted, "It's a little loss for myself, but I think it brings you closer together [as a team]. Problems like that, or turmoil, or whatever you want to call it, brings people together and I think that's what it did."

In the same way, Hawkeye fans will remain forever linked by the memory of a wonderful young man who left us far too soon.

Accolades

- Iowa basketball annually presents a Chris Street Award in his honor
- Led team in rebounding and field goal percentage (1992)
- Holds school record for consecutive free throws made
- No. 40 retired by Iowa basketball in his honor

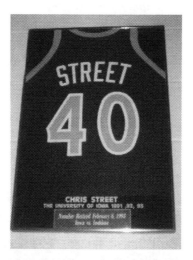

No. 40 CHRIS STREET									
Year	GP	FG-FGA	FG%	FT-FTA	FT%	Reb	Avg	Pts	Avg
1991	28	47-94	50%	44-68	65%	143	5.1	139	5.0
1992	30	114-202	56%	81-119	68%	247	8.2	319	10.6
1993	15	74-129	57%	66-74	89%	143	9.5	218	14.5
Totals	73	235-425	55%	191-261	73%	533	7.3	676	9.3

How He's Remembered

"He was an inspiration to his teammates. He was like that in life and obviously was like that in death. His life inspired us. I think that's why he captured the feelings of so many Iowans of all ages. He was a typical Iowan, but he also was somebody who represented the best of what Iowans are all about – the work ethic, the openness, the way we treat people. Chris was about all those things, a fun-loving and caring person."

Tom Davis

"Street was one of the nicest players anyone had known, making his death seem all the harder to understand…Street was the Iowa player who went out of his way to talk to strangers. Street was the player who stuck around to answer every reporter's question, win or lose. Street was the player who had the most impact on kids."

Chris Dufresne, *The Los Angeles Times*

"Chris had a great future and was one of the real outstanding kids and players in the Big Ten. What could be more tragic than to have something like this happen? He played hard every minute of the game and because of that, he was one of my favorite players in the Big Ten."

Bob Knight

"Chris was a coach's player. He was unselfish and did all the little things that helped you win. He was tough, hard-nosed, and put a premium on defense. He was the kind of player our coaching staff and all our players had the deepest respect for."

Jud Heathcote

"He had passion, heart, grit. He was humble but confident – not cocky. He made you respect him. He was exciting and intense. He wasn't flashy but still had a flair for the dramatic...Street's death, unfortunately, is what a lot of people think of when Street's name is mentioned. They'll remember his impassioned play and his smile. But his death they can't escape – a life cut short in the midst of his prime."

Kelly Terpstra, *Ottumwa Courier*

Jersey #40 Honorable Mention

Kevin Boyle – Basketball (1979-82)

Kevin Boyle burst onto the Iowa basketball scene in 1979. He started for Iowa's Big Ten championship team and was named the Big Ten Freshman of the Year. Boyle was a Second Team All-Big Ten selection in 1980 and a starter for Iowa's Final Four team. He was a First Team All-Big Ten choice in 1981 and a Third Team pick in 1982. Kevin Boyle is one of just nine Hawkeye basketball players to be a three-time All-Big Ten selection. He left Iowa as the school's all-time leader in starts with 118 and fourth in career points with 1,189. Boyle also started for USA Basketball at the World University Games, winning a gold medal in 1981.

#41: AN INSIDE PRESENCE

"Greg Stokes out of Ohio was a true-blue blue-chipper. He came to Iowa, and he turned out to be everything that label meant. He was Lute's prize, and he wound up being on my all-time team and Iowa's All-Century Team. He was just a really great player that I'll never forget."

- Ron Gonder

In Iowa football, there are Greenway and Hodge. In wrestling, there are Tom and Terry. In 1980s basketball, there are Stokes and Payne.

Collectively known as Iowa's Twin Towers of the 1980s, Greg Stokes and Michael Payne are forever linked with one another. They were the cornerstones of Lute Olson's 1981 freshman class, and they played side-by-side for the next four years.

In the beginning, it was Michael Payne who had an immediate impact while earning 1982 Big Ten Freshman of the Year honors. In the end, it was Greg Stokes who left the more prominent mark on the Iowa record books. He became the most dominant inside presence of the 1980s to wear the black and gold.

Greg Stokes attended high school in Hamilton, Ohio. In 1981, he was the Ohio Triple A Player of the Year, resulting in nearly 50 scholarship offers. In the end, his choice of colleges came down to two – Iowa and Michigan.

> **Greg Stokes made 11 out of 11 field goal attempts in a 1984 game against Georgia State.**

"Michigan just seemed like more of a football school," Stokes explained. "And Iowa was recently off the Final Four a couple seasons prior to that. Lute Olson had the program going, and that kind of swung the scales in Iowa's favor.

"I then came out to Iowa on a recruiting trip, and we went to a football game. The football team was pretty bad at the time, because Hayden Fry was rebuilding the program. Iowa hadn't scored and was losing by 30 points or so. With about two minutes to go, Iowa scored and the fans went nuts. The people seemed to love their Hawkeyes. It just so happens, ironically, the football team ended up going to the Rose Bowl the next year. At that point, I was part of the Hawkeye family, and I've been in love with it ever since. There's a tremendous Iowa fan base, and even now 20 years later, people still remember the old Twin Towers."

Like many high school stars, Stokes needed time to adjust to the next level of competition. Following an injury to teammate Mark Gannon, he broke into the starting lineup his freshman year and averaged almost nine points per game over his last seven games.

With a year of experience under his belt, Stokes' career began to blossom during his sophomore season. He averaged 17.7 points per game that year, earning him an invitation to the 1983 Pan-American Basketball Trials.

"We had the cream of the crop as far as the college players [in the Pan-Am Games]," Stokes said recently. "We had Michael Jordan, Patrick Ewing, Charles Barkley, Sam Perkins, and Chris Mullin. Playing against those guys three times a day for a period of about two weeks – you pretty much see what you're made of. I think they selected 13 guys from the camp, and I was one of them. That was, at that point, the highlight of my career. We ended up winning the gold medal for the United States, which was one of my proudest accomplishments."

His sophomore year of 1982-83 brought about a number of changes to the Iowa basketball program. In January, the first game in Carver-Hawkeye Arena was played. It was a significant upgrade in facilities from the Field House, but the Field House remained a sentimental favorite of many people.

"Just to be part of that move was awesome. But I loved the Field House; the atmosphere was just outstanding. I mean, the fans were right up on the court. They got those rafters vibrating, and you think the thing's gonna fall down. But the move was great because we had a new venue," said Stokes.

> **As Carver-Hawkeye Arena opened in late 1982 for its first basketball practice, players raced each other down the stairs to be the first to dunk the ball. Stokes won.**

In March of 1983, another significant change took place. Lute Olson announced he was leaving to become head coach at the University of Arizona.

"Just when you think things are going well, Lute Olson decides to leave," Stokes said. "That kind of took me back a little bit, and then George Raveling came in. We had a very shaky year that junior year. I think we were 13-15 overall."

More disappointment came when he was cut from the U.S. Olympic Team after the first set of workouts. Despite this, he entered his senior year with a new focus, determined to have a better year both personally and as a team. He did just that. The team rebounded with a 21-11 record and an NCAA Tournament berth.

"There's probably one game that really stands out for me personally, and that was a game against Ohio State," Stokes recalled. "I needed three or four points to break the Iowa all-time scoring record. When I got the record, they stopped the game. My grandmother was there who was very close to me; my aunt, little sister, and very first basketball coach all came out, along with my mom. I didn't know they were coming, so it was a really special time for me."

"That was probably the last time my grandmother, Irene Stokes, saw me play," Greg continued. "That was special for me, too, because we were very, very close growing up. She was my biggest supporter, and she raised me from a little tiny guy. She couldn't have been more proud of me for doing all the things I had done. Everything I am today, without a doubt, I owe to that lady. A lot of people don't really know my story and how I grew up. She's just a real special person."

That day was also special to Stokes for another reason. It came against his home-state Buckeyes.

"I always tried to play well against Ohio State," Stokes explained. As a junior in high school, he called Ohio State head coach Eldon Miller to inquire about a scholarship. "They must have thought I was some kind of nut case because here's a 16-year-old kid calling a college and asking if they'd be interested in me."

Miller indicated they would keep an eye on him, but Brad Sellers from the Cleveland area was their higher recruiting priority. After a tremendous senior year, Stokes garnered attention from nearly every Big Ten school.

"When Sellers committed to Wisconsin, Ohio State kind of came back and said, 'Hey, Greg, are you still interested?' I politely said, 'No, thank you.' So I really made an effort to put it on 'em every time I went there."

Stokes averaged 23.3 points per game his last three years against the Buckeyes, including games of 29 and 28.

When his eligibility at Iowa ended in spring 1985, Stokes was drafted by the Philadelphia 76ers. At the time, the likes of Julius Erving, Charles Barkley, and Moses Malone were on the roster.

"Just to be a part of that team was so incredible," Stokes said. "Toward the end of the year, I ended up actually starting several games. It was just a tremendous honor to be associated with those guys."

After his time with the 76ers, Stokes played European basketball in Italy and Spain for a few years. He had another brief stint in the NBA with the Sacramento Kings before he ended his playing career in Australia.

Today, Greg Stokes serves as an assistant basketball coach for Kirkwood Community College. His two children, Darius and Kiah, are talented basketball players themselves; Darius is walking on to the basketball program at Iowa. Greg Stokes continues to have fond memories of his playing days at Iowa and is very grateful for the opportunities basketball has presented him in life.

To Iowa fans, he will forever be remembered as the greatest of two towers.

Accolades
• First Team All-Big Ten (1985); Second Team All-Big Ten (1983, 84)
• Broke school record for career scoring
• Won gold medal with the USA Pan American team (1983)
• Selected to Iowa's All-Century basketball team (2002)
• No. 41 retired by Iowa basketball in his honor

No. 41 GREG STOKES								
Year	FG-FGA	FG%	FT-FTA	FT%	Reb	Avg	Pts	Avg
1982	61-128	48	43-77	56	123	4.2	165	5.7
1983	219-403	54	110-173	64	223	7.2	548	17.7
1984	163-284	57	91-134	68	193	6.9	417	14.9
1985	262-479	55	114-170	67	268	8.4	638	19.9
Totals	705-1294	55	358-554	65	807	6.7	1,768	14.7

How He's Remembered

"Stokes had this tremendous left-handed hook. I mean, he barely even needed to look at the basket. It was just a left-handed jump-hook and the amazing thing most people don't understand, Greg Stokes has pretty small hands for a guy his size. He really had the ball in the palm of his hand, and that's why he shot that hook shot; it was kind of like he was throwing it off the palm of his hand rather than the rotation out around the fingers. Not many people in the Big Ten have used it in the last 20 years as well as Greg Stokes did."

Mac McCausland

"Stokes was a left-hander, which made him doubly efficient because he shot from a different side than most of the guys, plus he was a great rebounder. He and Michael Payne were the Twin Towers. Payne was a good shooter, too, but I think Stokes got most of his baskets close in. They both had a lot of height, so they could dominate a game."

Buck Turnbull

"I'll always remember him being part of the Twin Towers. Not a lot of teams started two guys that were 6'10" and 6'11" up front. He was just such a good post player. I remember him in Lute's last tournament run when they beat Missouri and then lost to Villanova in the regional semifinals that year. Stokes was such a beast. Just a real polished and smooth post-up guy."

Tom Kakert

"Greg Stokes was a super talent."

Bump Elliott

Jersey #41 Honorable Mention

Eddie Vincent – Football (1953-55)

A member of the famed "Steubenville Trio" (with Cal Jones and Frank Gilliam), Eddie Vincent played halfback and defensive back for Forest Evashevski. He amassed a total of 1,373 yards rushing on 227 attempts, resulting in one of the highest career yard-per-carry averages (6.0) in Iowa history. Vincent scored on a 94-yard run versus Purdue in 1954; it is still the longest touchdown run in school history. He was selected First Team All-Midwest by *The New York Daily News* in both 1954 and 1955. In 1955, he was named All-Big Ten as a halfback.

Bob Stoops – Football (1979-82)

The oldest of three brothers to wear the Hawkeye uniform in the 1980s, Bob Stoops started at strong safety for three years. He was voted team captain, team MVP, and All-Big Ten his senior year. He amassed a total of 230 career tackles and eight interceptions, helping lead Iowa to two bowl games during his career. Stoops attended Cardinal Mooney High School in Youngstown, Ohio, where he starred in basketball, football, and track. After his playing career, Stoops went into coaching, leading Oklahoma University to six conference championships through 2009.

Mike Stoops – Football (1981, 1983-85)

Mike Stoops began his career as a reserve behind his elder brother for two years. He became the most decorated of the three Stoops brothers by the end of his career, earning All-Big Ten honors in both 1983 and 1984. He also achieved Honorable Mention All-American status his senior year. Mike played in four bowl games and totaled 180 career tackles. He also ranks 13th on Iowa's career interceptions list with nine. After graduation, Stoops became the head coach at the University of Arizona.

"Bobby Stoops and Mike Stoops were two of the most physical tacklers at safety that I've ever been around in college football. They're not trying to hurt people, but they were vicious hitters, physical hitters."

Dan McCarney

#42: PERSEVERANCE PAYS OFF

"It took quite a few evaluations to decide Ryan could play in the Big Ten; now I wonder what took me so long! I had seen him several times in the Iowa City summer league and wasn't convinced. But when I saw him playing pressure defense for Mac McCausland's summer AAU team, I knew instantly he would be a good fit. His enthusiasm and energy were apparent, and that led to a terrific college and NBA career."

- Dr. Tom Davis

It takes an exceptional athlete to star on a Division I college basketball team. It is a rare athlete who is able to continue on and make a living in sports professionally. It is an admirable athlete who appreciates where he grew up and gives back to the community.

Ryan Bowen passes all those criteria with flying colors. Unheralded and lightly recruited out of Fort Madison High School, this Iowa native starred for the Hawkeyes from 1995 through 1998. He is one of the best examples of player development under Coach Tom Davis.

While in high school, Bowen garnered interest from smaller Division I schools such as Northern Iowa and Wichita State. He had yet to receive an offer from a major Division I school. The summer before his senior year, he played on an AAU team with Raef LaFrentz, Klay Edwards, and Kent McCausland. Kent's dad, Mac McCausland, coached the team. It was this experience that caught the eye of Tom Davis.

"He saw me playing against some of the other great AAU teams across the country, and we did really well," Bowen explained. "When I got back from this AAU trip, Coach Davis finally thought I was good enough to play for him. He'd be the first to tell you that he'd watched me play probably 10 or 11 times and just didn't think I was quite there yet. For me, I wanted to be a Hawkeye since I was little, and to get the opportunity to do that was great. It just took a while for all the pieces to fall in place."

Ryan enrolled at Iowa the summer of 1994. He played as a true freshman, mostly in a reserve role behind teammates Jess Settles, Jim Bartels, and Kenyon Murray. "I'll never forget playing my first game at Carver. I actually started that game and jumped center," Bowen recalled. "I remember going up for the tip. Somebody has a picture of the ball going up, the other guy tipping the ball, and me cemented to the floor."

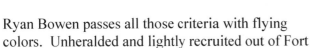

In Ryan Bowen's freshman year of 1994-95, Iowa lost four Big Ten Conference games each by a single point.

Bowen averaged five points per game his freshman year and led the team in blocked shots. He attributed much of his ability to adjust to the college game to Jess Settles. Settles had established himself as a force in the conference the season before, earning Big Ten Freshman of the Year honors. The 1994-95 team finished 21-12, earning seventh place in the Big Ten.

The following season, Bowen again started the year in a reserve role behind starters Settles, Murray, Russ Millard, Andre Woolridge, and Mon'ter Glasper. By February, Bowen had cracked into the starting lineup. Soon after he earned his big opportunity, however, he broke a bone in his left hand. The injury was supposed to take six to eight weeks to heal, which would have ended Bowen's season. Undeterred, Bowen wore a soft cast over his hand and returned for the NCAA Tournament less than three weeks later, helping Iowa advance to the second round.

In his junior season, Bowen led Iowa in rebounds and steals despite missing several games with an irregular heartbeat. He was a Third Team All-Big Ten selection and averaged 12 points per game for the Hawkeyes, who made it back to the NCAA Tournament. Bowen scored 15 points and added 16 rebounds in a first-round victory over Virginia, but the Hawkeyes fell in the second round to Kentucky, 75-69.

Ryan Bowen ended his Iowa career in style. He averaged 14 points per game and led the Hawkeyes in field goal percentage, blocked shots, rebounds, and steals. His 79 steals in 1998 set a school season record and boosted his career total to 208, another school record. Bowen's career field goal percentage of 57.5 remains a school record, and he became the 32nd Hawkeye player to score more than 1,000 points. He also ranked in Iowa's top ten in career blocked shots (third) and career rebounds (seventh). Although the Hawkeyes were denied an NCAA Tournament bid, Bowen was named First Team All-Big Ten.

"I think the biggest thing for me [was] to focus on what my strengths are and not try to make me out to be something that I wasn't. I'll never forget the day [Coach Davis] called me into his office. I think this was my senior year, talking about playing professionally. He said, 'You have to be a shooter, a good rebounder, and a good defender. But you have to be great at something, and I don't know why you can't be a great hustler and a great worker. I think that's going to be your niche to make it in the NBA.' And that's the one thing I've always fallen back on," Bowen said.

In the 1998 NBA Draft, the Denver Nuggets selected Ryan in the late second round. In what would have been his rookie year, a players' strike postponed the start of the season until February. Instead of taking most of a year off from competitive basketball, the Nuggets prompted Ryan to go play in Europe for a year. He played one season in Turkey, where he got his first taste of professional ball.

"That was probably the best thing for me, playing over there, being the star player, getting all the shot attempts and just playing basketball all season," Bowen recalled. "I would have only had two weeks to try to make the Nuggets, whereas I waited another year and actually got a whole summer to go through summer league and then show up early for camp."

> **Houston Rockets coach Jeff Van Gundy said, "Ryan Bowen, to me, is exactly what the NBA player should be. Self-motivated but not self-absorbed. And if I were a general manager, he would have a lifetime contract."**

When asked about the differences between college and professional basketball, Bowen said there are many. "It's still basketball, but it is an entirely different game. I can't believe the preparation that goes into games and how much they scout and how they really go at your weaknesses. I mean, they know what you can and can't do, and they do everything they can to exploit those differences. And just the size, the speed, and the strength of all the athletes; it's amazing the difference. You go to a Big Ten game and you think these are elite athletes; then you step on the court with some of these guys and it's like it's a whole new level."

Ryan Bowen played ten seasons in the NBA, five of them with the Nuggets. In 2010, Iowa head coach Fran McCaffery announced that Ryan Bowen had joined his staff as an administrative assistant. "I couldn't be more excited to be joining the Iowa basketball staff," Bowen said. "I had a great time as a student-athlete at Iowa and look forward to once again being part of the Hawkeye family."

Bowen is also well-known for his charitable work. In 2003, Ryan and his wife Wendy established the Ryan Bowen Foundation. This fund supports activities they were involved in while growing up in southeast Iowa. AAU teams, youth softball teams, and cheerleading squads have all received funding through the foundation. In addition, $1,000 college scholarships are distributed each year. Ryan himself reads through the applications to help select the recipients. This year, five scholarships were given. Bowen also holds basketball camps and golf outings, from which all proceeds go to the foundation.

For Ryan Bowen, Iowa's all-time steals leader and founder of the Ryan Bowen Foundation, his career has indeed been one of "give and take." It just hasn't been in that order.

Accolades
• First Team All-Big Ten (1998); Third Team All-Big Ten (1997)
• Team MVP (1998)
• Holds school record for career steals
• Ranks in the top ten at Iowa for career rebounds and blocked shots
• Played 11 seasons in the NBA

No. 42 RYAN BOWEN									
Year	GP	FG-FGA	FG%	FT-FTA	FT%	Reb	Avg	Pts	Avg
1995	33	58-110	53	35-59	59	148	4.5	151	4.6
1996	27	55-91	60	39-58	67	121	4.5	149	5.5
1997	29	120-217	55	93-135	69	264	9.1	343	11.8
1998	31	164-272	60	111-161	69	271	8.7	447	14.4
Totals	134	397-690	58	278-413	67	804	6.7	1,090	9.1

How He's Remembered

"Ryan always enjoyed practice and his teammates, so you can imagine how much fun he was to coach."

Tom Davis

"I thought Ryan Bowen brought as much enthusiasm to a basketball court as any player I've covered. He certainly played well enough as witnessed by the fact that he's been in the NBA *for several years. He was just always a fun guy to watch, and he was always a very easy person to deal with after a game as far as a reporter goes."*

Mike Hlas

"People weren't sure he could play in the Big Ten. Now he's played years in the NBA when people didn't know what kind of career he'd even have at Iowa. He proves you don't need to lead the league or even your team in anything, whether it's rebounding or scoring. If you just play the game right and you can add qualities to a team, you can win games. Nobody has given the effort that Ryan Bowen has every play and I'm talking whether it was practice or in a game."

Mac McCausland

"Ryan Bowen might be the nicest guy I've ever dealt with at Iowa. No matter the situation, he was always positive, he was always polite, he always had time. If he had an ego, I never saw it. But I think sometimes we took for granted his athletic ability. He was 6'8", could run like a guard, and he could defend all five positions on the court. That's why he's made it in the NBA. He had a specialty, and he took advantage of that. He was a great defensive player. I think his athleticism, his work ethic, and just his friendly demeanor are the three things I'll always think of when I think of Ryan Bowen. He epitomizes what college sports are supposed to be about."

Pat Harty

Jersey #42 Honorable Mention

Leven Weiss – Football (1976-79)

Leven Weiss was a 6'2", 215-pound linebacker from Detroit, Michigan. He started his career for Coach Bob Commings and recorded 128 tackles in his first three years. As a senior under first-year Iowa coach Hayden Fry, Weiss led the Hawkeyes with 112 tackles and also recovered three fumbles. In his final Hawkeye game in 1979, Weiss intercepted a pass to set up a touchdown in a 33-23 victory over Michigan State. He was an All-Big Ten selection and an Honorable Mention All-American as a senior. He currently ranks 31st with 240 career tackles at Iowa.

Michael Payne – Basketball (1982-85)

Michael Payne will always be known as one half of the "Twin Towers" of Iowa basketball in the 1980s. Michael's father, Tom, was a reserve letterman on Iowa's 1956 national runner-up squad. Michael, a McDonald's All-American from Quincy, Illinois, chose to become a Hawkeye like his father. Payne had a tremendous freshman season; he led the team in scoring and rebounding and earned Second Team All-Big Ten honors. He again led the team in rebounding as a sophomore and was named team MVP as a senior. Though Payne's scoring average dropped in each of his four seasons, he still scored well over 1,000 points and remains in Iowa's top 30 career scorers. He left school as Iowa's second-leading career rebounder behind Kevin Kunnert.

#43: A ROSY RETURN WEST

"I'm telling you, he's unreal. I've been coaching all my life and I've never had one like him…Nick could be an All-American tight end, but he wants to be a running back."
- Hayden Fry

Some of the greatest joys in the world are unexpected pleasures. Finding money in your pocket that you didn't even know you had lost or randomly overhearing a great song that you hadn't heard in years are examples of the joys that can spring up in an unanticipated moment. If serendipity is the aptitude for stumbling upon a desirable discovery by accident, then serendipity for a college football coach is discovering a player like Nick Bell. Bell became an unexpected star from 1988-1990 and helped the Hawkeyes rediscover Pasadena.

Nick Bell struggled to overcome a learning disability as a youngster in Las Vegas, Nevada, where he often mixed up words and suffixes. "It's not dyslexia, technically," Bell said. "There are some things that don't work correctly in my mind." Still, he had a gift for athletics. He was so big growing up that he was not allowed to play in the local youth football league. As a result, Bell did not take up football until high school, but he quickly became a First Team All-State football player. In addition to playing fullback, he won the state heavyweight wrestling championship as a junior. USC and UCLA took one look at Bell's strong, wide frame and extended him offers as a defensive tackle. However, he wanted to run with the football, and Coach Hayden Fry decided to give Bell that opportunity. That was enough to convince Nick Bell to move to the Midwest.

Bell did not make an immediate impact at Iowa, though. He was a Prop 48 player due to his learning disability, and nagging injuries cost him his entire freshman season. When the 1988 season began, Bell was buried on the team's depth chart. Midway through the year, the 4-2-2 Hawkeyes traveled to Bloomington to square off against a surprisingly powerful Indiana squad.

Bell was not even listed on the two-deeps prior to the game, but David Hudson, Iowa's starting fullback, was a late scratch with a foot injury. Hudson's backup, Richard Bass, got the start, but the Hoosiers quickly raced out to a 35-3 lead. Facing a huge deficit, Bell saw his first real action of the year, and Fry decided to let the passes fly. Though the Hawkeyes' furious comeback came up short with Iowa losing, 45-34, quarterback Chuck Hartlieb finished the game with 44 completions in 60 attempts for 558 yards.

> **Nick Bell made his mark in the record books by catching a school-record 13 passes for 128 yards and a touchdown against Indiana. "He had one of the greatest first games of any player I've ever been associated with," Fry gushed after the game.**

Running back Tony Stewart became the first sophomore in Iowa history to rush for 1,000 yards in 1988. However, he severely injured his knee late in the season against Ohio State and didn't regain his form for the 1989 season. That opened the door for Bell to take over the starting running back job for the Hawkeyes.

Yet the 1989 season did not go smoothly for Bell either, as he was injured in the season opener against Oregon. He was severely hampered for the first month of the season and rushed for just 91 yards combined in the first four games of the year. Bell recovered and broke out against Wisconsin, rushing for 217 yards and a touchdown in a 31-24 victory. It was the fourth-highest rushing total in school history at the time. He also caught a touchdown pass and scored the winning touchdown with 2:07 left in the game. But in the following game against Michigan, Bell twisted his knee and was hobbled for the rest of the season. Iowa missed a bowl game for the first time in nine years.

As Bell's senior season of 1990 approached, Iowa faced a running back controversy. Bell had shown what he could do, but Tony Stewart was finally back and fully healthy as well. Fry vowed to keep Bell involved in the offense. "You may see him line up any place – fullback, running back, tight end. He may even go in motion and become a wide receiver," Fry said. "What we are trying to do is get Nick one-on-one with someone not as talented on the defense. We're going to have a mismatch. We're going to try to feature Nick as much as we can to get everything possible out of him."

Nick Bell quickly established himself as Iowa's biggest scoring threat in his senior season. He scored a touchdown in the opener against Cincinnati and then rushed for 115 yards and a touchdown against Iowa State. He scored two touchdowns, including a 53-yard touchdown catch, in a loss against No. 9 Miami. Bell then caught a touchdown in a win at Michigan State. Though he had been dinged up by the Spartans, he rushed for 146 rushing yards and a touchdown the following week against Wisconsin. Michigan became the first team that season to keep Bell out of the end zone, but the Hawkeyes upset the Wolverines in Ann Arbor, 24-23. Bell only played in the first half the next week against Northwestern but still rushed for 136 yards and three touchdowns.

The biggest game of the 1990 season was a showdown with No. 5 Illinois. The 6-1 Hawkeyes went to Champaign to battle the 6-1 Fighting Illini, with the winner seizing an almost insurmountable lead in the Rose Bowl race. The Illini had the conference's top-rated defense, and Iowa had the Big Ten's top offense. "Football in the Big Ten starts with defense," snorted Illinois coach John Mackovic. "The Hawkeyes have run pretty effectively, but that doesn't mean they'll run up and down the field on us." When asked about Nick Bell, Mackovic replied dismissively, "Our strategy is we're gonna tackle him."

His team did, but not until after Bell had racked up 168 rushing yards (130 in the first quarter alone) and two touchdowns. The Hawks led 21-0 after one quarter and 35-7 late in the first half on their way to a convincing victory. "Iowa 54, Illinois 28, and who in their right mind believes it?" *The Cedar Rapids Gazette* asked. "Stunning. Fantastic. Unbelievable. Incredible. Pick a word."

> **"I wonder if anybody has seen anybody like Nick Bell at the college level,"**
> **Fry said after the game. "I thought I knew everything about Nick Bell, until**
> **the first half. He was incredible."**

Longtime Iowa broadcaster Frosty Mitchell recalled, "I remember after one of his touchdowns late in the second quarter, I jumped across the hallway to the men's room. I saw Keith Jackson, who was doing the game for ABC-TV. He looked at me and he just said, 'Holy moly.' That was the whole conversation, but it was all about Nick Bell."

Despite his amazing performance, Bell remained uncomfortable in the spotlight. "I don't want to be a star, but I am, unfortunately," he said. "I like being like everybody else, but you can't at this point." Fry appreciated Bell's desire just to fit in. "I guess some people would classify Nick Bell as an introvert," Fry said. "He is one of the most bright, refreshing personalities I've ever met. He just has that feeling that he doesn't want to be in the limelight when a lot of his buddies never are. He works real hard at being a member of the family, not somebody that's leading the family."

The victory over Illinois paced Iowa to the Big Ten championship and the Rose Bowl. The win over the Illini was also instrumental in Bell claiming the Chicago Tribune Silver Football that is awarded to the Big Ten's MVP. He ended his career with 149 total yards and two touchdowns in the 1991 Rose Bowl.

After three seasons in the NFL, Nick Bell retired to a private life. Art was his new passion. "Nick Bell is very attentive and sensitive," teammate Merton Hanks said. "He has tremendous artistic talent." Bell explained, "Art is one of the more inspirational aspects of my life. For me, art is a combination of expression and emotion. It is one way for me to express what I feel without words."

In retrospect, Bell's resounding success in that 1990 season almost made fans forget just how far Bell had come to even see the field for the Hawks. All Coach Fry was seeking two years earlier was someone who would continue to give maximum effort in the face of a blowout loss, but what he uncovered in his third-string fullback was so much more. It was truly a serendipitous find for both Hayden Fry and Hawkeye fans everywhere.

Accolades
• Big Ten MVP (1990)
• Second Team All-American (1990)
• Led Iowa in rushing (1989, 90)
• Ranks sixth in school history for rushing yards in a game
• Holds the school record for most receptions in a game

No. 43 NICK BELL								
Year	Att	Yards	Avg	Long	Recept	Yards	Avg	TDs
1988	28	136	4.9	19	22	220	10.0	3
1989	117	603	5.2	47	12	96	8.0	5
1990	166	1,009	6.1	44	21	308	14.7	14
Totals	311	1,748	5.6	47	55	624	11.3	22

How He's Remembered

"The thing you've got to do with Nick Bell is try to slow him down before he gets going. And then if you're a defensive back coming up once he starts going, I would suggest that you tackle him low. Very low."

Dennis Erickson, former Miami coach

"As far as a big, strong running back, I think Nick Bell had more gifts than Shonn Greene, who is certainly currently big and strong. Even if the hole wasn't there, Bell could break it wide open."

Frosty Mitchell

"Bell is a big, strong runner who's terrific in the open field. At that size, you don't expect him to be such a nifty runner."

John Mackovic, former Illinois coach

"Mackovic looked stricken following his team's 54-28 loss to Bell and the rest of the Hawkeyes. Bell had run over, through, past, and around the Illinois defenders – six of whom were All-Conference last year – and made them look like gnats trying to fell an elephant."

Douglas S. Looney, *Sports Illustrated*

"I'll tell you what, Bell can flat run. I can assure you of that. To see a guy that big be able to run like that is amazing. We haven't got guys that big on our offensive line."

Francis Peay, former Northwestern coach

Jersey #43 Honorable Mention

Chad Calabria – Basketball (1968-70)

Eighty colleges showed interest in Chad Calabria during his senior season of high school in Aliquippa, Pennsylvania, but he decided to attend the University of Iowa because he liked Coach Ralph Miller's aggressive style of play. Calabria started on the bench as a sophomore, but he quickly earned a starting role and was a Second Team All-Big Ten selection by the end of the 1968 season. The Hawkeyes won the Big Ten title that year, and Calabria would pick up another conference championship as a member of the "Six Pack" Iowa team that went undefeated in the Big Ten in 1970. He finished his career as Iowa's sixth-leading scorer with 1,168 career points.

Craig Clemons – Football (1969-71)

Craig Clemons was one of the most ferocious hitters to ever play for the Iowa football team. Clemons' career got off to a dubious start, as he was caught up in the "Black Boycott" of the 1969 Hawkeye football team. But Clemons was reinstated by a vote of the team for his sophomore season, and he quickly earned a starting spot at cornerback. He led the Hawkeyes in interceptions in each of his final two seasons, and he finished his career third on Iowa's all-time interceptions list with nine. He also finished his career with 261 career tackles, which was just three short of the school record at the time. Clemons was named team captain and MVP as a senior in 1971, and he was voted All-Big Ten and a First Team All-American that year. He was selected 12th overall in the 1972 NFL Draft by the Chicago Bears, and he played six seasons in the NFL. He was voted to the University of Iowa's all-time football team in 1989.

Earl Douthitt – Football (1972-74)

Earl Douthitt played defensive back for Iowa from 1972-1974. He came to Iowa from Cleveland, Ohio, to play for Coach Frank Lauterbur, and he made his biggest impact on the team by returning kicks. He averaged 24.6 yards per kick return as a sophomore, which ranked seventh in the nation. During Iowa's miserable 0-11 season in 1973, Douthitt set an NCAA record by racking up 994 kick return yards. He also led the team in interceptions as a junior. New Hawkeye head coach Bob Commings selected Douthitt as Iowa's team captain in 1974, and Douthitt earned All-Big Ten and Honorable Mention All-American honors that season. His 1,762 career kickoff return yards remain a school record. As a defensive back, Douthitt recorded 221 career tackles, which, at the time, ranked seventh in school history.

Pat Angerer – Football (2006-09)

Pat Angerer was an All-State linebacker as a junior and senior at Bettendorf High School. After playing sparingly his first two seasons, Angerer led the Hawkeyes with 107 tackles in 2008. He ranked second in the Big Ten in interceptions per game and sixth in tackles per game that season. As a senior, Angerer was a First Team All-American at middle linebacker. He helped lead the Hawkeyes to a 9-0 start and an Orange Bowl win over Georgia Tech. He ranked fourth in the nation in tackles per game in 2009.

#44: DOING IT FOR MOM

"That's the first thing to understand about Clark – the pain of that moment will never pass...If Jan Clark were alive, she would be delighted by how far her youngest son has come."

- Jeffri Chadiha, ESPN.com

Graduation day for most high school seniors is an exciting time. Feelings of relief, excitement, freedom, and an occasional "good riddance" enter a graduate's mind. Feelings of mourning are not supposed to be part of the moment.

For Dallas Clark, a feeling of tremendous loss *was* part of the moment. Just days before his graduation in spring 1998, his mom collapsed in their garage while preparing for his graduation open house. Jan Clark, at only 48, had succumbed to a massive heart attack and could not be revived. Dallas and his aunt were home when it happened.

In the town of Livermore, Iowa, as in many small towns, most people know almost everyone. The entire school was touched by the loss of Dallas' mother, so a packed gymnasium served as the funeral location. From that day on, Jan Clark served as Dallas' primary inspiration.

"Dallas had to overcome a lot," Pat Harty of the *Iowa City Press-Citizen* recalled. "His parents were divorced, and he overcame the death of his mother from a heart attack just days before he graduated from high school. It's like he dedicated his career as a football player to his mother's memory."

Dallas Clark did not take the usual route to having success on the football field. Though he lettered in four high school sports and earned Second Team All-State honors in football, he garnered little attention from college programs. Iowa maintained contact with him and offered him an opportunity to walk on the team. Dallas enrolled at Iowa and began practicing with the team the following spring. This was spring 1999, and Kirk Ferentz was conducting his first practices as head coach at the University of Iowa. Dallas spent most of the 1999 season in recovery from a collarbone injury and appendicitis.

> As a walk-on, Dallas Clark needed a side job to pay his college expenses. "I mowed Kinnick Stadium and mowed the baseball stadium, both softball fields, and both soccer fields," Clark said. "I fixed sprinkler heads. I mowed the complex. That helped me pay the bills."

In 2000, he saw his first playing time in Kinnick Stadium, serving as an integral part of the special teams and as a reserve linebacker. Since Clark arrived at Iowa under such sorrowful circumstances, he was forced to mature more quickly than most college students. "I was by myself, so I had to handle that. I had to grow up," Clark recalled. "I didn't get to enjoy the finer things in college. But to play even just one game at Kinnick Stadium, it was all worth it." After his freshman season, Coach Ferentz offered Clark a scholarship in appreciation of his efforts. Ferentz had observed a hard worker in practice and contributor on special teams. He imagined more.

The following spring, the coaching staff saw Clark catching passes from quarterback Kyle McCann. They were impressed by what they saw from Dallas and approached him with a potential move to the tight end position. He eventually agreed to give it a try and developed significantly during those few weeks of practices.

It was a brilliant move. Clark is perhaps the best of many examples of Ferentz's coaching staff finding the right position for a player. By fall, he earned a starting spot on offense, with McCann at quarterback and Ladell Betts in the backfield. They were coming off a 3-9 season but had made significant improvement from the previous season.

"Dallas was a guy that it was a matter of you just had to find the right position. He played about four or five positions in high school, much like Marv Cook. He reminded me a lot of Marv Cook years later. I wasn't sure what his position was going to be in college. Once he found it, you knew that he was going to excel," said former Iowa State head coach Dan McCarney.

2001 was a turnaround year for the Ferentz program. Their record improved to 7-5, with their five losses by a combined total of 27 points. The season ended with a 19-7 victory over Texas Tech in the Alamo Bowl and an All-Big Ten Honorable Mention for Clark. Perhaps the defining moment of Clark's 2001 season came at home versus Minnesota, where he dragged three or four Gophers for over ten yards at the end of a pass reception.

Iowa entered the 2002 season with a new starting quarterback, Brad Banks, and a new starter at running back in Fred Russell. The strength of the team was the offensive line, including Clark at tight end. It would prove to be one of Iowa's most magical years in football. Not a tremendous amount was expected of the team going into the season. One pre-season magazine boldly stated, "The Hawkeyes won't return to a bowl." In actuality, the team would nearly run the table in the regular season with a quarterback who almost won the Heisman Trophy.

There were many heroes that year, but few individual players were more important to Iowa's success than Dallas Clark. He was a defensive coordinator's worst nightmare. Iowa again had a tight end that could find the seam in opposing defensive coverages.

The season started off slowly for Clark; he caught only four passes in the first three games. The following game against Utah State, he would haul in five receptions. From then on, he remained an integral part of Iowa's potent offensive attack that averaged over 37 points per game.

Perhaps Clark's most memorable game as a Hawkeye came on Homecoming against Purdue. Iowa trailed, 14-3, before the Hawkeyes scored two touchdowns to take a 17-14 lead. Late in the third quarter, Iowa was stuck deep in their own territory. Banks completed a pass to Clark, who hurdled one would-be tackler and sprinted 95 yards for a touchdown, outrunning defensive backs along the way.

"I'll tell you one thing about Dallas, I don't think people understood just how fast he is," said WHO-Radio's Mark Allen. "But I remember a certain Purdue game where he went 95 yards. I don't think people respected Dallas' speed all that much, but I was on the sidelines. First of all, it was a great catch, and then he just barreled his head and outran the defense. I don't think people really realize just how quick Dallas was."

> Dallas Clark's 95-yard touchdown reception against Purdue in 2002 was the longest pass play in Kinnick Stadium history.

The score gave Iowa a seemingly comfortable 24-14 lead, but Purdue rushed for two touchdowns in the fourth quarter to grab a 28-24 advantage. With no timeouts and less than two minutes to play, the Hawks had one final scoring chance. Aided by a 14-yard pass reception by Clark, Iowa drove down the field and faced fourth and goal from the seven-yard line. Banks dropped back, held the ball until the last possible second before being hit by a defender, and floated a pass to a wide-open Clark in the right side of the end zone. Dallas caught the touchdown pass and reached his hands straight up in the air in celebration. It was only his third reception of the game, but his touchdown grab with 1:07 remaining provided the winning margin in Iowa's 31-28 victory.

"The two plays that will always stand out are the Purdue game where he goes 95 yards and outruns defensive backs down the sidelines," Tom Kakert said, "and then the late touchdown catch on the fourth-down play from Brad Banks. That was probably, in my opinion, his statement game where everybody knew about Dallas Clark."

Clark had more memorable games remaining that season, including five catches each in wins over Indiana, Michigan, and Wisconsin. Iowa completed their first undefeated Big Ten season in 80 years in 2002 and were invited to their first BCS bowl game. Clark ended the year by winning the Mackey Award as the nation's top tight end.

Dallas Clark was faced with a difficult choice after the 2002 season. He still had a remaining year of eligibility, but he was already 23 years old. He was a sure early-round NFL draft choice. Realistically, it would be difficult to top what he just experienced both from a team and an individual perspective. He opted to make himself available for the NFL draft. "When you come in as a walk-on, you don't even think about the NFL," Clark said. "It was never a dream of mine to play in the NFL. My dream was just to play football as long as I can."

Clark was selected with the 24th overall pick of the 2003 NFL Draft by the Indianapolis Colts, and he quickly earned a starting position. He had a breakout season in 2006, as the Colts went on to win Super Bowl XLI. Clark started all four games in the playoffs for the Colts and had

317 receiving yards. Those 317 yards were the most by a tight end in a single playoff season since the AFL-NFL merger of 1970.

In 2009, Clark became just the second tight end in NFL history to record 100 catches in a single season. He earned his first Pro Bowl berth and his first All-Pro selection, and he surpassed John Mackey for the Colts' franchise record for most catches by a tight end. Clark's 1,106 yards receiving helped lead the Colts to Super Bowl XLIV. In the process, he became the all-time career leader among tight ends in playoff receptions and playoff receiving yards. With his final touchdown catch of the season in the AFC Championship Game against the New York Jets, Clark surpassed Quinn Early and Ed Podolak for the most career touchdowns scored by a Hawkeye in the NFL.

As a player, Dallas Clark's rise from walk-on to All-American at Iowa was incredible. Tom Kakert summarized Clark's Iowa career by simply saying, "To me, he is the poster boy for the walk-on program of Iowa football."

At the very least, it can surely be assumed that he's made Mom proud.

Accolades
• Unanimous First Team All-American (2002)
• All-Big Ten (2002)
• Won Mackey Award as the nation's most outstanding tight end (2002)
• Has played seven seasons in the NFL; First Team NFL All-Pro (2009)

No. 44 DALLAS CLARK						
Year	Recept	Yards	Avg	TDs	Long	Tackles
2000	-	-	-	-	-	6
2001	38	539	14.2	4	40	5
2002	43	742	17.3	4	95	-
Totals	81	1,281	15.8	8	95	11

How He's Remembered

"Tremendous athlete, ran like a wide receiver with the body of a tight end. One of the most athletic tight ends that I've coached against. Tremendous set of hands, just a great receiver at tight end, and has really developed as a blocker, too. His forte used to be catching the ball early in his career, and then he really improved as a blocker as he's gone on."

Dan McCarney

"He's another one of those Robert Gallery-type stories. Clark played quarterback in high school. He kind of got lost in the recruiting shuffle living in a small town in Iowa. He came to Iowa, though, and like Ferentz and those coaches do, they found the best position for him and boy, did he blossom."

Pat Harty

"When I watched Dallas play the game, I knew that's the way you're supposed to do it. You're not supposed to show up the opponent. You're supposed to run your routes, make your catches, and throw your blocks. When you take a look at that class of Kirk Ferentz's, you look at an entire team that bought into the system and bought into a coaching staff."

Mark Allen

"He's really a small-town Iowa hero. There's so many things he's done…He made First Team All-American at Iowa and of course, he's an [NFL] All-Pro, you know. He's got a lot of things going for him…he's just a heck of a guy."

Bob Brown

Jersey #44 Honorable Mention

Dick Romey – Football (1923-25)

A native of Mason City, Iowa, Richard E. (Dick) Romey played for Coach Howard Jones in 1923 and Coach Burt Ingwersen in his junior and senior seasons. The 6'1", 186-pound end lettered three times during a successful three-year stretch that saw Iowa go 16-7-1. In 1924, Romey was named to the All-Western Second Team by a top eastern critic. As a senior the following year, he was named All-Big Ten. Romey recovered a fourth-quarter fumble that led to a touchdown in Iowa's 15-0 victory over Ohio State in 1925. He also earned First Team All-American honors that season. He played professionally for one year.

Francis Schammel – Football (1932-33)

Francis "Zud" Schammel was one of the toughest players to ever play for the Hawkeyes. He attended Waterloo East High School, where he captained the high school basketball team. He then spent his first two seasons of college eligibility at Northern Iowa before joining the Hawkeyes prior to his junior season. Schammel played right tackle and fullback in 1932, but Coach Ossie Solem moved him to the guard position for his senior season in 1933. It was at this position that Schammel shined and became a Hawkeye legend. He suffered from a painful leg infection during the entire 1933 season that kept him hospitalized and on crutches five days a week, yet every Saturday he managed to not only suit up but dominate. Schammel earned All-Big Ten and First Team All-American honors as a senior for helping lead Iowa to a 4-2-2 record. He served as Solem's line coach at Iowa from 1934-1936 before playing one season with the Green Bay Packers in 1937. Schammel was inducted into the University of Iowa Hall of Fame in 2003.

Glenn Vidnovic – Basketball (1968-70)

Glenn "The Stick" Vidnovic earned his nickname as a result of his 6'5", 150-pound frame. But the forward from McKeesport, Pennsylvania, was a sharpshooter for Coach Ralph Miller's most successful teams. His career average of 16.1 points per game ranks 12th in school history. Vidnovic led the team in free throw percentage as a junior and senior, and his career free throw percentage of 85.6 ranks third in school history. He was a Second Team All-Big Ten selection as a senior for Iowa's 1970 team that went 14-0 in Big Ten play.

Kevin Kunnert – Basketball (1971-73)
Greg Brunner – Basketball (2003-06)

Kevin Kunnert was a 6'10" center from Dubuque Wahlert High School. He averaged 15.9 points per game over his career and left Iowa as the seventh-leading scorer in school history. Kunnert was even more impressive on the boards. His career average of 12.7 rebounds per game is a school record, and he left as Iowa's all-time leading rebounder. It would be 33 years before another No. 44 broke his record for career rebounds. Kunnert led the Hawkeyes in rebounding all three seasons and led Iowa in scoring as a senior. He was twice named Second Team All-Big Ten, and he was a First Team All-American as a senior. Kunnert played nine seasons in the NBA and is a member of Iowa's All-Century Team.

Greg Brunner was a somewhat undersized forward at 6'7", and some questioned whether the product of Charles City High School could be effective in the Big Ten. Brunner answered those questions by starting as a true freshman and improving throughout his four-year career. He led the team in rebounding three straight seasons and led the team in scoring as a junior and senior. He was a Second Team All-Big Ten selection as a junior. In 2006, he led the Big Ten in rebounding and earned First Team All-Big Ten honors, leading Iowa to a second-place finish in the Big Ten. Brunner left Iowa ranked tenth in school history with 1,516 points and broke Kevin Kunnert's school record for career rebounds.

"Bru didn't have a whole lot of offers out of high school. It was like, 'He's a little short, he's not a great shooter, he's a little slow,' and so on. All he did was push himself to get the most out of it where other kids sometimes don't work that hard. Right there with Settles, Street, and Bowen was Greg Brunner. Put 'em all in the same bag, and you pulled out the same trick. You're getting great effort every day."

Mac McCausland

"I'm glad to see that a kid from Iowa is going to get the [career rebounding] record...Doesn't he wear No. 44? So 44's still got the record."

Kevin Kunnert

#45: COVER 1

"Merton Hanks had tremendous athleticism and talent; and what a classy young man. What a class act, and he went on to have a great career at Iowa and a great career in the NFL."

- Dan McCarney

TM

Great football players come in all shapes and sizes. Bob Sanders and Tim Dwight were short, compact, and powerful. Robert Gallery and Bryan Bulaga were lumbering giants. Then there's Merton Hanks.

Former Iowa assistant coach Dan McCarney remembers Hanks' frame when he arrived at Iowa. "Merton Hanks – he had the longest neck. I mean, long arms, long legs…I remember when he first came in, it looked like Merton had never lifted a weight," McCarney said. "You know, he probably hadn't. He was so tough, but I bet Merty wasn't 160 pounds dripping wet when he got here. And we were seriously always worried that Merton might break his neck. You talk about a pencil neck. We always worried about it."

Merton Hanks had a difficult childhood. He was born with a disorder of the central nervous system that causes his hands to shake. After his father was shot and killed while Merton was still a baby, he was raised by his single mother in Dallas, Texas.

> **Merton Hanks came to Iowa City in 1986 in large part due to an appreciation of Coach Hayden Fry. "Hayden was the first coach to have a minority player in the old Southwest Conference at SMU," Hanks said. "My mother remembered that and remembered that he stood up for minorities at a time when it was not always popular to do so and helped break that color barrier in the old Southwest Conference."**

Hanks played both cornerback and safety during his career, and he excelled on special teams. In fact, special teams play is where Hanks first made his mark as a Hawkeye freshman. The 1987 Holiday Bowl matched Iowa with the Wyoming Cowboys in San Diego. It was a low-scoring affair which Wyoming led, 19-7, at halftime. Iowa's lone touchdown in the first half came on a blocked punt by Hanks, which the Hawkeyes returned for a touchdown. Iowa eventually pulled ahead, 20-19, in the fourth quarter before Wyoming attempted a 52-yard field goal as time expired. But Greg Worker's attempt was blocked by Hanks, and Iowa earned their second straight Holiday Bowl victory. Merton had established himself as an impact player with a flair for the dramatic.

Many defenses play with two defensive backs assigned to deep coverage (known as "Cover 2") or sometimes three ("Cover 3"). Because Merton Hanks always displayed great range in the defensive backfield, he gave Iowa defensive coordinator Bill Brashier the luxury of being able to cover a wide area of the field with one person. It was like having Willie Mays in center field.

"I just remember the range he had," recalled McCarney. "When the ball was thrown, you'd say, 'There's no way he could get to that,' but he'd find a way because of tremendous anticipation and timing coming out of a back pedal. He'd make a break on a throw and use the unbelievable range he had to get to the ball when it was in the air."

Hanks attended Iowa at a time of great change in the program. The stability of the 1980s' coaching staff finally gave way to changes. Kirk Ferentz, Dan McCarney, Bernie Wyatt, Bill Dervrich, and Bill Snyder were among Hayden Fry's longtime assistant coaches who left over the span of Hanks' career. But all of Iowa coaches, old and new, loved Hanks' talent and personality.

"Merton Hanks was an absolute favorite of the defensive coordinator, Bill Brashier," longtime Iowa broadcaster Frosty Mitchell said. "Merton Hanks was a riot in the locker room. He would loosen up the team at tense times, because he would do an impersonation in the locker room of Bill Brashier chewing out Merton Hanks. And it would break up the whole defensive team at a real tense time, like when they needed to relax before a game."

Iowa's run of bowl games came to an end in 1989. However, led by Hanks' senior class, Iowa bounced back in a big way in 1990. Wins at Michigan State, at Michigan, and at Illinois highlighted an 8-3 regular season. The 1990 team became Hayden Fry's third and final Rose Bowl team.

Although they again lost to Washington in Pasadena, it was a satisfying culmination to Merton Hanks' time at Iowa. The Hawkeyes were back on the college football landscape as they had been throughout the 1980s. Hanks was named All-Big Ten and a First Team All-American as a senior in 1990. As evidence of his great range defensively, he caught ten interceptions at Iowa and also blocked a school-record seven kicks on special teams.

Hanks went on to a very successful professional career. He was expected by some to go in the first few rounds of the 1991 NFL Draft, but he had an unexpectedly slow 40-yard dash at the NFL scouting combine. This dropped him to a fifth-round selection by the San Francisco 49ers. He was named to the Pro Bowl four times and recorded 33 career interceptions during his nine-year career. He also helped the 49ers to victory in Super Bowl XXIX.

> **Merton Hanks became known for his "Funky Chicken" dance after key touchdowns or interceptions. "It came from watching Bert and Ernie on Sesame Street with my daughters," Hanks said. "We were playing around with it and then…it popped up on game day."**

Merton Hanks currently works as Director of Football Operations and Development for the National Football League. His wife, Marva, earned four letters in women's basketball for the Hawkeyes. Their daughter, Milan, was diagnosed with autism when she was four years old, and the Hanks' spend much of their free time doing charitable work for autism foundations.

Many Iowa fans remember Merton Hanks for his excellent special teams play. Others remember him for his defensive play. Still others remember him for his stellar play as a professional. Regardless of what an individual fan may first recall, Hanks will be remembered by all as one of the great defensive backs in the Hayden Fry era.

Accolades
- First Team All-American (1990)
- All-Big Ten (1990)
- Team MVP (1990)
- Played nine seasons in the NFL; First Team NFL All-Pro (1995)

No. 45 MERTON HANKS

Year	Solo Tackles	Assisted	Total	Interceptions
1987	39	21	60	2
1988	54	32	86	1
1989	39	17	56	3
1990	34	12	46	4
Totals	**166**	**82**	**248**	**10**

How He's Remembered

"One of the things that everyone remembers about Merton was his long neck and the dance he did when he played for the 49ers in the NFL. But the real story about Hanks was that he was one of those players that got better each and every year as a defensive back."

Tom Kakert

"Mert covers more ground than anyone else at his position, and his quick changes of direction surprise a lot of quarterbacks."

Steve Young

"He's like a smaller Ronnie Lott. He doesn't mind sticking his head in there."

Jerry Rice

"He was a great secondary player and went on to a fine pro career with San Francisco. He was definitely an all-timer at Iowa in the secondary. And in the locker room, he was just a team favorite."

Frosty Mitchell

"I'd love to have a football team where all of them emulated Merton Hanks as a person, as a Christian, and as a football player, having the enthusiasm and energy he has."

Hayden Fry

Jersey #45 Honorable Mention

George Peeples – Basketball (1964-66)

George Peeples, a 6'8" center from the Detroit suburb of Ecorse, Michigan, led the freshman basketball team in scoring in 1963 before starting on the varsity team for three seasons. He was a physical player for new coach Ralph Miller in 1965, suffering a broken nose in a win over No. 5 Indiana before returning to help the Hawkeyes upset No. 1 UCLA the following game. He led Iowa in rebounding that year and was a Third Team All-Big Ten pick. As a senior, Peeples again led Iowa in rebounding and helped the Hawkeyes rise to No. 4 in the national rankings. On January 24, 1966, Peeples became the only Hawkeye basketball player ever featured on the cover of *Sports Illustrated* magazine. He was a Second Team All-Big Ten selection as a senior and ranks 39th all-time with 1,025 career points. Peeples played six professional seasons in the ABA, participating in the 1969 ABA Finals as a member of the Indiana Pacers.

Jay Norvell – Football (1982-85)

Jay Norvell was a 6'4", 207-pound strong safety from Madison, Wisconsin. His cousin, Bruce Gear, also started on defense at Iowa for coordinator Bill Brashier. Norvell was a reserve his first two years before becoming Iowa's top special teams player in his junior season. In 1985, he made 76 tackles and led the Big Ten with seven interceptions. He earned All-Big Ten honors that season and shared the team MVP award. He was named Big Ten Player of the Week after intercepting two passes against his hometown Badgers in 1985. Norvell played one season with the Chicago Bears and then began a long career as an assistant coach in college football and in the NFL.

Jonathan Babineaux – Football (2000, 2002-04)

Jonathan Babineaux was a linebacker, fullback, and punter as a high school senior in Port Arthur, Texas. He started three games at fullback for Iowa in 2000 before missing the 2001 season with a broken leg. Babineaux moved to the defensive line prior to the 2002 season, and at that position, he helped lead Iowa to the Big Ten title as a sophomore. He was off to an excellent start in 2003 when his junior season was cut short by another broken leg. As a senior, however, Babineaux bounced back to lead the Big Ten with 11 sacks and finish second in the nation with 25 tackles for loss, a mark that set a modern school record. He was an All-Big Ten selection in 2004 after guiding Iowa to a second conference title. Jonathan Babineaux was named team captain and MVP in 2004. He has played five NFL seasons with the Atlanta Falcons.

#46: SOLID BETTS

"Our first couple years, it was very difficult to block…thank goodness Ladell Betts was a tough back. I'm still trying to figure out how he made the yards he did."

- Kirk Ferentz

A running back is often only as good as the offensive line he has blocking for him. A great offensive line can give an average running back numerous opportunities to make seemingly spectacular plays. But very few running backs are talented enough to stand out without the benefit of a solid offensive line. Ladell Betts was one of those running backs.

Ladell Betts was a star athlete at Blue Springs High School in Missouri. He was named a Parade All-American and the USA Today Missouri Player of the Year. As a senior, he rushed for 2,183 yards and 32 touchdowns while leading his team to a 10-1 record.

> **Ladell Betts played most of his senior season in high school with a broken right hand.**

As a freshman at Iowa, Betts made an immediate impact. He led the team in rushing and set school records for rushing yards in a game and a season by a freshman. After the season, Hall of Fame coach Hayden Fry retired and was replaced by Kirk Ferentz. The coaching change, coupled with injuries and transfers, decimated the offensive line. Betts, a highly-regarded high school prospect, could have considered a transfer himself. He clearly did not expect to play for a struggling, rebuilding team. But abandoning his teammates wasn't Betts' style.

In his first year under Ferentz, Betts led the team in rushing with 857 yards and was named team MVP. *The Kansas City Star* wrote, "Most of Betts' 857 rushing yards…weren't covered with sunshine on his face. Often, he was pushing a lineman or breaking a tackle or finding a detour. His may have been the most punishing 857 yards in Big Ten history. The Hawkeyes had only 1,026 rushing yards for the season. If Betts didn't get them, they pretty much weren't got."

That statement would prove to be prophetic the following season. As a junior in 2000, Ladell Betts accounted for Iowa's *entire* rushing offense. Betts rushed for 1,090 yards, which equaled the entire total of the Hawkeye team. It was the first time in school history that a Hawkeye running back had all of the team's rushing yards for the entire season. If Betts didn't get them, they literally weren't got.

Yet even as Iowa won only seven games in his first three seasons, Betts never complained about the lack of talent around him. He was taking a tremendous physical pounding, but he never called out his teammates who were working hard to improve. With that kind of team-first attitude, it's only fitting that Betts went out a winner.

In his senior season in 2001, Ladell Betts led Iowa in rushing for the fourth straight season. Only this time, the Hawkeyes turned the corner as a team as well. Iowa opened the Big Ten slate against Penn State. Early in the second quarter, Betts injured his left knee and spent the rest of the game limping in and out of the game. Still, he gritted out 95 yards and two touchdowns in a 24-18 win. "Once I get the ball in my hands and the play goes, I don't feel anything," Betts said afterwards.

Iowa stood at 5-4 late in the season, needing just one more win to become bowl-eligible for the first time since 1997. Betts wasn't going to miss his chance to lead his team to a bowl game.

> **In his final conference game against Minnesota, Ladell Betts led Iowa with 171 rushing yards, as Iowa picked up a 42-24 victory, took back Floyd of Rosedale, and clinched an Alamo Bowl berth.**

"He's fast and he hits hard. He makes people miss, and it always takes more than one guy to tackle him. Every yard he's gained, he's earned," teammate Dallas Clark remarked. "Throughout his career, he could have easily pointed fingers when his offensive line was young and immature. But he just kept running hard. His character and personality is what you want as a player."

Though Betts finally succumbed to his injuries in Iowa's Alamo Bowl victory over Texas Tech, he left Iowa with the program back on solid ground. The underappreciated Betts was never named All-Big Ten, but he graduated as Iowa's second-leading rusher with 3,686 career yards. "It's just a privilege, honor, and blessing to wear the black and gold. I'm really grateful for the opportunity to be a Hawkeye," Betts said.

Ladell Betts was drafted by the Washington Redskins in 2002. He was used as a reserve running back for years in Washington, playing behind backs like Stephen Davis, Trung Canidate, and Clinton Portis. An injury to Portis midway through the 2006 season gave Betts a starting spot a year before Betts was due to be a free agent. With the spotlight finally on him, Betts sparkled. He had five straight 100-yard games and became the first Redskin to ever rush for 150 yards in consecutive games. After such a tremendous season, Betts could have sought a starting job in the NFL, with all the money and fame that accompanies such a job.

Instead, Betts surprised many by re-signing for less money with Washington, willingly agreeing to remain in relative anonymity as Clinton Portis' backup. "I like the group of guys we have in the locker room," Betts explained. "I didn't feel like relocating...I just felt comfortable here. To me, being comfortable is more important than the money. That's just me, though."

Yes, that's just Ladell. Hawkeye fans already knew Betts was a loyal, team-oriented guy that supported his teammates, no matter what. Playing behind an overmatched offensive line is a tough job, but thankfully for Iowa, Ladell Betts was one of the toughest and most durable backs in school history. For that, he remains one of the most admired backs to ever play for the Hawkeyes.

Accolades

• Team captain (1999, 2001)
• Led team in rushing (1998, 99, 00, 01)
• Ranks second in school history in career rushing yards
• Has played seven seasons in the NFL

No. 46 LADELL BETTS

Year	Att	Yards	Avg	TDs	Long	Recept	Yards	TDs
1998	188	679	3.6	5	40	20	259	0
1999	189	857	4.5	5	74	20	195	1
2000	232	1,090	4.8	10	42	17	111	0
2001	222	1,060	4.8	10	42	15	137	1
Totals	831	3,686	4.4	30	74	72	702	2

How He's Remembered

"Betts is part mule, part armadillo. He's durable, stubborn, impenetrable."

Marc Morehouse

"I'll say this, he slammed that thing against Minnesota about as hard as I've seen anybody run. I told Ladell... 'Look at the whole year, what you did. You didn't say squat, you played special teams, you ran back kicks, [and] when you got an opportunity, you rushed for over [100] yards.' Ladell, I sure like him as a football player. I think there's a lot of stuff to him."

Joe Gibbs

"I'll always wonder what kind of numbers Betts could have put up if he would have had a better offensive line during his career, especially as a sophomore and a junior. Those were the early years for Kirk Ferentz and the line was pretty thin and small, yet Betts was always grinding out yards, which was pretty amazing. He was a real tough runner who had a lot of heart."

Tom Kakert

"Ladell Betts could make the first tackler miss better than anyone. It was a good thing because we didn't open many holes until his senior year. Even when there was no hole, he found a way to make positive yards. He was very unselfish and did his job without complaining. He was a team guy."

Ken O'Keefe

"He's a guy you want when you're up by four with four minutes left – you give the ball to him five straight times and run the clock out. He's that type of back. He runs hard, gets extra yards, falls forward, catches the ball out of the backfield...He's a very smart football player, and he's a very good guy. He's a good teammate. I mean, what more do you want?"

Matt Bowen

<u>Jersey #46 Honorable Mention</u>

Sharm Scheuerman – Basketball (1954-56)
Milton "Sharm" Scheuerman was a member of the "Fabulous Five" that played in the 1955 and 1956 Final Fours. He was a Second Team All-Big Ten selection in 1955, and he played three seasons of baseball in addition to basketball. His number 46 was retired at Iowa. When his playing career ended, Scheuerman became Iowa's freshman basketball coach and was promoted to head coach after Bucky O'Connor's untimely death in 1958. Scheuerman coached Iowa for six seasons; his 1961 team finished No. 8 in the final AP rankings. He was later an analyst for Hawkeye basketball, on the radio with Jim Zabel and on television alongside Bob Hogue. Scheuerman was also the assistant coach for Team USA in the 1995 Pan American Games.

#47: A ROYAL DISRUPTION

"That kid King is a really good football player – maybe as good of a defensive lineman as we've played against."

- Joe Paterno (2008)

It's good to be King.

In 2008, the Big Ten Conference named Mitch King their Defensive Lineman of the Year. But if you ask the former linebacker-turned-defensive tackle, he'd say he had lots of help along his way to being named tops in the Big Ten trenches. His teammate and close friend Matt Kroul started 50 consecutive games at the other tackle spot. Together, they epitomized Norm Parker's simple defensive philosophy of "six seconds of hell" each and every play.

King signed with Iowa in 2004 as a three-star linebacker out of Burlington High School. He saw his first action as a redshirt freshman in 2005. Instead of patrolling the field as a linebacker, however, he began playing with one hand on the ground. The stout 2004 defensive line was senior-laden, anchored by Matt Roth and Jonathan Babineaux. This opened it up to underclassmen the following year when King and Kroul became the two primary defensive tackles.

Early in the 2005 season, the defensive front had clearly taken a step back from 2004's dominant unit. As the year progressed, however, this young group began to gain its own identity as a scrappy bunch. They were undersized as far as Big Ten defensive tackles go, but they were showing potential. Mitch King first made a name for himself at Wisconsin that year. He was downright disruptive to the Badger offense during Barry Alvarez's last home game in Madison.

> **Mitch King finished with two quarterback sacks and four tackles for loss against Wisconsin in 2006, which earned him Big Ten Defensive Player of the Week honors.**

His impact late that season didn't go unnoticed. No less than four media outlets named King to their Freshman All-American Team. He was even named Honorable Mention All-Big Ten that year. The Hawkeyes finished with a 7-5 record and a loss in the Outback Bowl.

King began the 2006 season firmly entrenched in the starting lineup. Though he missed some time due to an injury, he had a solid year with 56 tackles and seven quarterback sacks. One of the most memorable moments in the 2006 season occurred in a non-conference game against Syracuse. The Hawkeyes and Orange battled to two overtimes, and in the second overtime, Iowa held a 20-13 lead. Syracuse needed a touchdown to extend the game to a third overtime period, and they had first and goal from the two-yard line. King and the Iowa defense repelled the Orange offense for three plays before being called for a pass interference penalty, giving Syracuse another first down at the two-yard line. That penalty might have demoralized some defenses, but King and his teammates were undeterred. The Hawks held Syracuse out of the end zone on four more plays, stopping the opposition on a total of eight consecutive plays inside their own five-yard line to win, 20-13.

Iowa went 6-7 in 2006, ending the season with a loss in the Alamo Bowl. After six consecutive bowl appearances, the 2007 season was disappointing to many. The Hawkeyes finished 6-6 in King's junior season and missed an opportunity for a seventh straight bowl game when they lost to Western Michigan at home in the final game of the season. Individually, King was named All-Big Ten in his junior season.

2008 brought about lower expectations for Iowa in King's senior season, and for the first half of the year, the Hawks lived up to them. Close losses to Pittsburgh, Northwestern, and Michigan State left Iowa at 3-3. Time and again, however, Coach Kirk Ferentz spoke highly of the leadership being provided from seniors such as King and insisted that they were close to turning things around.

He was right, and Iowa rebounded to win five of their next six games. While Shonn Greene bowled over opponents on his way to the Doak Walker Award, it was Iowa's defense that sealed the deal against most opponents. Iowa gave up only 13 points per game, and nobody played a bigger role than King. With his 15.5 tackles for loss, he was the heart and soul of the defense. Even prior to taking the field every game, the entire team circled around King for his pregame pep talk. With his Samson-like long blonde hair flowing, King rallied the troops.

> **In the week leading up to Senior Day 2008, Mitch King's long, blonde locks of hair were cropped to a very short haircut. Going into the Purdue game, he seemingly transformed his appearance from a biblical Sampson to that of an oversized Opie Taylor.**

Iowa finished the regular season by defeating Minnesota, 55-0, in the Gophers' final game ever played in the Metrodome. The win set the stage for a New Year's Day game against South Carolina in the Outback Bowl. In the Hawkeye Huddle pep rally before the game, King exuded emotion as he said, "I'm more of a Hawkeye this week than I have ever been." He then mentioned that unlike South Carolina, the Iowa team had been proudly wearing their school colors all weekend. King then screamed, "That's what Hawkeye pride is!" Iowa continued its end-of-season momentum and took a 31-0 lead in the game before winning, 31-10.

"I knew we'd win last week," said King in early January. "We knew if we prepared well, if we played well and mistake-free, we had this game won. I cannot wait to sit in my living room next year and watch [Iowa] play. They'll be a great team."

Mitch King didn't have eye-popping statistics in any of his four years, but his persistence and incessant pressure on the opposing offense set him apart. He countered his lack of size with quickness. By spinning and twisting his way through blockers, King was like the Tasmanian Devil on Saturday cartoons with a voracious appetite for the ball carrier.

Even if he didn't make the play, he absorbed double-teams so another defender could; he was that one player who every opposing coach had to account for.

One coach who didn't have to account for him was Kirk Ferentz. Ferentz praised King for how he had made himself accountable to his team for four years at Iowa. "For Mitch to do what he did is absolutely phenomenal," said Ferentz. "Maybe the thing I appreciate most about him is the work behind the scenes. Mitch was out there setting a great example."

Accolades
• Second Team All-American (2008)
• All-Big Ten (2007, 08)
• Team captain and MVP (2008)
• Big Ten Defensive Lineman of the Year (2008)

No. 47 MITCH KING

Year	Solo Tackles	Assisted	Total	Tackle/loss	Sacks	PBU
2005	36	24	60	11/28	2/7	3
2006	35	21	56	14/49	7/35	2
2007	25	33	58	14.5/77	4.5/45	7
2008	27	27	54	15.5/65	4/37	0
Totals	123	105	228	55/219	17.5/124	12

How He's Remembered

"He's as good a college football player as we've had since we've been here on defense."

Norm Parker

"He's the toughest kid I've ever played against, I'll be honest with you. As a defensive tackle, he's got everything you want. He's got a great motor, plays with intensity, strong as an ox. He's big, he's fast, he never quits."

A.Q. Shipley, Penn State center

"They broke the mold after Mitch. He's one of a kind. He's always got something to say."

A.J. Edds

"Mitch King is a heavy-metal concert locked inside a 280-pound bowling ball. From the long, blond hair that tips his shoulders to his on-field swagger, King breathes real life into University of Iowa football with a wild streak that stretches from Iowa City to his hometown of Burlington. He'll say anything or do anything to get the job done."

Scott Dochterman, *The Cedar Rapids Gazette*

Jersey #47 Honorable Mention

Homer Harris – Football (1935-37)

Homer Harris was a trailblazer at Garfield High School in Seattle, where he was the first African-American to captain his high school's football team. Since black football players were not welcomed at the University of Washington at the time, Harris went to Iowa on the advice of his coach, Leon Brigham, who had earned four letters at Iowa in track and baseball from 1918-1920. Harris started a few games at end as a sophomore, helping Iowa to a 4-2-2 record. He was a defensive mainstay as a junior, and he was voted 1936 team MVP over Ozzie Simmons by one vote. That led to Harris being named as the Hawkeyes' team captain in 1937 and becoming the first African-American to captain a Big Ten football team. Unfortunately, injuries to his teammates forced him to shift to tackle and play out of position for most of his final season. Harris coached North Carolina A&T in 1940 while he earned his medical degree. He later became a well-known Seattle dermatologist. Harris was inducted into the University of Iowa Hall of Fame in 2002.

Tom Rusk – Football (1975-78)

Tom Rusk was a First Team All-State fullback at Dubuque Hempstead High School, and he also won the state championship in wrestling at 185 pounds. Although he played fullback as a freshman at Iowa, Coach Bob Commings moved him to the middle linebacker position prior to his sophomore season. Rusk promptly led the Hawkeyes in tackles for the next three seasons, becoming one of the most fearsome tacklers the Hawkeyes have ever had. He was an All-Big Ten selection as a junior and was named team captain the following year.   Rusk left Iowa ranked second in career tackles with 361. He then spent one season wrestling at heavyweight for Dan Gable before playing three seasons in the Canadian Football League.

#48: HODGE BALL

"The one thing that Howard learned to do is take his athletic ability and put together technique, understanding pad level, and hand placement, as opposed to being caught up in how much he weighs."

- Ron Aiken

Great defensive ends often have large statures and even larger personalities. Though Howard Hodges possessed neither of these qualities, he nevertheless developed into one of the best players the Hawkeyes have ever had at the position and challenged the stereotype of what a great defensive end must be.

Howard Hodges was raised in Copperas Cove, Texas. Coach Kirk Ferentz brought Hodges to Iowa as part of his first recruiting class. Hodges was initially an outside linebacker for the Hawkeyes. After redshirting in 1999, he joined Aaron Kampman in making the move from linebacker to defensive end. As with Kampman, the move would pay off for Hodges.

Hodges made his presence felt almost immediately. In his first career game, he recorded five tackles and one tackle for loss. He appeared to force a fumble against Kansas State quarterback Michael Beasley before the officials ruled Beasley down. The game foreshadowed a promising career for the freshman, who had not yet played extensive minutes. Though Hodges' sophomore year in 2001 was cut short by a foot injury suffered against Wisconsin, the graduation of Kampman opened up a starting spot on the defensive line. Hodges would quickly claim the starting spot as his own.

> As a junior in 2002, Howard Hodges earned All-Big Ten honors as a key member of Iowa's Big Ten championship team that ranked fifth in the nation in rushing defense.

Hodges made a habit of coming up big in Iowa's biggest games. He had six tackles, three tackles for loss, two quarterback sacks, and three quarterback pressures in Iowa's 34-9 victory at Michigan in 2002. It was the Wolverines' largest margin of defeat at home in 35 years.

With the conference championship on the line, Iowa traveled to Minnesota, hoping to seal Iowa's first undefeated Big Ten season since 1922. Hawkeye fans invaded the Metrodome to see the Hawkeyes hold the top rushing offense in the conference to 80 rushing yards. "I looked to my left during warm-ups, and all I saw was black and gold," Hodges remarked about the Hawkeye fans. Hodges didn't disappoint those fans.

With Iowa leading, 14-7, he forced a fumble while sacking the Gopher quarterback and recovered it himself to set Iowa up with a short field. That led to a 15-yard drive for a touchdown and gave Iowa a two-touchdown lead. In the second half with Iowa leading, 28-14, Hodges forced another turnover in Minnesota territory. The fumble was recovered by Derek

Pagel and eventually led to another Iowa touchdown, putting the game out of reach. Iowa defeated the Gophers, 45-21, to clinch the Big Ten title.

Howard Hodges spent his senior season in 2003 paired at defensive end with Matt Roth. Their two personalities could not have been more different. Roth had a classic defensive end's attitude – excitable, colorful, and just a little bit crazy. Naturally, Roth grabbed the spotlight and quickly became a fan favorite. By contrast, Hodges was an easygoing Texan off the field. Only when the whistle sounded did Hodges' relentless energy come to the forefront. For all their differences, Roth and Hodges became a perfect pair.

Hodges' final game at Kinnick Stadium was a rematch with the Golden Gophers. Minnesota had a 9-2 record and another highly-regarded rushing offense. While Bob Sanders stole the show on that day for the Hawkeyes, Hodges also haunted the Gophers again by recording 12 tackles on Senior Day. Iowa held the potent Minnesota offense without a touchdown for the first 55 minutes of the game while building an insurmountable 40-6 lead. "I don't think we really cared too much about people hyping them up on offense," Hodges responded. "It was more like – they're coming into Kinnick and they wanted to run across the field and take Floyd from us. You don't come into Kinnick thinking you're going to just get a win. You're going to have to work for a win." Overall, Hodges placed third in the Big Ten in sacks in 2003 with 12, tied with Matt Roth.

> **The final sack of Howard Hodges' Hawkeye career came against Chris Leak of Florida, as Iowa's defense held the Gators to just 57 rushing yards in a 37-17 win in the 2004 Outback Bowl.**

Hodges spent years bouncing around professional football, playing for the NFL, NFL Europe, the Arena Football League, and the Canadian Football League. Hodges signed with the Calgary Stampeders of the CFL in 2008, starting 15 games. He started at defensive tackle for the Stampeders as Calgary defeated Montreal, 22-14, for the 2008 Grey Cup.

Howard Hodges was not a prototypical defensive end. While he was cool and laidback off the field, he played with a focused aggressiveness on it. Hodges displayed a passion and intensity that negated what some critics had dismissed as a small frame. Howard Hodges overcame that skepticism and proved, once again, that it's the size of a player's heart that truly counts.

Accolades
- All-Big Ten (2002)
- Team captain (2003)
- Recorded 142 career tackles and 21 career sacks
- Started for Calgary's Grey Cup championship team (2008)

No. 48 HOWARD HODGES						
Year	Solo Tackles	Assisted	Total	Tackle/loss	Sacks	PBU
2000	10	8	18	¼	0/0	4
2001	4	5	9	½	0/0	4
2002	42	20	62	11/56	9/52	17
2003	42	11	53	13/61	12/58	3
Totals	98	44	142	26/123	21/110	28

How He's Remembered

"Hodges' trip to First Team All-Conference has been unconventional, to say the least...Hodges was another Ferentz recruit that ignored measurements and played way bigger than his 6'2", 250 [-pound frame]."

Marc Morehouse

"Are they going to double Howard, or are they going to double Matt Roth? That can cause problems for people when they start to scheme and set up a gameplan for protecting the quarterback."

Ron Aiken

"I came in with this class when Iowa wasn't doing too good. I always knew I was in a good program. But it takes time to win a championship and win big games."

Howard Hodges

#49: A HOOSIER STATE HAWKEYE

"I don't know if I've ever coached an athlete as good as he is. He can do so many things, and he can do a lot of things that guys his size just normally can't do."
                         - Rick Wimmer, Edds' high school coach

True leadership is exhibited by those who step up in those critical times when they are needed most. From 2006-2009, A.J. Edds provided the Hawkeyes with intelligent, steady leadership, and his largely unheralded play at outside linebacker was a key ingredient in Iowa's first BCS-level bowl win in 51 years.

A.J. Edds grew up in Greenwood, Indiana, and had excellent guidance on his path to college football. His father, David, lettered in football at Indiana University in 1972. A.J.'s coach at Greenwood High School was Rick Wimmer. Wimmer had coached Jamel Williams, who went on to win two mythical national championships with the Nebraska Cornhuskers, and Eugene Wilson, who won two Super Bowls with the New England Patriots. With his father and coach guiding him, A.J. Edds committed to Iowa over offers from Purdue and Georgia Tech.

Edds was both a linebacker and a tight end in high school, and he was recruited to Iowa as a tight end. But with Scott Chandler, Ryan Majerus, and Tony Moeaki ahead of him on the depth chart, Edds quickly shifted to the linebacker position. Learning defense at the college level was a trial by fire for Edds. "It was touch and go for awhile, but I got my feet on the ground eventually. There were a couple of times…in practice I would look around, find Mike Humpal, and say, 'What just happened?' There were definitely days like that," Edds remarked.

A.J. Edds played as a true freshman on special teams and backup linebacker, and he made his first start in a 47-17 win over his former suitor – Purdue. He was named as an Honorable Mention Freshman All-American after the season by *The Sporting News*. Coach Kirk Ferentz had been hesitant earlier in his coaching career to rely on true freshmen, but he would later point to Edds' rapid improvement in play as one of the major reasons why he changed his philosophy on utilizing first-year players.

Edds secured a starting linebacker spot as a sophomore. He had a great year individually in 2007, recording 80 tackles, but the Hawkeyes missed a bowl game for the first time in seven years. After the season, Ferentz told the team that their off-season workouts would be tougher than anything they had ever experienced. "He told us if you weren't all in, you're not going to make it," Edds recalled. "Our coaches laid it out there and gave us an ultimatum. You're going to figure it out, or you're not going to be part of this team."

The coaches called upon Edds to assume a leadership role, and that's exactly what he did. "I need to step up," he said at the time. "The team's kind of looking around for leadership. It's on me to make sure everyone is on the same page." Part of that leadership role involved approaching his linebacking mate, Pat Angerer.

Angerer possessed a world of talent, but he needed to focus harder to realize his full potential. Edds was one of the players that challenged Angerer to get serious about football. "I think I helped a little, just talking to him and knowing how good he could be," Edds admitted. Angerer and Edds developed into a ferocious tandem at linebacker for the next two seasons.

As part of a revamped defense, Edds immediately helped get the Hawkeyes back on the right track in 2008. In the first half of Iowa's 2008 season opener, he sacked Maine quarterback Adam Farkes for a safety, the only points of Edds' career. Edds was named Honorable Mention All-Big Ten, as he led the Hawkeyes to a 9-4 record and a January bowl berth.

> **In 2008, A.J. Edds recorded a career-high eleven tackles in a 24-23 upset of second-ranked Penn State, and he recovered two fumbles in an Outback Bowl win over South Carolina.**

Edds' senior season in 2009 was a special one. Iowa's first conference game was a road match against No. 4 Penn State. The Nittany Lions had been undefeated a season earlier before being upset in Iowa City, and they were looking to exact some revenge on the Hawkeyes. But Edds intercepted a pass with less than four minutes remaining to help lead Iowa to a 21-10 win. It was Iowa's first road win over a team ranked in the top four in the nation since winning at Wisconsin in 1958.

The Hawkeyes' next road game in 2009 was, coincidentally, in Madison against the 5-1 Badgers. A win would give Iowa its seventh victory to start the season, tying the school record. The Hawkeye defense limited Wisconsin to just 87 rushing yards and 243 yards total, and Edds came up with another fourth-quarter interception to clinch a 20-10 victory.

The fourth-ranked Hawks still had a perfect record two weeks later when they hosted Indiana. It looked as though the streak would be shattered when the Hoosiers jumped out to a 21-7 lead midway through the third quarter. Indiana had the ball on the Hawkeye two-yard line when Hoosier quarterback Ben Chappell dropped back to pass. Edds deflected the pass, which bounced off of the arm of defensive lineman Christian Ballard. The ball then ricocheted off of two Hoosier defenders before bouncing off of Edds' back and into the arms of Hawkeye safety Tyler Sash, who ran the interception back 86 yards for a touchdown. The "pinball interception" kept Iowa in the game, and the Hawkeyes scored 28 unanswered fourth-quarter points to win, 42-24, and run their record to 9-0.

Iowa later lost the de facto Big Ten title game at Ohio State in overtime. Edds made a career-high seven solo tackles in the loss. Still, the Hawkeyes defeated Minnesota the following week to move within one victory of the single-season school record for wins. The final game of Edds' collegiate career would be the 2010 Orange Bowl against Georgia Tech, another of the schools Edds considered attending coming out of high school.

The Hawkeyes' last four appearances in BCS-level bowl games had been disasters. Iowa had lost the 1982, 1986, and 1991 Rose Bowls and the 2003 Orange Bowl, allowing a combined 157 points in those four games. The Hawkeyes had trailed at some point in each of those games by at least 25 points. Not only was Iowa 0-4 in their last four BCS-level bowl appearances, but they had been blown out in each one. Edds and his defensive teammates were determined to rewrite that history against a potent triple-option Georgia Tech offense.

> **For the third time in the 2009 season, A.J. Edds picked off a key fourth-quarter pass, and the Hawkeye defense held the Yellow Jackets to just 155 yards of offense in a 24-14 win.**

Georgia Tech had averaged 35.3 points per game in the 2009 regular season, but the Iowa defense limited them to just one offensive touchdown. The Yellow Jackets' 12 yards passing were the fewest in an Orange Bowl in 49 years. Tech had only had 14 three-and-out possessions in the regular season; Iowa forced five in the first half alone. No. 9 Georgia Tech was the highest-ranked bowl opponent Iowa had ever defeated, and the Hawks ended the year ranked seventh in the country, Iowa's highest final ranking since 1960.

Edds was a three-time Academic All-Big Ten selection, and he was also instrumental in helping his friend Pat Angerer blossom into a First Team All-American. Edds and Angerer developed a close friendship, despite some good-natured needling. "He doesn't have a lot of friends, so I've got to help him out, you know?" Angerer laughed. "He's fun to play with and obviously a good player," Edds admitted. "That said, he's short, dumb, and ugly." Angerer countered, "I'm better looking than he is. I think the biggest surprise is that a guy that ugly managed to get a girlfriend."

Defensive end Adrian Clayborn has admiration for both men. "They provide a lot of leadership," the Orange Bowl MVP said. "Pat, he's a crazy, crazy person, but he keeps us up. A.J., he's so smart, and he just gives us knowledge throughout the game and in practice."

A.J. Edds' leadership and intelligence helped right the ship of Iowa football and lead the Hawks to a 20-6 record over his final two seasons. As an outside linebacker, Edds' impact cannot be measured in mere statistics. "A.J.'s playing out there at a position that's so key to our defense, yet it's not as pronounced because statistically, that's just how it works out. But we can't play good defense without somebody in that position," Ferentz observed.

"Our defense is kind of built for our inside guys and the safeties to make plays," said Edds. "The outside linebacker, in theory, is kind of an edge defender, kind of an outside guy to force it all back in, which seems pretty mundane. If you can do it the right way, you can still find a way to make some plays out there, I guess."

A.J. Edds is living proof of that.

Accolades
• Team captain (2009)
• Recorded 226 career tackles and seven career interceptions
• Made 38 consecutive career starts
• Selected for the Senior Bowl (2010)

No. 49 AJ EDDS

Year	Solo Tackles	Assisted	Total	Tackle/loss	Sacks	Int
2006	4	5	9	0.5/0	0	0
2007	29	51	80	3.5/5	0	1
2008	18	41	59	4.5/19	2	1
2009	25	53	78	4.5/8	0.5	5
Totals	76	150	226	13/32	2.5	7

How He's Remembered

"He's a great player, and he's a good friend. It's so fun playing out there with him. He's done such a great job for this team, and his career's been unbelievable. You can't script it up any better. I mean, he started as a true freshman, and he's started every year. You know, you go out there and you want to fight for guys like that, fight for guys you care about a lot."

Pat Angerer

"Edds is probably going after Gary Barta's job as soon as he gets out of football. Fortunately, he wants to go into administration, not coaching, or maybe he'll be president of a bank or something like that. That's what he looks like."

Kirk Ferentz

"Edds was a three-year starter who was a virtuoso at outside linebacker. Everything about [him] was sound...Filling Edds' shoes is going to be a gigantic challenge. Edds was the gold standard at this position."

Marc Morehouse

"The biggest thing is it's easy to talk the talk, if you will, but the way you really earn respect...as far as your teammates valuing what you do is by showing up and working everyday and doing what you need to on a daily basis."

A.J. Edds

#50: POINT FORWARD

"I was a point forward before they called it a point forward. I ran the show – took all the weight off the guards."
                                          - John Johnson

John Johnson was the original "point forward," a player whose skills were so unique that the NBA defined a whole new position for him. In the process, he literally changed the way the pro game is played. Long before that, Johnson had his own definition of "point forward," rewriting the Iowa record books as one of the greatest scorers the University of Iowa has ever seen.

John Johnson was a key contributor to Iowa head coach Ralph Miller's successful teams in the late 1960s. Like Sam Williams and Fred Brown, John Johnson also came to Miller's teams via junior college. He attended Powell Junior College in Wyoming for two years prior to arriving in Iowa City. Both he and Fred Brown were Milwaukee, Wisconsin, natives.

> **John Johnson signed a letter of intent with the Hawkeyes in May 1968 but nearly switched his commitment to Utah State a few weeks later. After two tense months of waiting, J.J. decided to stick with his decision to attend Iowa.**

Only three games into his Iowa career, his home state of Wisconsin saw first-hand what they missed out on. On December 7, 1968, Johnson scored 46 points in a 116-80 trouncing of the University of Wisconsin-Milwaukee. It set a single-game scoring record for Iowa, topping Dick Ives' 43 points in 1944. Coach Miller knew early on that he had gained someone special. "John is an extraordinary player, and I expected him to have a great year," said Coach Miller, "but his shooting has been close to fantastic."

Ironically enough, it was his shot that many people – his coach included – wanted to change. Longtime Iowa announcer Ron Gonder remembers Johnson's shooting style very well. "The thing that was most remarkable about him was that for a player who was such an accurate shooter and such a high-scoring player, he had a very, very flat shot," said Gonder. "For a player to have that accuracy with a flat shot, could you imagine what he would have done with an elevated shot…that has the proper arch on it? That's the most distinguishing thing about Johnson."

Iowa's team of 1968-69 was dominated by juniors, Johnson included. They had moderate success that season. They started 10-4, but once they got into the heart of the Big Ten season, they only won two of their last ten to finish at 12-12. Scoring points was clearly not their problem; they scored 90 points or greater eight times. Unfortunately, their opponents were keeping pace.

Individually, it was a wildly successful debut season for Johnson. He averaged 20 points per game to lead Iowa in scoring, just ahead of Chad Calabria and Glenn Vidnovic. Johnson also averaged more than ten rebounds a game. All that remained was to improve the team's performance in the Big Ten.

As the calendar turned to another season, the four junior starters became seniors with one addition. Miller had successfully recruited Fred Brown to join the team from Southeastern Community College in Burlington, Iowa. The pieces seemed to be in place for an improved finish in the Big Ten.

The season of 1969-70 began much like the previous season ended. By the end of December, the Hawkeyes sat at 4-4 with the Big Ten slate awaiting them. League-favorite Purdue was Iowa's next opponent, and they featured the great Rick Mount. Despite Mount's 53 points, Iowa defeated the Boilermakers in Iowa City, 94-88. It was an encouraging win, but hardly anyone could have imagined that this Hawkeye squad wouldn't lose again until March.

Iowa began to roll through the Big Ten schedule – 107 points against Michigan; 119 points against Wisconsin; 115 points against Northwestern. They simply outscored people with their multifaceted offense of Johnson, Brown, Calabria, and Vidnovic. Even Ben McGilmer, Iowa's sixth man, averaged over 10 points per game. Teams could stop one of Coach Miller's "Six Pack" on a given night, but another would step up in his place.

John Johnson was the highest scorer of them all, averaging 27.9 points per game. It still remains the highest season scoring average in Iowa history. Johnson took a lot of shots, but they were quality attempts, as he set a school record for shooting percentage (57 percent) in a season. He scored 31 points or greater nine times that year. Coupled with his ten rebounds per game, it was as fine a season as a Hawkeye has ever had.

"Probably the most proficient and efficient offensive player I've ever seen at Iowa," said basketball analyst Mac McCausland. "There wasn't much he couldn't do with his game...he was one of the first players I saw go between his legs and behind his back but always progressing to the basket to score. He had some definite 'playground' shots, which most people would think were a little awkward, but his efficiency was unbelievable."

Iowa went on to set a Big Ten record by scoring 102.9 points per game in 1969-70. Their run of 16 straight wins came to an unfortunate end early in the NCAA Tournament. Jacksonville edged the Hawkeyes, as a last-second basket gave Jacksonville the 104-103 win. Jacksonville was the eventual NCAA runner-up, but it was a crushing defeat for Iowa. Hawkeye fans, players, and coaches alike felt this team could have brought home Iowa's first national championship.

> **Despite scoring 27.9 points per game as a senior (and 31.8 in Big Ten play), John Johnson did not lead the Big Ten in scoring. That honor went to Rick Mount of Purdue and his amazing 39.4 points per game.**

In those days, teams played consolation games in the tournament, and the Hawks drew Notre Dame. They blew out the Irish, 121-106, in John Johnson's final game as a Hawkeye. Iowa's 121 points set an NCAA Tournament record for a regulation game, and it remains the fifth-most points ever scored in a regulation NCAA Tournament game. "When I walked in the building, I saw the score was 34-13," Kentucky coach Adolph Rupp said. "Then I sat down and watched it. They should have stopped that game and said, 'That's enough. You've convinced everybody.' That Iowa is a hell of a team."

John Johnson finished just one-tenth of a point behind Sam Williams for the highest career scoring average at Iowa. He also earned First Team All-American honors as a senior. By all measures, it was a remarkable career.

John Johnson was drafted seventh overall by the expansion Cleveland Cavaliers in the 1970 NBA Draft; he was the first Hawkeye basketball player drafted in the top ten and the first ever draft choice of the Cavs. He was an NBA All-Star in his first two seasons with the Cavaliers. It was with Cleveland that Johnson first played with Hall of Fame point guard Lenny Wilkens. J.J. would play with and under Wilkens in 1975 with the Portland Trail Blazers, where Wilkens was the team's player-coach.

Wilkens moved on to become the director of player personnel with the Seattle Supersonics. He made a trade to acquire John Johnson a week into the 1977-78 season, where J.J. was reunited with Fred Brown. After Seattle coach Bob Hopkins started the year 5-17, Wilkens fired him and named himself head coach. Wilkens immediately altered the offense, starting Johnson at small forward and giving him instructions to distribute the ball. "I knew J.J. had a great understanding of the game," Wilkens said, "and so, after he'd rebound, I'd tell our guards, 'Just take off, and he'll find you.'"

The "point forward" position was born. The new offense confounded opponents. Johnson's ball handling and rebounding abilities allowed the Sonics' guards to race down the floor on the fast break. The Sonics went 42-18 the rest of the year and made it all the way to the NBA Finals. The following season, Seattle won their only NBA championship in franchise history. J.J. led the team in assists while "Downtown" Freddie Brown poured in 14 points per game.

Years later, "point forwards" like Larry Bird and Scottie Pippen would popularize the notion of having a forward handle the ball and initiate the offense. The idea originated, however, when the Supersonics wisely adapted to John Johnson's unique skills and zoomed to consecutive NBA Finals appearances. J.J. was unlike anything the NBA had ever seen before. Hawkeye fans already knew that feeling well.

Accolades
• First Team All-American (1970)
• First Team All-Big Ten (1970)
• Holds school records for points in a game and a season
• Played 12 seasons in the NBA; NBA All-Star (1971, 72)
• Selected to Iowa's All-Century basketball team (2002)

No. 50 JOHN JOHNSON

Year	GP	FG-FGA	FG%	FT-FTA	FT%	Reb	Avg	Pts	Avg
1969	24	174-344	51%	125-186	63%	256	10.7	473	19.7
1970	25	289-508	57%	121-161	75%	253	10.1	699	27.9
Totals	49	463-852	54%	246-347	71%	509	10.4	1,172	23.9

How He's Remembered

"John Johnson was the leader. He scored an Iowa-record 49 points in a conference game against Northwestern. It's still the Iowa record. There used to be a trivia question when Babe Ruth held the home run record at 60, who was No. 2? Well, that was Babe Ruth also – he had 59. This was the same in John Johnson's case. Who has the second-highest game point total? John Johnson does – he had 46 the season before."

Ron Gonder

"John Johnson was a great all-around player. He was a great shooter and a great passer. He and Fred Brown together were probably the best twosome that Iowa ever had. They were a dynamic twosome in the pros, too."

Buck Turnbull

"John was real smooth. He and Freddy Brown were really two great ones for Iowa at the same time. John was a really fine passer, too, along with being a good shooter, and he had a nice career in the NBA, too."

Sharm Scheuerman

"Johnson is the best all-around forward in the country...There is no doubt in my mind that John could score 40 points a game. But he knows we would not be a consistent winner that way, and above all else, he is a team player."

Ralph Miller

Jersey #50 Honorable Mention

William "Bill" Van Buren – Football (1955, 1960-61)

Bill Van Buren played linebacker and center for Coach Forest Evashevski's Hawkeye football team. A product of Lorain, Ohio, Van Buren suffered through ankle injuries during his sophomore season in 1955. He soon dropped out of school and joined the Army, and he spent four years in Germany playing and coaching football. Van Buren returned to Iowa as a junior in 1960 and was a starter for Evashevski's 1960 Big Ten championship team. As a senior under new coach Jerry Burns, Van Buren served as the Hawkeyes' team captain and was selected as a First Team All-American after the 1961 season.

Howard "Hap" Peterson – Football (1982-85)

Hap Peterson was a football player and wrestler at Bettendorf High School, earning All-State honors in both sports and winning the state heavyweight wrestling title as a senior. Peterson played nine games as a freshman before being sidelined with a leg injury. He earned a starting spot as a sophomore at nose guard, and he would start for his final three years with the Hawkeyes. Peterson had a fine year as a sophomore, winning defensive MVP honors in Iowa's 1983 victory over Ohio State. He was hampered in his junior season by a knee injury, but he returned for the 1984 Freedom Bowl against Texas, where he posted three tackles for loss, two sacks, a forced fumble, and a fumble recovery. Peterson was a team captain of the 1985 Hawkeyes that won the Big Ten title. He was an All-Conference selection and an Honorable Mention All-American as a senior.

The End Zone

1: Heisman Trophy winner at Iowa

2: Rose Bowl victories

3: Iowa's appearances in the basketball Final Four

4: Heisman runners-up

5: Number of future Big Ten or Big XII head coaches on Hayden Fry's 1985 staff

6: Touchdowns thrown by Chuck Long versus Texas in 1984 Freedom Bowl

7: Number of months it took to build Kinnick Stadium

8: Final national ranking after the 2002, 2003, and 2004 football seasons

9: Blocked shots by Acie Earl versus Wisconsin on January 29, 1992

10: Points scored versus Nebraska in September 12, 1981, upset in Iowa City

11: Number of weeks the Iowa football team has spent at No. 1 in the nation

12: State high school track championships won by Tim Dwight

13: In 1981, Iowa's football opponents averaged 13 points per game; in 1973, opponents averaged 36 points per game.

14: The Hawkeyes had a 14-0 Big Ten basketball record in 1970.

15: Number of consecutive home Big Ten wins by 2001-2005 football teams

16: Iowa wrestling was named the 16th best dynasty of the 20th century by *Sports Illustrated* in 1999.

17: Conference game winning streak of Ohio State ended by the 1956 Hawkeyes in football

18: Career interception record held by Nile Kinnick

19: Number of three-pointers attempted by Chris Kingsbury in a 1994 game against Long Island

20: Years Hayden Fry coached at Iowa

21: Dual meet losses under Dan Gable in 21 years; in 15 of those years, Iowa won the NCAA championship.

22: Straight completions by Chuck Long versus Indiana in 1985

23: Roy Marble's first-round draft pick by Atlanta Hawks in 1989, matching his Iowa jersey number

24: Sam Williams averaged 24 points per game in his Hawkeye career, a school record.

25: Wrestling dual meet wins in 1991

26: Age at which Kirk Ferentz joined Hayden Fry's coaching staff

27: Touchdowns thrown by Chuck Long in 1985

28: Yard pass completion on fourth and 23 with 16 seconds left from Chuck Hartlieb to Marv Cook at Ohio State in 1987

29: Rob Houghtlin hit a 29-yard field goal with two seconds left as No. 1 Iowa defeated No. 2 Michigan in 1985.

30: Combined Iowa football wins in 1970s

31: Combined Iowa football wins in 2002, 2003, and 2004 seasons

32: A total of 32 fumbles occurred during a snowy 1925 game between Iowa and Wisconsin.

33: Iowa wrestlers won 33 matches in the 1985 Big Ten Tournament; they lost only two.

34: Consecutive free throws made by Chris Street prior to tragically being killed in 1993

35: Number of school football records broken by Iowa's offense in 1983

The End Zone

36: Length in inches of the Heartland Trophy

37: Wins by Iowa football from 2002-2005

38: Aubrey Devine drop-kicked a field goal from the 38-yard line in a 10-7 win that broke Notre Dame's 20-game unbeaten streak.

39: Number of Hawkeye football games that have ended in a tie

40: Number of football games Iowa has won by 50 or more points

41: Yard field goal by Rob Houghtlin as time expired in the 1986 Holiday Bowl win over San Diego State

42: Consecutive wins by Iowa wrestling team during a span from 1994-1997

43: Rushing touchdowns scored by Tim Dwight his senior year at Iowa City High

44: Passes thrown by Iowa's leading passer in 1953; Chuck Hartlieb threw 460 times in 1988.

45: Reggie Roby's career punting average at Iowa was over 45 yards per punt.

46: Iowa points scored in shutout win over Monmouth in Iowa (Kinnick) Stadium's first game in 1929

47: Games started by Chuck Long in his Iowa career

48: Number of points Iowa scored against Notre Dame in 1956, the seventh-most ever allowed by the Irish

49: John Johnson scored a school-record 49 points against Northwestern on February 24, 1970.

50: Horse and mule teams brought in to build Iowa (Kinnick) Stadium

51: Rebounds by Reggie Evans in four games in the 2001 Big Ten Tournament

52: Career coaching victories at Iowa by Forest Evashevski

53: In 2006, Fox Sports ranked the 1985 Iowa-Michigan game as the 53rd best college football finish ever.

54: Field goals kicked by Rob Houghtlin in his career

55: Yard field goal on the last play of the first half by Nate Kaeding versus Penn State in 2002

56: Yard pass from Drew Tate to Warren Holloway as time expired in 2005 Capital One Bowl

57: Points Iowa scored against Iowa State in a 1985 football game

58: Tim Douglas made a school-record 58-yard field goal against Illinois in 1998

59: In 2006, Fox Sports ranked the 1987 Iowa-Ohio State game as the 59th best college football finish ever.

60: Number of touchdowns scored by Iowa in 2002

61: Words in "On Iowa"

62: Number of times Iowa has scored 50 or more points in football

63: Consecutive football sellouts over a span of 12 years in 1980s and 1990s

64: Iowa players drafted to the NFL during Hayden Fry's tenure

65: Chuck Long completed 65 percent of his passes at Iowa.

66: Chuck Long engineered a 66-yard fourth-quarter drive to beat Michigan in 1985.

67: Field goals kicked by Nate Kaeding in his career

68: Kilogram weight class in which Dan Gable won a gold medal in the 1972 Olympics

69: Passes Jim Gibbons caught in his Hawkeye career

70: Points scored by Iowa versus Utah State in 1957 football game

71: Iowa football wins over opponents ranked in the top 20

72: Gordon Locke scored 72 conference points in 1922, the most by a Big Ten back until 1943.

73: Career pins by wrestler Ed Banach

74: Career touchdowns thrown by Chuck Long at Iowa

75: Shonn Greene spun a 360 and ran 75 yards for a touchdown against Purdue in 2008.

The End Zone

76: Jason Baker had a 76-yard punt versus Arizona State in the 1997 Sun Bowl.
77: Wins by Hayden Fry's Hawkeyes in the 1980s
78: Points the 1913 Iowa football team scored against Northwestern, the most points the Wildcats have ever allowed

79: Rows in Kinnick Stadium
80: Total touchdowns scored by Tim Dwight at Iowa City High
81: Bob Jeter set a Rose Bowl record by running 81 yards for a touchdown in 1959 against California.
82: In 1939, Nile Kinnick was instrumental in 82 percent of team's total points.
83: Points by which Nate Kaeding leads all other Iowa Hawkeyes in career scoring
84: Points given up by 1956 Iowa football team through the end of the season
85: The last points scored on Iowa Field were on an 85-yard interception return for a touchdown by Gerhard Hauge of Iowa in 1929.
86: Ryan Donahue punted an Iowa-record 86 times in 2007.
87: Approximate cost (in millions) to renovate Kinnick Stadium from 2004 to 2006
88: Number of tackles by freshman Larry Station in 1982, leading the team
89: Consecutive wrestling matches won by Jim Zalesky
90: Herkys on parade
91: Iowa beat Iowa Wesleyan, 91-0, in an 1890 football game.
92: In 2007, ESPN.com ranked "Tate-to-Holloway" as the 92nd best play in college football history.
93: Yard touchdown reception by Quinn Early against Northwestern in 1986
94: Weight in pounds of Floyd of Rosedale

95: Yard touchdown reception by Dallas Clark in a 2002 Homecoming victory over Purdue
96: Points scored by running back Dennis Mosley in 1979
97: Iowa held Ohio State to only 97 yards passing in a 1991 win in Columbus.
98: Consecutive Big Ten wins by the Iowa wrestling team from 1975 through 1989
99: Norm Granger returned a kickoff 99 yards for a touchdown against Indiana in 1981.

1985 Iowa Football Coaching Staff

Player Index

Note: if a player wore multiple numbers in his career, the number he wore during his most decorated season was selected as that player's "primary" number. Players are listed by their primary jersey numbers below.

No.	Athlete and Sport	Years	Hometown	Other Nos. Worn
1	**Aubrey Devine - FB**	**1919-21**	**Des Moines, IA**	
	Quinn Early - FB	1984-87	Great Neck, NY	
	Adam Haluska - BB	2005-07	Carroll, IA	
2	**Gordon Locke - FB**	**1920-22**	**Denison, IA**	6
	Robert Smith - FB	1983-86	Dallas, TX	
	Fred Russell - FB	2000-03	Inkster, MI	
	Jeff Horner - BB	2003-06	Mason City, IA	
3	**Danan Hughes - FB**	**1989-92**	**Bayonne, NJ**	
	Tom Nichol - FB	1981-84	Green Bay, WI	
	Kerry Burt - FB	1984-87	Waterloo, IA	6
	Damien Robinson - FB	1993-96	Dallas, TX	
4	**Jess Settles - BB**	**1994-97,99**	**Winfield, IA**	
	Chris Pervall - BB	1965-66	Newark, NJ	32
5	**Sedrick Shaw - FB**	**1993-96**	**Austin, TX**	
	Andre Woolridge - BB	1995-97	Omaha, NE	
	Drew Tate - FB	2003-06	Baytown, TX	
6	**Tim Dwight - FB**	**1994-97**	**Iowa City, IA**	
	Leland Parkin - FB	1922-24	Waterloo, IA	22, 43
	Ben Stephens - BB	1937-39	Cambridge, IL	
7	**Reggie Roby - FB**	**1979-82**	**Waterloo, IA**	
	Dick Ives - BB	1944-47	Diagonal, IA	
	Rob Houghtlin - FB	1985-87	Glenview, IL	
	Brad Banks - FB	2001-02	Belle Glade, FL	10
8	**Chuck Hartlieb - FB**	**1986-88**	**Woodstock, IL**	
	Leroy Smith - FB	1988-91	Sicklerville, NJ	34
9	**Matt Bowen - FB**	**1997-99**	**Glen Ellyn, IL**	
	Ben Selzer - BB	1932-34	Passaic, NJ	5
	Maurice Brown - FB	2002-03	Ft. Lauderdale, FL	
10	**B.J. Armstrong - BB**	**1986-89**	**Detroit, MI**	
	Dave Danner - BB	1944,46,47	Iowa City, IA	4
11	**Ken Ploen - FB**	**1954-56**	**Clinton, IA**	
	Lester Belding - FB	1918-21	Mason City, IA	
	Bob Jeter - FB	1957-59	Weirton, WV	
12	**Ronnie Lester - BB**	**1977-80**	**Chicago, IL**	
	Gary Snook - FB	1963-65	Iowa City, IA	11
13	**Rick Bayless - FB**	**1984-87**	**Hugo, MN**	
14	**Ed Podolak - FB**	**1966-68**	**Atlantic, IA**	
	Chris Kingsbury - BB	1994-96	Hamilton, OH	

No.	Athlete and Sport	Years	Hometown	Other Nos.
15	**Duke Slater - FB**	**1918-21**	**Normal, IL**	
	Willie Fleming - FB	1958	Detroit, MI	
	Don Nelson - BB	1960-62	Rock Island, IL	
	Jimmy Rodgers - BB	1963-65	Franklin Park, IL	
16	**Chuck Long - FB**	**1981-85**	**Wheaton, IL**	
	Paul Krause - FB	1961-63	Flint, MI	
	Deven Harberts - FB	1986-88	Walnut, IA	
17	**Murray Wier - BB**	**1945-48**	**Muscatine, IA**	**3**
	Willis Glassgow - FB	1927-29	Shenandoah, IA	
18	**Chad Greenway - FB**	**2002-05**	**Mt. Vernon, SD**	
	Lowell Otte - FB	1922-24	Sidney, IA	15, 28
	Dennis Mosley - FB	1976-79	Youngstown, OH	
19	**Larry Ferguson - FB**	**1959-62**	**Madison, IL**	
	Karl Noonan - FB	1963-65	Davenport, IA	
	Keith Chappelle - FB	1979-80	Inglewood, CA	82
20	**Dean Oliver - BB**	**1998-01**	**Mason City, IA**	
	Dick Crayne - FB	1933-35	Fairfield, IA	
	Wilburn Hollis - FB	1959-61	Boys Town, NE	
	Andre Jackson - FB	1973-75	Dixmoor, IL	
21	**Carl Cain - BB**	**1954-56**	**Freeport, IL**	
	Devon Mitchell - FB	1982-85	Brooklyn, NY	
	Tony Stewart - FB	1987-90	Vauxhall, NJ	
22	**Bill Seaberg - BB**	**1954-56**	**Bettendorf, IA**	
	Eddie Phillips - FB	1980-83	Chicago, IL	18
	Tavian Banks - FB	1994-97	Moline, IL	
23	**Roy Marble - BB**	**1986-89**	**Flint, MI**	
	Bob Clifton - BB	1950-52	Boone, IA	
	Gerry Jones - BB	1965-67	Chicago, IL	
	Shonn Greene - FB	2005-06,08	Sicklerville, NJ	
24	**Nile Kinnick - FB**	**1937-39**	**Adel, IA**	
	Bobby Hansen - BB	1980-83	Des Moines, IA	
	James Moses - BB	1989-92	Gardena, CA	
	Luke Recker - BB	2001-02	Auburn, IN	
25	**Randy Duncan - FB**	**1956-58**	**Des Moines, IA**	
	Ed Horton - BB	1986-89	Springfield, IL	
	Dave Gunther - BB	1957-59	Le Mars, IA	57
26	**John Hancock - FB**	**1922-24**	**Marshfield, WI**	**14, 32**
	Norm Granger - FB	1980-83	Newark, NJ	
	Jovon Johnson - FB	2002-05	Erie, PA	
27	**Chuck Darling - BB**	**1950-52**	**Helena, MT**	
28	**Herb Wilkinson - BB**	**1945-47**	**Salt Lake City, UT**	
29	**Bill Diehl - FB**	**1939-41**	**Cedar Rapids, IA**	

No.	Athlete and Sport	Years	Hometown	Other Nos.
30	**Bill Reichardt - FB**	**1949-51**	**Iowa City, IA**	
	Al Couppee - FB	1939-41	Council Bluffs, IA	
	Kenny Arnold - BB	1979-82	Chicago, IL	
31	**Ronnie Harmon - FB**	**1982-85**	**Laurelton, NY**	
	Bill Logan - BB	1954-56	Keokuk, IA	
	Mel Cole - FB	1978-81	Elgin, IL	
	John Derby - FB	1988-91	Oconomowoc, WI	
	Matt Roth - FB	2001-04	Villa Park, IL	
32	**Fred Brown - BB**	**1970-71**	**Milwaukee, WI**	
	Emlen Tunnell - FB	1946-47	Garrett Hill, PA	44
	Mike Saunders - FB	1988-91	Milton, WI	
	Reggie Evans - BB	2001-02	Pensacola, FL	
33	**Bob Sanders - FB**	**2000-03**	**Erie, PA**	
	Michael Enich - FB	1938-40	Boone, IA	
	William Kay - FB	1945-48	Walnut, IA	
	Bill Schoof - BB	1954-56	Chicago Heights, IL	
	Owen Gill - FB	1981-84	Brooklyn, NY	
34	**Jack Dittmer - FB**	**1946-49**	**Elkader, IA**	
	Scott Thompson - BB	1974-76	Moline, IL	
	Jonathan Hayes - FB	1981-84	South Fayette, PA	
35	**Joe Laws - FB**	**1931-33**	**Colfax, IA**	
	Kevin Gamble - BB	1986-87	Springfield, IL	
	Brad Quast - FB	1986-89	Des Plaines, IL	
36	**Larry Station - FB**	**1982-85**	**Omaha, NE**	
	Peter Westra - FB	1927-29	Sheldon, IA	
37	**Erwin Prasse - FB**	**1937-39**	**Chicago, IL**	
	Matt Hughes - FB	1995-98	Eastland, TX	
38	**Zach Bromert - FB**	**1995-98**	**Pensacola, FL**	
39	**Ken Pettit - FB**	**1938-40**	**Logan, IA**	
40	**Chris Street - BB**	**1991-93**	**Indianola, IA**	
	Kevin Boyle - BB	1979-82	Chicago, IL	
41	**Greg Stokes - BB**	**1982-85**	**Hamilton, OH**	
	Eddie Vincent - FB	1953-55	Steubenville, OH	
	Bob Stoops - FB	1979-82	Youngstown, OH	
	Mike Stoops - FB	1981,83-85	Youngstown, OH	2
42	**Ryan Bowen - BB**	**1995-98**	**Fort Madison, IA**	
	Leven Weiss - FB	1976-79	Detroit, MI	
	Michael Payne - FB	1982-85	Quincy, IL	
43	**Nick Bell - FB**	**1988-90**	**Las Vegas, NV**	
	Chad Calabria - BB	1968-70	Aliquippa, PA	
	Craig Clemons - FB	1969-71	Sidney, OH	
	Earl Douthitt - FB	1972-74	Cleveland, OH	42
	Pat Angerer - FB	2006-09	Bettendorf, IA	

No.	Athlete and Sport	Years	Hometown	Other Nos.
44	**Dallas Clark - FB**	**2000-02**	**Livermore, IA**	
	Dick Romey - FB	1923-25	Mason City, IA	4, 23
	Francis Schammel - FB	1932-33	Waterloo, IA	
	Glenn Vidnovic - BB	1968-70	McKeesport, PA	
	Kevin Kunnert - BB	1971-73	Dubuque, IA	
	Greg Brunner - BB	2003-06	Charles City, IA	
45	**Merton Hanks - FB**	**1987-90**	**Dallas, TX**	
	George Peeples - BB	1964-66	Ecorse, MI	
	Jay Norvell - FB	1982-85	Madison, WI	89
	Jonathan Babineaux - FB	2000,02-04	Port Arthur, TX	49
46	**Ladell Betts - FB**	**1998-01**	**Blue Springs, MO**	
	Sharm Scheuerman - BB	1954-56	Rock Island, IL	
47	**Mitch King - FB**	**2005-08**	**Burlington, IA**	
	Homer Harris - FB	1935-37	Seattle, WA	
	Tom Rusk - FB	1975-78	Dubuque, IA	
48	**Howard Hodges - FB**	**2000-03**	**Copperas Cove, TX**	
49	**A.J. Edds - FB**	**2006-09**	**Greenwood, IN**	
50	**John Johnson - BB**	**1969-70**	**Milwaukee, WI**	
	William Van Buren - FB	1955,60-61	Lorain, OH	
	Howard Peterson - FB	1982-85	Bettendorf, IA	

Up Next!

We hope you enjoyed reading Volume I of *Hawkeye Greats, By the Numbers* as much as we enjoyed writing it. There is a lot to agree or disagree with. (If we still haven't convinced you Duke Slater really tops Don Nelson, we can agree to disagree.)

We're pleased to announce this is only the beginning. An extended Volume II of *Hawkeye Greats, By the Numbers* (Nos. 51-99) is in the works! Not to worry, Alex Karras, Sam Williams, and Andre Tippett will make their appearances, and the same type of debates will linger. How do you decide whether Jerry Hilgenberg or Abdul Hodge reigns at No. 52? Would you select Jared DeVries or Adrian Clayborn at No. 94? We'll make our case and see what you think. In *Big Ten Greats, By the Numbers*, we open it up to the Big Ten Conference as a whole. Nile Kinnick will take his place alongside the likes of Earvin "Magic" Johnson, Archie Griffin, and Dick Butkus.

For more information on these and other books, please visit our website at www.singlewingpress.com.

"We're such a unique state in that we don't have professional sports to speak of. It basically is the Hawks, the Cyclones, the Panthers, and the Bulldogs. That's not to slight the Iowa Conference or any other schools in the state, because it's a wonderful college atmosphere in the state of Iowa. But the epicenter is around our college athletics, and I think that's not an accident. I think people really latch onto their teams, and of course I'm a little bit partial, but I think the No. 1 story in Iowa is the Iowa Hawkeyes."

- Gary Dolphin

Preview

Credits

Photos provided by:

Bob Rasmus: Pages 30, 31, 42, 49, 78, 87, 89, 97, 100, 113, 118, 132, 150, 159, 161, 173, 207, 208, 217, 221, 222, 225, 226, 228, 237 (bottom photo), 238 (bottom photo)

Artwork by Heuss Printing/Stuart Baldwin: Pages 7, 12, 27, 37, 53, 64, 68, 73, 82, 92, 127, 154, 188, 193, 202

Single Wing Press, LLC: Pages 48, 66, 75, 131, 184, 191, 227, 230, 236, 237 (top photo), 238 (top and middle photos), 243

University of Iowa Photo Services: Pages 136, 139

University of Iowa Library Special Collections, University of Iowa Archives, Iowa City, Iowa: Page 169

The Daily Iowan: Pages 61, 192

Al Goldis: Pages 17, 19

State Historical Society of Iowa (Des Moines): Pages 58, 119 (drawing by Robert Mills)

Bob Horner: Page 16

Murray Wier: Page 85

Bill Seaberg: Pages 105, 108

Canadian Football League Hall of Fame: Page 56

Darren Miller: Page 125

Some of the quotes contained in this book were first reported by *the Des Moines Register*, *the Iowa City Press-Citizen*, *the Cedar Rapids Gazette*, *the Waterloo Courier*, *the Burlington Hawk Eye*, *the Oelwein Daily Register*, and *the Mason City Globe-Gazette*.